PAUL VALÉRY, born in Cette (Sète) on France's western Mediterranean coast in 1871, studied law at Montpellier before coming to Paris in 1892. He had a few pieces published in the small poetry magazines but then stopped writing poetry for some fifteen years. Valéry came to general notice in 1895 when *La Nouvelle Revue* published "Introduction à la méthode de Léonard de Vinci," but from that period, which also saw the publication of "Monsieur Teste" in *Le Centaure,* until the first World War, Valéry wrote little creatively, his time away from his work at the War Office and then at the Havas news agency being spent in studying mathematics and compiling notes on his developing philosophy of spirit and mind and their relationship to the universe at large.

In 1917, with the publication of "La jeune parque," on which he had been working for years as an addition to a suggested volume of his collected poems, Valéry became famous; the *Album des vers anciens: 1890–1900* appeared in 1920 and was followed in 1922 by *Charmes,* which included "Le Cimitière marin." By 1923 Valéry was able to turn completely to literature, in particular to investigation of the philosophical problems that always remained his chief preoccuption. *Eupalinos* (1923), *Propos sur l'intelligence* (1925), *Regards sur le monde actuel* (1933), display Valéry's sparkling epigrammatic style. Five volumes of critical essays, *Variété,* appeared between 1924 and 1944, as well as other volumes of art criticism and philosophy. He was elected to the Académie in 1925, and from 1937 until his death in Paris in 1945 he held the specially created chair of poetry at the Sorbonne.

Paul Valéry has been called the greatest poet of the half-century, and certainly the influence of his musical, allusive, abstract, magical poetry has grown with the years. Valéry was almost completely the intellectual, mistrusting anything but conscious and deliberate effort and denying that the spontaneous was truly creative; yet in *Monsieur Teste* he recognized the inherent dangers in his views by indicating how sterile the completely intellectual might be.

THE TRANSLATORS

DENIS DEVLIN

C. DAY LEWIS

LIONEL ABEL

JANET LEWIS

LÉONIE ADAMS

JAMES KIRKUP

BARBARA GIBBS

C. F. MacINTYRE

ANTHONY BOWER

LOUISE VARÈSE

W. J. STRACHAN

DOROTHY BUSSY

JAMES LAUGHLIN

MALCOLM COWLEY

LLOYD ALEXANDER

THOMAS McGREEVY

JACKSON MATHEWS

WILLIAM McC. STEWART

VERNON WATKINS

PAUL VALÉRY

SELECTED WRITINGS

A New Directions Book

Published by arrangement with Librairie Gallimard

Translations by Malcolm Cowley, from *Variety,* Copyright, 1927,
by Harcourt, Brace & World, Inc.; renewed, 1954, by
Malcolm Cowley. Reprinted by permission of the publishers.
Translations by C. Day Lewis, from *Poems 1943–1947,* Copyright
1948 by Oxford University Press, Inc.
Translations from The Teste Cycle by Jackson Mathews, from
Monsieur Teste, Copyright 1947 by Alfred A. Knopf, Inc.

Library of Congress catalog card number: 50-7546

ISBN: 0-8112-0213-5

First paperbook edition 1964

MANUFACTURED IN THE UNITED STATES OF AMERICA

New Directions Books are published for James Laughlin by
New Directions Publishing Corporation, 80 Eighth Avenue,
New York 10011

SIXTH PRINTING

CONTENTS

POEMS

PROSE WRITINGS

ON POETRY

ON ARCHITECTURE

ON THE DANCE

ESSAYS ON VARIOUS SUBJECTS

THE TESTE CYCLE

THEATER

PUBLISHER'S NOTE

This selection from the writings of Paul Valéry is published by arrangement with Librairie Gallimard, Paris. With the exception of the poetry section, the selection is identical with the Gallimard *Morceaux Choisis* volume, which was chosen by Valéry himself. In the poetry section it was felt advisable to substitute certain short poems for which good English translations already exist in place of others of a similar kind and length for which no acceptable translations were available. These substitutions are as follows: Poems dropped—"Féerie," "Poésie," "Les Grenades," "Sinistre," "Heure," and "Le Philosophe et la 'Jeune Parque.'" Poems added—"Cantique des Colonnes," "L'Abeille," "Au Bois Dormant," "Intérieur," "La Fausse Morte," "La Fileuse," "Les Pas," and "Le Rameur."

The editing of the English texts was begun by Anthony Bower and completed by J. Laughlin. Many admirers of Valéry assisted with suggestions to the editors, but particular thanks are due to Mrs. Louise Varèse, Wallace Fowlie, Jackson Mathews, Vernon Watkins, T. Weiss (whose Valéry issue of *The Quarterly Review of Literature* was a helpful source for translations), Malcolm Cowley, and Francis Golffing.

We are especially grateful to the translators who generously permitted us to use their translations, and to their publishers, among whom are: The Oxford University Press, Harcourt, Brace & World, Alfred A. Knopf, and John Rodker.

POETRY

POEMS
PROSE POEMS

LA FILEUSE

Assise, la fileuse au bleu de la croisée
Où le jardin mélodieux se dodeline;
Le rouet ancien qui ronfle l'a grisée.

Lasse, ayant bu l'azur, de filer la câline
Chevelure, à ses doigts si faibles évasive,
Elle songe, et sa tête petite s'incline.

Un arbuste et l'air pur font une source vive
Qui suspendue au jour, délicieuse arrose
De ses pertes de fleurs le jardin de l'oisive.

Une tige, où le vent vagabond se repose,
Courbe le salut vain de sa grâce étoilée,
Dédiant magnifique, au vieux rouet, sa rose.

Mais la dormeuse file une laine isolée;
Mystérieusement l'ombre frêle se tresse
Au fil de ses doigts longs et qui dorment, filée.

Le songe se dévide avec une paresse
Angélique, et sans cesse, au doux fuseau crédule,
La chevelure ondule au gré de la caresse . . .

Derrière tant de fleurs, l'azur se dissimule,
Fileuse de feuillage et de lumière ceinte:
Tout le ciel vert se meurt. Le dernier arbre brûle.

Ta sœur, la grande rose où sourit une sainte,
Parfume ton front vague au vent de son haleine
Innocente, et tu crois languir . . . Tu es éteinte

Au bleu de la croisée où tu filais la laine.

THE SPINNER

The garden rocks in a melodious swell.
Beside the open sash a woman spins
And grows bewildered by her snoring wheel.

Tired, having drunk the azure, she begins
To dream, guiding the evasive, wheedling hair
With feeble hands; her little head inclines.

By falling flowers formed, and the pure air,
A living spring suspended to the day
Waters her garden while she idles there.

A stem the restless wind lingers to sway
Inclines a vain salute of starry grace—
Its rose before the ancient wheel to lay.

The sleeper spins a single thread. The lace
Of fragile shadow strangely interweaves,
Spun with the thread her sleeping fingers trace.

The gentle spindle endlessly receives
The lazy-winding dream with a caress
That stirs the credulous skein which it relieves.

Beyond so many flowers the blue is less
Than blue, spinner bound by leaves and light:
The last tree burns. The green sky perishes.

The rose, your sister, where a saint delights,
Perfumes your vague brow with her innocent breath;
You languish . . . you are an extinguished light

At the blue window, where you spun the thread.

Translated by Barbara Gibbs

FRAGMENTS DE "LA JEUNE PARQUE"

Qui pleure là, sinon le vent simple, à cette heure
Seule avec diamants extrêmes? . . . Mais qui pleure,
Si proche de moi-même au moment de pleurer?

Cette main, sur mes traits qu'elle rêve effleurer,
Distraitement docile à quelque fin profonde,
Attend de ma faiblesse une larme qui fonde,
Et que de mes destins lentement divisé,
Le plus pur en silence éclaire un cœur brisé.
La houle me murmure une ombre de reproche,
Ou retire ici-bas, dans ses gorges de roche,
Comme chose déçue et bue amèrement,
Une rumeur de plainte et de resserrement . . .
Que fais-tu, hérissée, et cette main glacée,
Et quel frémissement d'une feuille effacée
Persiste parmi vous, îles de mon sein nu? . . .
Je scintille, liée à ce ciel inconnu . . .
L'immense grappe brille à ma soif de désastres.

Tout-puissants étrangers, inévitables astres
Qui daignez faire luire au lointain temporel
Je ne sais quoi de pur et de surnaturel;
Vous qui dans les mortels plongez jusques aux larmes
Ces souverains éclats, ces invincibles armes,
Et les élancements de votre éternité,
Je suis seule avec vous, tremblante, ayant quitté
Ma couche; et sur l'écueil mordu par la merveille,
J'interroge mon cœur quelle douleur l'éveille,
Quel crime par moi-même ou sur moi consommé? . . .
. . . Ou si le mal me suit d'un songe refermé,
Quand (au velours du souffle envolé l'or des lampes)
J'ai de mes bras épais environné mes tempes,
Et longtemps de mon âme attendu les éclairs?

FRAGMENTS FROM "THE YOUNGEST OF THE FATES"

Who, if not the single wind, is sighing
Alone here with distant diamonds dying?
Whose sob so near myself is taking place?

This hand whose touch is dreaming of my face,
Absently answering some deep call,
Awaits the tear my frailty will let fall
When the clearest of my destinies, apart
In silence brings to light a broken heart.
The mounting wave murmurs, obscurely mocks
At me and withdraws into its gullet of rocks
Plaintively, in rumors of restraint,
Like something bitter swallowed with complaint . . .
Whose cold hand? What bristles beyond the reef?
And what is this flutter of a faded leaf
Sustained among you, isles of my naked breast?
I glisten, toward this unknown heaven pressed . . .
Great clusters glitter to my thirst for dangers.

All powerful, inescapable astral strangers,
Deigning to let shine far off in time
Something supernaturally sublime;
You that plunge in mortals to the depth of tears
These sovereign beams, these invincible spears,
Impulses from your eternity,
I am alone with you, tremblingly
Risen from my couch; and on this reef
Worn with wonder, ask my heart what grief
Wakes it? Have I done, or suffered, wrong?
. . . Or did I keep a dream locked in too long
When (lamp's gold to velvet breath had fled)
I folded heavy arms about my head
And lay awaiting lightning from my soul?

Toute? Mais toute à moi, maîtresse de mes chairs,
Durcissant d'un frisson leur étrange étendue,
Et dans mes doux liens, à mon sang suspendue,
Je me voyais me voir, sinueuse, et dorais
De regards en regards, mes profondes forêts.

J'y suivais un serpent qui venait de me mordre.

* * *

Quel repli de désirs, sa traîne! . . . Quel désordre
De trésors s'arrachant à mon avidité,
Et quelle sombre soif de la limpidité!

O ruse! . . . A la lueur de la douleur laissée
Je me sentis connue encor plus que blessée . . .
Au plus traître de l'âme, une pointe me naît;
Le poison, mon poison, m'éclaire et se connaît:
Il colore une vierge à soi-même enlacée,
Jalouse . . . Mais de qui, jalouse et menacée?
Et quel silence parle à mon seul possesseur?

Dieux! Dans ma lourde plaie une secrète sœur
Brûle, qui se préfère à l'extrême attentive.

* * *

Harmonieuse MOI, différente d'un songe,
Femme flexible et ferme aux silences suivis
D'actes purs! . . . Front limpide, et par ondes ravis,
Si loin que le vent vague et velu les achève,
Longs brins légers qu'au large un vol mêle et soulève,
Dites! . . . J'étais l'égale et l'épouse du jour,
Seul support souriant que je formais d'amour
A la toute-puissante altitude adorée . . .

Quel éclat sur mes cils aveuglément dorée,
O paupières qu'opprime une nuit de trésor,

All? All mine, yes, mistress to control
At a quiver all this strange extent of flesh;
Suspended in my blood, caught in my mesh,
I saw me see myself as sinuous, strewed
Golden glances deep in my deep wood.

A serpent there had bit me, and I followed.

          *   *   *

Ah, what coils of desire where he wallowed!
What riot of riches fled my avidity,
And O the dark thirsting for lucidity!

A trick! . . . By the faint light of pain alert
Suddenly I felt more known than hurt.
Deep in my treachery a sting was growing;
Its poison, my poison, lit me with its knowing,
Clarified in me a virgin, found
Wound round herself, in her embraces bound,
And jealous . . . But of whom? Dreading what stroke?
What silence to my sole possessor spoke?

Gods, in my wound a secret sister woke,
Preferring herself to the extreme attentive.

          *   *   *

Harmonious Self, but different from a vision,
Flexible firm woman, whose silent hands
Are pure acts! . . . Limpid brow, and floating strands
Wave-woven so far out the velvet winds
Offer to the open sea their ends,
Listen! . . . I was the equal spouse of day
Forming with love a sole smiling stay
To the adored almighty altitude . . .

What splendors on my lashes blindly brood!
O eyelids laden from night's treasure rooms,

Je priais à tâtons dans vos ténèbres d'or!
Poreuse à l'éternel qui me semblait m'enclore,
Je m'offrais dans mon fruit de velours qu'il dévore;
Rien ne me murmurait qu'un désir de mourir
Dans cette blonde pulpe au soleil pût mûrir:
Mon amère saveur ne m'était point venue.
Je ne sacrifiais que mon épaule nue
A la lumière; et sur cette gorge de miel,
Dont la tendre naissance accomplissait le ciel,
Se venait assoupir la figure du monde.
Puis dans le dieu brillant, captive vagabonde,
Je m'ébranlais brûlante et foulais le sol plein,
Liant et déliant mes ombres sous le lin.
Heureuse! A la hauteur de tant de gerbes belles,
Qui laissais à ma robe obéir les ombelles,
Dans les abaissements de leur frêle fierté;
Et si, contre le fil de cette liberté,
Si la robe s'arrache à la rebelle ronce,
L'arc de mon brusque corps s'accuse et me prononce,
Nu sous le voile enflé de vivantes couleurs
Que dispute ma race aux longs liens de fleurs!

Je regrette à demi cette vaine puissance . . .
Une avec le désir, je fus l'obéissance
Imminente, attachée à ces genoux polis;
De mouvements si prompts mes vœux étaient remplis
Que je sentais ma cause à peine plus agile!
Vers mes sens lumineux nageait ma blonde argile,
Et dans l'ardente paix des songes naturels,
Tous ces pas infinis me semblaient éternels.
Si ce n'est, ô Splendeur, qu'à mes pieds l'Ennemie,
Mon ombre! la mobile et la souple momie,
De mon absence peinte effleurait sans effort
La terre où je fuyais cette légère mort.
Entre la rose et moi, je la vois qui s'abrite;
Sur la poudre qui danse, elle glisse et n'irrite

I prayed, groping in your golden glooms!
The eternal found me porous, could permeate,
I offered him my velvet fruit, he ate;
Nothing whispered that a wish to die
In this blond pulp in the sun might fructify:
My bitter savor had not yet appeared.
I offered nothing but my shoulder bared
To the light; upon my breast, so honey-sweet
That when it was born heaven was complete,
The world's face finally drowsed and slept.
Then in the god's nimbus roving rapt,
Shaken, burning, pacing the firm ground,
My shadows under the flax I bound, unbound.
Happily umbels on their tall stalk,
Obedient to my garment as I walk,
Bend before my pace their fragile pride;
And if, against the freedom of my stride
My robe is by the rebel briar flounced,
The arc of my sudden body is pronounced
Naked beneath the veil of living colors
Won by my tribe from long lines of flowers!

Now I half regret those idle powers . . .
Blent with desire, I was obedience's
Self, imminent on candid knees;
My wishes were fulfilled by impulses
So quick my cause was hardly quick as they!
Toward luminous senses swam my fair clay,
And as in ardent natural peace I dreamed,
All these infinite steps eternal seemed.
Until, O Splendor, the enemy at my feet,
My shadow, mummy changeable and fleet,
The color of my absence, skimmed like a breath
The land where I was fleeing that frail death.
Between the rose and me I see it hiding;
Over the dancing dust it glides, and gliding

Nul feuillage, mais passe, et se brise partout . . .
Glisse! Barque funèbre . . .

* * *

Grands dieux! Je perds en vous mes pas déconcertés!

Je n'implorerai plus que tes faibles clartés,
Longtemps sur mon visage envieuse de fondre,
Très imminente larme, et seule à me répondre,
Larme qui fais trembler à mes regards humains
Une variété de funèbres chemins;
Tu procèdes de l'âme, orgueil du labyrinthe.
Tu me portes du cœur cette goutte contrainte,
Cette distraction de mon suc précieux
Qui vient sacrifier mes ombres sur mes yeux,
Tendre libation de l'arrière-pensée!
D'une grotte de crainte au fond de moi creusée
Le sel mystérieux suinte muette l'eau.
D'où nais-tu? Quel travail toujours triste et nouveau
Te tire avec retard, larme, de l'ombre amère?
Tu gravis mes degrés de mortelle et de mère,
Et déchirant ta route, opiniâtre faix,
Dans le temps que je vis, les lenteurs que tu fais
M'étouffent . . . Je me tais, buvant ta marche sûre . . .
—Qui t'appelle au secours de ma jeune blessure?

Mais blessure, sanglots, sombres essais, pourquoi?
Pour qui, joyaux cruels, marquez-vous ce corps froid,
Aveugle aux doigts ouverts évitant l'espérance!
Où va-t-il, sans répondre à sa propre ignorance,
Ce corps dans la nuit noire étonné de sa foi?
Terre trouble . . . et mêlée à l'algue, porte-moi,
Porte doucement moi . . . Ma faiblesse de neige
Marchera-t-elle tant qu'elle trouve son piège?
Où traîne-t-il, mon cygne, où cherche-t-il son vol?

20

Shakes no leaf, but passes, and everywhere
Breaks . . . Glide, O funeral bark! . . .

* * *

You gods! My baffled steps are lost in you!

Your feeble light alone I shall pursue
Henceforth, impending tear, the only trace
Of myself, longing to melt upon my face,
Tear that mirrors to my human gaze
A trembling number of funereal ways:
You issue from the soul, the labyrinth's pride.
You bring me this drop from the heart pried,
This extract of my precious juice to rise
And sacrifice my darkness on my eyes,
Tender libation of my hidden thought!
From a cave of fear deep in me wrought
A mysterious salt oozes this mute dew.
Whence were you born? What labor sad and new
Draws you so late, tear, from the bitter dark?
You climb the steps of my motherhood, and mark
Your own path, stubborn burden, through the days
That I must live, and choke me with your delays . . .
My silence drinks your footstep, is alert . . .
Who called you to the help of my young hurt?

But why these sobs, dark groping efforts, and
For whom, O cruel jewels, do you brand
This cold body, blind, extending a hand?
Whither, with fingers spread, evading hope,
Ignoring its own ignorance, does it grope
In the dark night, astonished at its faith?
Bear me, turbid and seaweedy earth,
Gently . . . My frailty of snow will dare
Walk until it walk into its snare?
Whither draws my swan? To what flight bound?

. . . Dureté précieuse . . . O sentiment du sol,
Mon pas fondait sur toi l'assurance sacrée!
Mais sous le pied vivant qui tâte et qui la crée
Et touche avec horreur à son pacte natal,
Cette terre si ferme atteint mon piédestal.
Non loin, parmi ces pas, rêve mon précipice . . .
L'insensible rocher, glissant d'algues, propice
A fuir, (comme en soi-même ineffablement seul),
Commence . . . Et le vent semble au travers d'un linceul
Ourdir de bruits marins une confuse trame,
Mélange de la lame en ruine, et de rame . . .
Tant de hoquets longtemps, et de râles heurtés,
Brisés, repris au large . . . et tous les sorts jetés
Éperdument divers roulant l'oubli vorace . . .

Hélas! De mes pieds nus qui trouvera la trace
Cessera-t-il longtemps de ne songer qu'à soi?

Terre trouble, et mêlée à l'algue, porte-moi!

* * *

Hier la chair profonde, hier, la chair maîtresse
M'a trahie . . . Oh! sans rêve, et sans une caresse! . . .
Nul démon, nul parfum ne m'offrit le péril
D'imaginaires bras mourant au col viril;
Ni, par le Cygne-Dieu, de plumes offensée
Sa brûlante blancheur n'effleura ma pensée . . .

Il eût connu pourtant le plus tendre des nids!
Car toute à la faveur de mes membres unis,
Vierge, je fus dans l'ombre une adorable offrande . . .
Mais le sommeil s'éprit d'une douceur si grande,
Et nouée à moi-même au creux de mes cheveux.
J'ai mollement perdu mon empire nerveux.
Au milieu de mes bras, je me suis faite une autre . . .
Qui s'aliène? . . . Qui s'envole? . . . Qui se vautre? . . .
A quel détour caché, mon cœur s'est-il fondu?
Quelle conque a redit le nom que j'ai perdu?

. . . Precious firmness . . . O the feel of ground,
My step had found in you its blessèd stay!
But under the living foot that feels its way,
Knowing its natal pact is near and dreadful,
This firm earth has touched my pedestal.
Not far, among these steps, my precipice,
Slick with seaweed, dreams on the abyss,
Favoring fall, ineffably alone . . .
As through a shroud, it seems, the wind's moan
Is weaving a vague web of the sounds of shore,
A jumble of the ruined wave and the oar . . .
Years of coughing, with death-rattles clashing,
Broken, far out, into echoes . . . dashing
The dice beyond hope, rolling oblivion . . .

Will he that finds my bare footprint be one
To cease for long from dreaming of himself?

O bear me, turbid and seaweedy shelf!

　　　　　　　　* * *

Yesterday the deep flesh had left me
Dreamless, and of all caress bereft me! . . .
No perfume offered the peril of implying
My arms about a manly neck dying;
Nor did the Swan-God with rude feathers find
And burning in his whiteness skim my mind . . .

Yet he would have found the softest nest!
For I was all embodied in my breast,
A virgin, offered in a dark retreat . . .
But sleep then fell in love with all that sweet;
And bodied in me, bedded in my hair,
Quietly I felt my nerves despair.
Within my own arms I became another . . .
But who was estranged? Who's gone? Who's left to hover? . . .
Did my heart melt upon the road it came?
What seashell was it murmured my lost name?

Le sais-je, quel reflux traître m'a retirée
De mon extrémité pure et prématurée,
Et m'a repris le sens de mon vaste soupir?
Comme l'oiseau se pose, il fallut m'assoupir.

Ce fut l'heure, peut-être, où la devineresse
Intérieure s'use et se désintéresse:
Elle n'est plus la même . . . Une profonde enfant
Des degrés inconnus vainement se défend,
Et redemande au loin ses mains abandonnées.
Il faut céder aux vœux des mortes couronnées
Et prendre pour visage un souffle . . .

                              Doucement,
Me voici: mon front touche à ce consentement . . .
Ce corps, je lui pardonne, et je goûte à la cendre.
Je me remets entière au bonheur de descendre,
Ouverte aux noirs témoins, les bras suppliciés,
Entre des mots sans fin, sans moi, balbutiés.
Dors, ma sagesse, dors. Forme-toi cette absence;
Retourne dans le germe et la sombre innocence,
Abandonne-toi vive aux serpents, aux trésors . . .
Dors toujours! Descends, dors toujours! Descends, dors, dors!

(*La porte basse c'est une bague . . . où la gaze*
Passe . . . Tout meurt, tout rit dans la gorge qui jase . . .
L'oiseau boit sur ta bouche et tu ne peux le voir . . .
Viens plus bas, parle bas . . . Le noir n'est pas si noir . . .)

* * *

Délicieux linceuls, mon désordre tiède,
Couche où je me répands, m'interroge et me cède,
Où j'allai de mon cœur noyer les battements,
Presque tombeau vivant dans mes appartements,
Qui respire, et sur qui l'éternité s'écoute,
Place pleine de moi qui m'avez prise toute,
O forme de ma forme et la creuse chaleur

What treacherous tow caught and contrived to bend
Me from my pure and premature last end,
And took the sense of sighs out of my breast?
Ah, like a homing bird I needed rest.

It was the time of day when the clairvoyant
In us wearies, is no longer buoyant,
Loses interest . . . And deep within our care
A child is helpless on an unknown stair,
Begging the distance to give back his hands.
We grant the crowned dead their last demands,
And put on, for a face, a breath . . .

Content,
My head already nodding toward consent,
My body I forgive. Ah, ash's scent!
I'm wholly given over to descent,
Laid open to dark witnesses, arms dead,
Words without end about me, but unsaid.
Now sleep, my conscience; take the shape of absence,
Go back into the seed's dark innocence,
Give yourself alive to serpents. Sleep
Forever now. Down . . . Down . . . Now sleep, now sleep.

(*The low door is a ring . . . where gauzes float . . .*
All things dying laugh in the gurgling throat . . .
Unseen but drinking from your mouth, a lark . . .
Come low, talk low . . . The dark is not so dark . . .)

* * *

Sweet winding sheet, O warm disorder, Bed
Wherein I stretch, wonder, yield, and was led
To let the beatings of my heart consume,
Here in my room almost a living tomb
Where eternity hears its own pulse beat,
O place that needs me all to be replete,
Shape of my shape, and, ah the warm contours

Que mes retours sur moi reconnaissaient la leur,
Voici que tant d'orgueil qui dans vos plis se plonge
A la fin se mélange aux bassesses du songe!
Dans vos nappes, où lisse elle imitait sa mort
L'idole malgré soi se dispose et s'endort,
Lasse femme absolue, et les yeux dans ses larmes,
Quand, de ses secrets nus les antres et les charmes,
Et ce reste d'amour que se gardait le corps
Corrompirent sa perte et ses mortels accords.

Arche toute secrète, et pourtant si prochaine,
Mes transports, cette nuit, pensaient briser ta chaîne;
Je n'ai fait que bercer de lamentations
Tes flancs chargés de jour et de créations!
Quoi! mes yeux froidement que tant d'azur égare
Regardent là périr l'étoile fine et rare,
Et ce jeune soleil de mes étonnements
Me paraît d'une aïeule éclairer les tourments,
Tant sa flamme aux remords ravit leur existence,
Et compose d'aurore une chère substance
Qui se formait déjà substance d'un tombeau! . . .
O, sur toute la mer, sur mes pieds, qu'il est beau!
Tu viens! . . . Je suis toujours celle que tu respires,
Mon voile évaporé me fuit vers tes empires . . .

. . . Alors, n'ai-je formé, vains adieux si je vis,
Que songes? . . . Si je viens, en vêtements ravis,
Sur ce bord, sans horreur, humer la haute écume,
Boire des yeux l'immense et riante amertume,
L'être contre le vent, dans le plus vif de l'air,
Recevant au visage un appel de la mer;
Si l'âme intense souffle, et renfle furibonde
L'onde abrupte sur l'onde abattue, et si l'onde
Au cap tonne, immolant un monstre de candeur,
Et vient des hautes mers vomir la profondeur
Sur ce roc, d'où jaillit jusque vers mes pensées

That you, my convolutions, knew were yours,
This pride that plunges in your matrix seems
At last to be mixing with the dross of dreams!
The idol in your covers, playing dead,
Dozes despite herself and lolls her head,
Weary and all woman, tears for eyes;
The secret of her grottoes naked lies,
And love left in her body like a germ
Has stalled her ruin, forestalled her mortal term.

Most secret arch, and yet so near, so plain,
This night my rapture meant to break your chain,
But all I could was lull with lamentation
Your deep sides heavy with day and creation!
Coldly my eyes, lost in so much blue,
Watch a single star die from view,
And this young sun of my astonishment
Clears up, it seems, an ancestress' torment:
Its beams all matter from remorse have drawn,
And now compose a dear substance out of dawn
That was just now the substance of a grave! . . .
How beautiful, on my feet and on that wave!
You come! . . . And I am still the breath you require,
My veil the vapor of your vast empire . . .

Was this all dream? But there is no farewell
If I am still alive . . . and can compel
Myself in ravished garments to this brink
To take the high foam, with the eyes to drink
The immense and laughing bitterness, to bare
Being to the wind, the very quick of the air,
Taking full in the face the sea's blare;
If the *animus* blow, and the abrupt wave
Rave on the broken wave, and if the wave
Thunder on the cape to sacrifice
A monstrous candor, if the deep seas rise
And vomit up pure depth upon these rocks,

Un éblouissement d'étincelles glacées,
Et sur toute ma peau que morde l'âpre éveil,
Alors, malgré moi-même, il le faut, ô Soleil,
Que j'adore mon cœur où tu te viens connaître,
Doux et puissant retour du délice de naître,

Feu vers qui se soulève une vierge de sang
Sous les espèces d'or d'un sein reconnaissant!

* * *

L'ABEILLE

Quelle, et si fine, et si mortelle,
Que soit ta pointe, blonde abeille,
Je n'ai, sur ma tendre corbeille,
Jeté qu'un songe de dentelle.

Pique du sein la gourde belle,
Sur qui l'Amour meurt ou sommeille,
Qu'un peu de moi-même vermeille
Vienne à la chair ronde et rebelle!

J'ai grand besoin d'un prompt tourment:
Un mal vif et bien terminé
Vaut mieux qu'un supplice dormant!

Soit donc mon sens illuminé
Par cette infime alerte d'or
Sans qui l'Amour meurt ou s'endort!

Flashing upon my mind their dazzling shocks
Of spray, my skin bitten with bitter waking,
Then, in spite of all I am forsaking,
I will adore my heart, wherein you burn,
O sun, sweet joy of being born, return!

O fire, whose virgin in my blood has blest
The golden coins of a grateful breast.

Translated by Jackson Mathews

THE BEE

So deadly delicate your sting!
Yet, O golden bee, I place
Over this soft curve, saddening,
Nothing but a dream of lace.

Prick the breast's fine gourd and press
Home where love dies, where sleeps his spell!
Thus may some of my rosiness
Rise to the round and stubborn flesh!

I need a hurt that's keen and swift.
A torment prompt and soon done with
Is better than one that sleeping lies.

O may my body be made warm
By this tiny gold alarm
Without which love sleeps or dies!

Translated by Lionel Abel

FRAGMENTS DU "NARCISSE"

Vous attendiez, peut-être, un visage sans pleurs,
Vous calmes, vous toujours de feuilles et de fleurs,
Et de l'incorruptible altitude hantées,
O Nymphes! . . . Mais docile aux pentes enchantées
Qui me firent vers vous d'invincibles chemins,
Souffrez ce beau reflet des désordres humains!

Heureux vos corps fondus, Eaux planes et profondes!
Je suis seul! . . . Si les Dieux, les échos et les ondes
Et si tant de soupirs permettent qu'on le soit!
Seul! . . . mais encor celui qui s'approche de soi
Quand il s'approche aux bords que bénit ce feuillage . . .

Des cimes, l'air déjà cesse le pur pillage;
La voix des sources change, et me parle du soir;
Un grand calme m'écoute, où j'écoute l'espoir.
J'entends l'herbe des nuits croître dans l'ombre sainte,
Et la lune perfide élève son miroir
Jusque dans les secrets de la fontaine éteinte . . .
Jusque dans les secrets que je crains de savoir,
Jusque dans le repli de l'amour de soi-même,
Rien ne peut échapper au silence du soir . . .
La nuit vient sur ma chair lui souffler que je l'aime.
Sa voix fraîche à mes vœux tremble de consentir;
A peine, dans la brise, elle semble mentir,
Tant le frémissement de son temple tacite
Conspire au spacieux silence d'un tel site.

O douceur de survivre à la force du jour,
Quand elle se retire, enfin rose d'amour,

FRAGMENTS FROM "NARCISSUS"

(From Part I)

Some face that never wept you hoped perchance to see,
You who are calm, who are with petals changelessly
Haunted, and leaves, O nymphs! and corruptionless altitude . . .
But yieldingly of those charmed downward leanings wooed,
Which were my roads to you unconquerably, this
Fair mirroring suffer you now of human ravages.

Joyous your mingled selves, O Waters deeply planed!
I am alone . . . If Gods, if streams, and echoed sound,
And so much sighing breath can leave one so! Yet here
Still he who nears himself, nearing your verges where
A benediction falls, of these leaved branches sent.

So early on the crests air fails of her sheer ravishment;
Altering, the voice of waters speaks nightfall at my ear;
Wide quiet lies listening for me, there where I would hear
Hope. I hear night's grass in the sacred shade increase,
And the perfidious moon uplifts her mirror upon
Even the secrecies within the shrouded fount; . . .
Upon even the secrecies I shrink to confront,
And even the fold where self desires self alone,
Till nothing shall elude evening and silentness . . .
Night moves upon my flesh, whispering my love is hers.
The cool tones tremble to shape them to my sighs;
It scarcely seems beguilement upon the shaken airs,
For so these tremors within her tacit temple are wrought
One with the spaciousness of silence in such a spot.

O grateful! to live out day's force and still to be
At her withdrawals, then when, with her last ardency

Encore un peu brûlante, et lasse, mais comblée,
Et de tant de trésors tendrement accablée,
Par de tels souvenirs qu'ils empourprent sa mort,
Et qu'ils la font heureuse agenouiller dans l'or,
Puis s'étendre, se fondre, et perdre sa vendange
Et s'éteindre en un songe en qui le soir se change.

Quelle perte en soi-même offre un si calme lieu!
L'âme, jusqu'à périr, s'y penche pour un Dieu
Qu'elle demande à l'onde, onde déserte, et digne,
Sur son lustre, du lisse effacement d'un cygne . . .
A cette onde jamais ne burent les troupeaux!
D'autres, ici perdus, trouveraient le repos,
Et dans la sombre terre, un clair tombeau qui s'ouvre . . .
Mais ce n'est point le calme, hélas! que j'y découvre!
Quand l'opaque délice où dort cette clarté,
Cède à mon corps l'horreur du feuillage écarté,
Alors, vainqueur de l'ombre, ô mon corps tyrannique,
Repoussant aux forêts leur épaisseur panique,
Tu regrettes bientôt leur éternelle nuit!
Pour l'inquiet Narcisse, il n'est ici qu'ennui!
Tout m'appelle et m'enchaîne à la chair lumineuse
Que m'oppose des eaux la paix vertigineuse!

Que je déplore ton éclat fatal et pur,
Si mollement de moi Fontaine environnée,
Où puisèrent mes yeux dans un mortel azur
Les yeux mêmes et noirs de leur âme étonnée!

Profondeur, profondeur, songes qui me voyez,
    Comme ils verraient une autre vie,
Dites, ne suis-je pas celui que vous croyez,
    Votre corps vous fait-il envie?

Cessez, sombres esprits, cet ouvrage anxieux
    Qui se fait dans l'âme qui veille;
Ne cherchez pas en vous, n'allez surprendre aux cieux
    Le malheur d'être une merveille:
Trouvez dans la fontaine un corps délicieux . . .

Unspent, wearied, but brimmed, love-flushed at length with rose,
Gently, and by such riches overheaped she goes,
Through such rememberings as empurple her dying,
Happy to kneel her in a golden space, then lying
Her length, to miss the fruiting of her vines, and dimmed,
Changed, to melt, into a day the dusk has dreamed.

What loss to self is offered within such quietude!
The soul leans forth upon it mortally. She would
Have a god of you waters, abandoned waters, on
Which lustre seems sleeked for the gliding effacement of a swan.
No gullet among the herds has watered at your pure
Stream. Another, lost as I, would find repose
And opened of sad ground a shining sepulture;
For me it is not calm, alas! your deeps unclose.
Rent now, that undergrowth of an unlit delight,
Which lulls your brilliance, its whole shudder to flesh had
Yielded, and thou, the very vanquisher of shade,
Spurning the panic mass of forests, would have again,
O my tyrannic body! how soon, their incessant night!
Narcissus, restless one, for thee, here is only pain
Of longing. All things to that luminous flesh enchain,
Entice, which fronts me, waters, from your giddying peace!

And I lament, how bitterly, these lucencies
Of yours, fateful and pure. Fountain, my tenderness
Of being encircles, where in a deathly azure my eyes
Drain of their startled soul the same and nighted eyes!

Deeps, deeps, dreamings which perceive me,
    As on another life turned wondering,
Tell me, am I not he whom you believe me?
    Has your own body set you languishing?

Give up, dark wits, these nervous toils which rise
    Out of a ridden soul, wakeful by night;
And hunt no more within, nor set off to surprise
Of heaven the plight of being a wonder; look there lies
    Within the fount a body for delight.

Prenant à vos regards cette parfaite proie,
Du monstre de s'aimer faites-vous un captif;
Dans les errants filets de vos longs cils de soie
Son gracieux éclat vous retienne pensif;

Mais ne vous flattez pas de le changer d'empire.
    Ce cristal est son vrai séjour;
    Les efforts mêmes de l'amour
Ne le sauraient de l'onde extraire qu'il n'expire . . .

PIRE.
    Pire? . . .
            Quelqu'un redit *Pire* . . . O moqueur!
Écho lointaine est prompte à rendre son oracle!

II

Claire, mais si profonde, une nymphe toujours
Effleurée, et vivant de tout ce qui l'approche,
Nourrit quelque sagesse à l'abri de sa roche,
A l'ombre de ce jour qu'elle peint sous les bois.
Elle sait à jamais les choses d'une fois . . .

O présence pensive, eau calme qui recueilles
Tout un sombre trésor de fables et de feuilles,
L'oiseau mort, le fruit mûr, lentement descendus,
Et les rares lueurs des clairs anneaux perdus.
Tu consommes en toi leur perte solennelle;
Mais, sur la pureté de ta face éternelle,
L'amour passe et périt . . .
Et dans ce corps caché tout marqué de l'amour,
Que porte amèrement l'âme qui fut heureuse
Brûle un secret baiser qui la rend furieuse . . .
Mais moi, Narcisse aimé, je ne suis curieux
    Que de ma seule essence;
Tout autre n'a pour moi qu'un cœur mystérieux,
    Tout autre n'est qu'absence.

Fix with thy gazes then this flawless prize,
    Make thine the monster catch thou hast,
Of self-desire. Netted in the long lashes of thine eyes
    His gracious luster, fast
And silkenly, binds thee to reveries.

But dream no shifting of his mastery.
    This mirror of waters is his only stay;
Not even love's ardency
    Can strain him forth, but he is sighed away.

Away.
    Someone repeats; Away. *Away.* Again,
The tease! Echo, aloof and brisk with oracle!

(From Part II)

Nymph all encounters will flutter, live with all which
Nears, how deep in her transparency she lies,
Nursing some wisdom in the stone keeping of her niche,
In covert of her day through the wood's darkness shed,
With things which are but once become forever wise . . .

Gathered, musing presence, within thy calm is heaped
A treasure of sad tone: legends and leaves; the dead
Bird, the ripe fruit, lingeringly descended; rare
Glimmers sometimes of lost rings from the fingers slipt
Untarnished; whose ceremonial loss has there
All consummation; but on thy taintlessness, o face
From the eternals, love's passings die. . . .
Within that body in hiding, scarred over with love, which turns
So wry a charge on the once happy spirit, there burns
Always and hiddenly the kiss that is frenzying it.
But I, Narcissus, who am cherished, only this,
    My solitary essence interests me.
Another is but absence, another is,
    For me, offering only of a heart's mystery.

35

III

Formons, toi sur ma lèvre, et moi, dans mon silence,
Une prière aux dieux qu'émus de tant d'amour
Sur sa pente de pourpre ils arrêtent le jour! . . .
Faites, Maîtres heureux, Pères des justes fraudes,
Dites qu'une lueur de rose ou d'émeraudes
Que des songes du soir votre sceptre reprit,
Pure, et toute ⁓areille au plus pur de l'esprit,
Attende, au sein des cieux, que tu vives et veuilles,
Près de moi, mon amour, choisir un lit de feuilles,
Sortir tremblant du flanc de la nymphe au cœur froid,
Et sans quitter mes yeux, sans cesser d'être moi,
Tendre ta forme fraîche, et cette claire écorce . . .
Oh! te saisir enfin! . . . Prendre ce calme torse
Plus pur que d'une femme et non formé de fruits . . .
Mais, d'une pierre simple est le temple où je suis,
Où je vis . . . Car je vis sur tes lèvres avares! . . .
        O mon corps, mon cher corps, temple qui me sépares
De ma divinité, je voudrais apaiser
Votre bouche . . . Et bientôt, je briserais, baiser,
Ce peu qui nous défend de l'extrême existence,
Cette tremblante, frêle, et pieuse distance
Entre moi-même et l'onde, et mon âme, et les dieux! . . .

        Adieu . . . Sens-tu frémir mille flottants adieux?
Bientôt va frissonner le désordre des ombres!
L'arbre aveugle vers l'arbre étend ses membres sombres,
Et cherche affreusement l'arbre qui disparaît . . .
Mon âme ainsi se perd dans sa propre forêt,
Où la puissance échappe à ses formes suprêmes . . .
L'âme, l'âme aux yeux noirs, touche aux ténèbres mêmes,
Elle se fait immense et ne rencontre rien . . .
Entre la mort et soi, quel regard est le sien!

Come, thou upon my lips, within my silence, I,
Compose such prayer together, that the gods, by
Passion shaken, on its purple slopes will halt the day! . . .
Do it, felicitous Masters, Fathers who can deceive
By such just cheats, say, rose, emeralds, one ray
Among all those that evening muses, your sceptres reprieve,
Pure, with the purest of spirit matched, at heaven's breast
Lingering, till thou art live, till thou preferest thy rest
Near me, upon some couch of leaves, till thou art come,
My love, tremulous forth from the cold Naiad womb,
And not gone from my sight, not ceasing to be I,
Proffer this form of freshness, this the lustrous shell . . .
After all, to grasp thee! . . . Calm torso, purer than one`
Of woman, not ripened of fruits . . . Of a single and a simple stone
This temple is, in which I am, in which I dwell . . .
For I dwell on thy avid lips! . . .
                              Dear body, my
Body, temple that from a god disjoins me, I
Would appease thy mouth . . . And soon, crush out, O kiss,
This little that closes us all the reach of being, this
Tenuous, shaken and pious distance there is
Of self from waters, spirit from the gods! . . .

                              Farewell . . .
Through thee, thrill now the thousand driftings of farewell?
Confusion of the shadows sets all shuddering! Tree
Eyeless towards the tree there are reachings, horribly
Of the darkened limbs which grope for the tree that disappears . . .
And so my soul within the forest which is hers,
There where all force escapes its supreme forms, has strayed . . .
Soul, soul of night-black eyes, she has touched at very shade,
And has made her one measureless, and encounters none . . .
Death and itself at gaze, what interchange is theirs!

Dieux! de l'auguste jour, le pâle et tendre reste
Va des jours consumés joindre le sort funeste;
Il s'abîme aux enfers du profond souvenir!
Hélas! corps misérable, il est temps de s'unir . . .
Penche-toi . . . Baise-toi. Tremble de tout ton être!
L'insaisissable amour que tu me vins promettre
Passe, et dans un frisson, brise Narcisse, et fuit . . .

LE BOIS AMICAL

Nous avons pensé des choses pures
Côte à côte, le long des chemins,
Nous nous sommes tenus par les mains
Sans dire . . . parmi les fleurs obscures;

Nous marchions comme des fiancés
Seuls, dans la nuit verte des prairies;
Nous partagions ce fruit de féeries
La lune amicale aux insensés.

Et puis, nous sommes morts sur la mousse,
Très loin, tout seuls parmi l'ombre douce
De ce bois intime et murmurant;

Et là-haut, dans la lumière immense,
Nous nous sommes trouvés en pleurant
O mon cher compagnon de silence!

A tender vestige soon of the august day is gone,
How pale, O Gods, to the funest portion of spent days;
Engulfed within the hell of profound remembrances!
Alas! wretched flesh, it is time to be at one . . .
Lean! Tremble in all thou art! Kiss! Never to be
Possessed, the love it has been thine to promise me
Is passing; its tremor shatters Narcissus and fails . . .

Translated by Léonie Adams

THE FRIENDLY WOOD

We were thinking of things pure,
side by side, along the paths,
we were holding hands
without speaking . . . among the dark flowers.

We strolled like a couple betrothed,
alone, in the green night of the fields,
sharing the fruit of fairyland
the moon friendly to madness.

And then we lay dead on the moss,
far away, all alone, in the soft shadows
of the intimate murmuring wood;

And above us, in the immense light,
we found ourselves weeping
oh my dear companion of silence!

Translated by C. F. MacIntyre and J. Laughlin

LE CIMETIÈRE MARIN

Ce toit tranquille, où marchent des colombes,
Entre les pins palpite, entre les tombes;
Midi le juste y compose de feux
La mer, la mer, toujours recommencée!
O récompense après une pensée
Qu'un long regard sur le calme des dieux!

Quel pur travail de fins éclairs consume
Maint diamant d'imperceptible écume,
Et quelle paix semble se concevoir!
Quand sur l'abîme un soleil se repose,
Ouvrages purs d'une éternelle cause,
Le temps scintille et le songe est savoir.

Stable trésor, temple simple à Minerve,
Masse de calme, et visible réserve,
Eau sourcilleuse, Œil qui gardes en toi
Tant de sommeil sous une voile de flamme,
O mon silence! . . . Édifice dans l'âme,
Mais comble d'or aux mille tuiles, Toit!

Temple du Temps, qu'un seul soupir résume,
A ce point pur je monte et m'accoutume,
Tout entouré de mon regard marin;
Et comme aux dieux mon offrande suprême,
La scintillation sereine sème
Sur l'altitude un dédain souverain.

THE GRAVEYARD BY THE SEA

This quiet roof, where dove-sails saunter by,
Between the pines, the tombs, throbs visibly.
Impartial noon patterns the sea in flame—
That sea forever starting and re-starting.
When thought has had its hour, oh how rewarding
Are the long vistas of celestial calm!

What grace of light, what pure toil goes to form
The manifold diamond of the elusive foam!
What peace I feel begotten at that source!
When sunlight rests upon a profound sea,
Time's air is sparkling, dream is certainty—
Pure artifice both of an eternal Cause.

Sure treasure, simple shrine to intelligence,
Palpable calm, visible reticence,
Proud-lidded water, Eye wherein there wells
Under a film of fire such depth of sleep—
O silence! . . . Mansion in my soul, you slope
Of gold, roof of a myriad golden tiles.

Temple of time, within a brief sigh bounded,
To this rare height inured I climb, surrounded
By the horizons of a sea-girt eye.
And, like my supreme offering to the gods,
That peaceful coruscation only breeds
A loftier indifference on the sky.

Comme le fruit se fond en jouissance,
Comme en délice il change son absence
Dans une bouche où sa forme se meurt,
Je hume ici ma future fumée,
Et le ciel chante à l'âme consumée
Le changement des rives en rumeur.

Beau ciel, vrai ciel, regarde-moi qui change!
Après tant d'orgueil, après tant d'étrange
Oisiveté, mais pleine de pouvoir,
Je m'abandonne à ce brillant espace,
Sur les maisons des morts mon ombre passe
Qui m'apprivoise à son frêle mouvoir.

L'âme exposée aux torches du solstice,
Je te soutiens, admirable justice
De la lumière aux armes sans pitié!
Je te rends pure à ta place première,
Regarde-toi! . . . Mais rendre la lumière
Suppose d'ombre une morne moitié.

O pour moi seul, à moi seul, en moi-même,
Auprès d'un cœur, aux sources du poème,
Entre le vide et l'événement pur,
J'attends l'écho de ma grandeur interne,
Amère, sombre, et sonore citerne,
Sonnant dans l'âme un creux toujours futur!

Sais-tu, fausse captive des feuillages,
Golfe mangeur de ces maigres grillages,
Sur mes yeux clos, secrets éblouissants,
Quel corps me traîne à sa fin paresseuse,
Quel front l'attire à cette terre osseuse?
Une étincelle y pense à mes absents.

Fermé, sacré, plein d'un feu sans matière,
Fragment terrestre offert à la lumière,

Even as a fruit's absorbed in the enjoying,
Even as within the mouth its body dying
Changes into delight through dissolution,
So to my melted soul the heavens declare
All bounds transfigured into a boundless air,
And I breathe now my future's emanation.

Beautiful heaven, true heaven, look how I change!
After such arrogance, after so much strange
Idleness—strange, yet full of potency—
I am all open to these shining spaces;
Over the homes of the dead my shadow passes,
Ghosting along—a ghost subduing me.

My soul laid bare to your midsummer fire,
O just, impartial light whom I admire,
Whose arms are merciless, you have I stayed
And give back, pure, to your original place.
Look at yourself . . . But to give light implies
No less a somber moiety of shade.

Oh, for myself alone, mine, deep within
At the heart's quick, the poem's fount, between
The void and its pure issue, I beseech
The intimations of my secret power.
O bitter, dark, and echoing reservoir
Speaking of depths always beyond my reach.

But know you—feigning prisoner of the boughs,
Gulf which eats up their slender prison-bars,
Secret which dazzles though mine eyes are closed—
What body drags me to its lingering end,
What mind draws *it* to this bone-peopled ground?
A star broods there on all that I have lost.

Closed, hallowed, full of insubstantial fire,
Morsel of earth to heaven's light given o'er—

43

Ce lieu me plaît, dominé de flambeaux,
Composé d'or, de pierre et d'arbres sombres,
Où tant de marbre est tremblant sur tant d'ombres;
La mer fidèle y dort sur mes tombeaux!

Chienne splendide, écarte l'idolâtre!
Quand solitaire au sourire de pâtre,
Je pais longtemps, moutons mystérieux,
Le blanc troupeau de mes tranquilles tombes,
Éloignes-en les prudentes colombes,
Les songes vains, les anges curieux!

Ici venu, l'avenir est paresse.
L'insecte net gratte la sécheresse;
Tout est brûlé, défait, reçu dans l'air
A je ne sais quelle sévère essence . . .
La vie est vaste, étant ivre d'absence,
Et l'amertume est douce, et l'esprit clair.

Les morts cachés sont bien dans cette terre
Qui les réchauffe et sèche leur mystère.
Midi là-haut, Midi sans mouvement
En soi se pense et convient à soi-même . . .
Tête complète et parfait diadème,
Je suis en toi le secret changement.

Tu n'as que moi pour contenir tes craintes!
Mes repentirs, mes doutes, mes contraintes
Sont le défaut de ton grand diamant! . . .
Mais dans leur nuit toute lourde de marbres,
Un peuple vague aux racines des arbres
A pris déjà ton parti lentement.

Ils ont fondu dans une absence épaisse,
L'argile rouge a bu la blanche espèce,
Le don de vivre a passé dans les fleurs!
Où sont des morts les phrases familières,

This plot, ruled by its flambeaux, pleases me—
A place all gold, stone, and dark wood, where shudders
So much marble above so many shadows:
And on my tombs, asleep, the faithful sea.

Keep off the idolaters, bright watch-dog, while—
A solitary with the shepherd's smile—
I pasture long my sheep, my mysteries,
My snow-white flock of undisturbéd graves!
Drive far away from here the careful doves,
The vain daydreams, the angels' questioning eyes!

Now present here, the future takes its time.
The brittle insect scrapes at the dry loam;
All is burnt up, used up, drawn up in air
To some ineffably rarefied solution . . .
Life is enlarged, drunk with annihilation,
And bitterness is sweet, and the spirit clear.

The dead lie easy, hidden in earth where they
Are warmed and have their mysteries burnt away.
Motionless noon, noon aloft in the blue
Broods on itself—a self-sufficient theme.
O rounded dome and perfect diadem,
I am what's changing secretly in you.

I am the only medium for your fears.
My penitence, my doubts, my baulked desires—
These are the flaw within your diamond pride . . .
But in their heavy night, cumbered with marble,
Under the roots of trees a shadow people
Has slowly now come over to your side.

To an impervious nothingness they're thinned,
For the red clay has swallowed the white kind;
Into the flowers that gift of life has passed.
Where are the dead?—their homely turns of speech,

L'art personnel, les âmes singulières?
La larve file où se formaient les pleurs.

Les cris aigus des filles chatouillées,
Les yeux, les dents, les paupières mouillées,
Le sein charmant qui joue avec le feu,
Le sang qui brille aux lèvres qui se rendent,
Les derniers dons, les doigts qui les défendent,
Tout va sous terre et rentre dans le jeu!

Et vous, grande âme, espérez-vous un songe
Qui n'aura plus ces couleurs de mensonge
Qu'aux yeux de chair l'onde et l'or font ici?
Chanterez-vous quand serez vaporeuse?
Allez! Tout fuit! Ma présence est poreuse,
La sainte impatience meurt aussi!

Maigre immortalité noire et dorée,
Consolatrice affreusement laurée,
Qui de la mort fais un sein maternel,
Le beau mensonge et la pieuse ruse!
Qui ne connaît, et qui ne les refuse,
Ce crâne vide et ce rire éternel!

Pères profonds, têtes inhabitées,
Qui sous le poids de tant de pelletées,
Êtes la terre et confondez nos pas,
Le vrai rongeur, le ver irréfutable
N'est point pour vous qui dormez sous la table,
Il vit de vie, il ne me quitte pas!

Amour, peut-être, ou de moi-même haine?
Sa dent secrète est de moi si prochaine
Que tous les noms lui peuvent convenir!
Qu'importe! Il voit, il veut, il songe, il touche!
Ma chair lui plaît, et jusque sur ma couche,
A ce vivant je vis d'appartenir!

The personal grace, the soul informing each?
Grubs thread their way where tears were once composed.

The bird-sharp cries of girls whom love is teasing,
The eyes, the teeth, the eyelids moistly closing,
The pretty breast that gambles with the flame,
The crimson blood shining when lips are yielded,
The last gift, and the fingers that would shield it—
All go to earth, go back into the game.

And you, great soul, is there yet hope in you
To find some dream without the lying hue
That gold or wave offers to fleshly eyes?
Will you be singing still when you're thin air?
All perishes. A thing of flesh and pore
Am I. Divine impatience also dies.

Lean immortality, all crêpe and gold,
Laurelled consoler frightening to behold,
Death is a womb, a mother's breast, you feign—
The fine illusion, oh the pious trick!
Who does not know them, and is not made sick—
That empty skull, that everlasting grin?

Ancestors deep down there, O derelict heads
Whom such a weight of spaded earth o'erspreads,
Who *are* the earth, in whom our steps are lost,
The real flesh-eater, worm unanswerable
Is not for you that sleep under the table:
Life is his meat, and I am still his host.

'Love,' shall we call him? 'Hatred of self,' maybe?
His secret tooth is so intimate with me
That any name would suit him well enough,
Enough that he can see, will, daydream, touch—
My flesh delights him, even upon my couch
I live but as a morsel of his life.

47

Zénon! Cruel Zénon! Zénon d'Élée!
M'as-tu percé de cette flèche ailée
Qui vibre, vole, et qui ne vole pas!
Le son m'enfante et la flèche me tue!
Ah! le soleil . . . Quelle ombre de tortue
Pour l'âme, Achille immobile à grands pas!

Non, non! . . . Debout! Dans l'ère successive!
Brisez, mon corps, cette forme pensive!
Buvez, mon sein, la naissance du vent!
Une fraîcheur, de la mer exhalée,
Me rend mon âme . . . O puissance salée!
Courons à l'onde en rejaillir vivant.

Oui! grande mer de delires douée,
Peau de panthère et chlamyde trouée,
De mille et mille idoles du soleil,
Hydre absolue, ivre de ta chair bleue,
Qui te remonds l'étincelante queue
Dans un tumulte au silence pareil

Le vent se leve! . . . il faut tenter de vivre!
L'air immense ouvre et referme mon livre,
La vague en poudre ose jaillir des rocs!
Envolez-vous, pages tout éblouies!
Rompez, vagues! Rompez d'eaux rejouies
Ce toit tranquille où picoraient des focs!

Zeno, Zeno, cruel philosopher Zeno,
Have you then pierced me with your feathered arrow
That hums and flies, yet does not fly! The sounding
Shaft gives me life, the arrow kills. Oh, sun!—
Oh, what a tortoise-shadow to outrun
My soul, Achilles' giant stride left standing!

No, no! Arise! The future years unfold.
Shatter, O body, meditation's mould!
And, O my breast, drink in the wind's reviving!
A freshness, exhalation of the sea,
Restores my soul . . . Salt-breathing potency!
Let's run at the waves and be hurled back to living!

Yes, mighty sea with such wild frenzies gifted
(The panther skin and the rent chlamys), sifted
All over with sun-images that glisten,
Creature supreme, drunk on your own blue flesh,
Who in a tumult like the deepest hush
Bite at your sequin-glittering tail—yes, listen!

The wind is rising! . . . We must try to live!
The huge air opens and shuts my book: the wave
Dares to explode out of the rocks in reeking
Spray. Fly away, my sun-bewildered pages!
Break, waves! Break up with your rejoicing surges
This quiet roof where sails like doves were pecking.

Translated by C. Day Lewis

PALME

À JEANNIE

De sa grâce redoutable
Voilant à peine l'éclat,
Un ange met sur ma table
Le pain tendre, le lait plat;
Il me fait de la paupière
Le signe d'une prière
Qui parle à ma vision:
—Calme, calme, reste calme!
Connais le poids d'une palme
Portant sa profusion!

Pour autant qu'elle se plie
A l'abondance des biens,
Sa figure est accomplie,
Ses fruits lourds sont ses liens.
Admire comme elle vibre,
Et comme une lente fibre
Qui divise le moment,
Départage sans mystère
L'attirance de la terre
Et le poids du firmament!

Ce bel arbitre mobile
Entre l'ombre et le soleil,
Simule d'une sibylle
La sagesse et le sommeil.
Autour d'une même place

PALM

TO JEANNIE

In the shadow of the blaze
Of his grace informed with dread,
An angel on my table lays
A bowl of milk, a loaf of bread;
And in his eyes reveals to me
The signal of a sacred plea
That speaks to my inner sight:
   Calm, calm, O stay calm!
Think how the heavy palm
Carries all her breadth and height!

In such measure as she may yield
To world's abundant benefits,
Her bodily form becomes fulfilled,
Her fruitfulness her bondage is.
Oh, admirable! that vibrant head!
How she, like slow fiber-thread
Partitioning its time of growth,
Divides without let or halt
The burden of the starry vault,
The fascination of the earth!

Beautiful, moving arbiter
Between the shadow and the sun,
She simulates the sybil, her
Sleep and sagacity in one.
The same place all surrounding,

51

L'ample palme ne se lasse
Des appels ni des adieux . . .
Qu'elle est noble, qu'elle est tendre!
Qu'elle est digne de s'attendre
A la seule main des dieux!

L'or léger qu'elle murmure
Sonne au simple doigt de l'air,
Et d'une soyeuse armure
Charge l'âme du désert.
Une voix impérissable,
Qu'elle rend au vent de sable
Qui l'arrose de ses grains,
A soi-même sert d'oracle,
Et se flatte du miracle,
Que se chantent les chagrins.

Cependant qu'elle s'ignore
Entre le sable et le ciel,
Chaque jour qui luit encore
Lui compose un peu de miel.
Sa douceur est mesurée
Par la divine durée
Qui ne compte pas les jours,
Mais bien qui les dissimule
Dans un suc où s'accumule
Tout l'arome des amours.

Parfois si l'on désespère,
Si l'adorable rigueur
Malgré tes larmes n'opère
Que sous ombre de langueur,
N'accuse pas d'être avare
Une Sage qui prépare
Tant d'or et d'autorité:
Par la sève solennelle

The full-blown palm accepts the abounding
Salutations and farewells . . .
What noble, what tender states!
With what good warrant she awaits
None but the god's sap in her cells!

The slight gold that is her murmur
Rings to the finger of the air,
And with plates of silken armor
Dresses the desert's soul for fair.
And the voice, time out of mind,
She gives back to the sandy wind
That sprinkles her with all its grain,
Becomes its own self's oracle,
And boasts about the miracle
Chanted by self-consuming pain.

While never she her self defines,
Between the sky and desert floor,
Every further day that shines
Accumulates her honey store.
Her sweetness is the piecemeal ration
Of all that divine duration
Which keeps no day-book of the days,
But dissembles them instead
In a juice that brings to a head
All love's aroma, all love's ways.

If that discipline, your cult,
From time to time, thawed in despair,
In spite of all your tears default
    Save in boredom's darkened air
Yet no miser is that wise
Tree that makes and multiplies
Such gold profusion with such sway:
Through the ceremonial sap

Une espérance éternelle
Monte à la maturité!

Ces jours qui te semblent vides
Et perdus pour l'univers
Ont des racines avides
Qui travaillent les déserts.
La substance chevelue
Par les ténèbres élue
Ne peut s'arrêter jamais
Jusqu'aux entrailles du monde,
De poursuivre l'eau profonde
Que demandent les sommets.

Patience, patience,
Patience dans l'azur!
Chaque atome de silence
Est la chance d'un fruit mûr!
Viendra l'heureuse surprise:
Une colombe, la brise,
L'ébranlement le plus doux,
Une femme qui s'appuie,
Feront tomber cette pluie
Où l'on se jette à genoux!

Qu'un peuple à présent s'écroule,
Palme! . . . irrésistiblement!
Dans la poudre qu'il se roule
Sur les fruits du firmament!
Tu n'as pas perdu ces heures,
Si légère tu demeures
Après ces beaux abandons;
Pareille à celui qui pense
Et dont l'âme se dépense
A s'accroître de ses dons!

To its fulfillment rises up
Hope that is of eternity!

These days that seem vain, all vain,
For all the universe, all lost,
Have roots that with their might and main
Labor through the sandy waste.
Substance, tough like hair created,
By dark chaos designated,
Never can its course prevent
To earth's very entrails, but
Those deep waters searches out
Which the lofty summits want.

Patience, patience be
In the blue vaults of the sky!
In each mote of silence see
The chance of its own ripeness lie!
Expect the fortunate surprise:
A dove, a light wind to rise,
The slightest variance from ease,
A woman leaning, the least strain,
Will release that blessed rain
In which we fall upon our knees!

Though a nation now collapse,
O Palm! . . . nor hope to rise again!
But down into the dust lapse
Among the shorn empyrean!
You have not lost this day and hour,
If you survive in buoyant flower
The negligence to which you bowed;
Like the man of thought whose soul
Consumes itself in growing whole
From gifts with which it is endowed!

Translated by Denis Devlin

CANTIQUE DES COLONNES

Douces colonnes, aux
Chapeaux garnis de jour,
Ornes de vrais oiseaux
Qui marchent sur le tour,

Douces colonnes, ô
L'orchestre de fuseaux!
Chacun immole son
Silence à l'unisson.

—Que portez-vous si haut,
Égales radieuses?
—Au désir sans défaut
Nos grâces studieuses!

Nous chantons à la fois
Que nous portons les cieux!
O seule et sage voix
Qui chantes pour les yeux!

Vois quels hymnes candides!
Quelle sonorité
Nos éléments limpides
Tirent de la clarté!

Si froides et dorées
Nous fûmes de nos lits

SONG OF THE COLUMNS

Sweet columns, with
Chaplets adorned with day,
Crowned with true birds, no myth,
That walk the stone-fledged way,

Sweet columns, O
The bobbins' orchestra!
Each one confides its own
Hush to the unison.

—What do you bear so high
Equal in radiance?
—For desire's faultless eye
Our studious elegance.

We sing by mutual choice
That we bear up the skies.
O sage and single voice
Singing for the eyes!

See what clear hymns!
What sonority
Our light-enamoured limbs
Draw from limpidity!

So chill, chased with dawn,
We from our beds early

Par le ciseau tirées,
Pour devenir ces lys!

De nos lits de cristal
Nous fûmes éveillées,
Des griffes de métal
Nous ont appareillées.

Pour affronter la lune,
La lune et le soleil,
On nous polit chacune
Comme l'ongle de l'orteil!

Servantes sans genoux,
Sourires sans figures,
La belle devant nous
Se sent les jambes pures,

Pieusement pareilles,
Le nez sous le bandeau
Et nos riches oreilles
Sourdes au blanc fardeau,

Un temple sur les yeux
Noirs pour l'éternité,
Nous allons sans les dieux
A la divinité!

Nos antiques jeunesses,
Chair mate et belles ombres,
Sont fières des finesses
Qui naissent par les nombres!

Filles des nombres d'or,
Fortes des lois du ciel,
Sur nous tombe et s'endort
Un dieu couleur de miel.

By the chisel were drawn
To become these lilies!

From our beds of cold crystal
We were awakened
Talons of metal
Gripped us and slackened.

To face the moon,
The moon and sun-glow,
We were polished each one
Like a nail of the toe!

Servant-maids inflexuous,
Smiles with no viewer,
The girl before us
Feels her legs pure.

Piously matched peers,
The nose beneath the string-course
And our rich ears
Deaf to the white load's force,

A temple on our eyes,
Dark for eternity,
Without the gods we rise
To that divinity!

Our antique youths,
Dull flesh, fair shades of mirth,
Are bright with subtle truths
Which numbers bring to birth.

Girls of the golden numbers,
Strong with heaven's laws and rod,
On us there falls and slumbers
A honey-colored god.

Il dort content, le Jour,
Que chaque jour offrons
Sur la table d'amour
Etale sur nos fronts.

Incorruptibles sœurs,
Mi-brûlantes, mi-fraîches,
Nous prîmes pour danseurs
Brises et feuilles sèches,

Et les siècles par dix,
Et les peuples passés,
C'est un profond jadis,
Jadis jamais assez!

Sous nos mêmes amours
Plus lourdes que le monde
Nous traversons les jours
Comme une pierre l'onde!

Nous marchons dans le temps
Et nos corps éclatants
Ont des pas ineffables
Qui marquent dans les fables . . . .

He sleeps at ease, the Day,
Whom every day with vows
We on love's table lay,
Slack-tided on our brows.

Incorruptible sisters,
Half fire, half cool as eves,
We took for dancers
Breezes and dry leaves,

And the centuries, by ten,
And the past peoples' tide,
It is a deep-found Then,
Then never satisfied!

Beneath our loves that raise
A weight than Earth more grave
Silent we cross the days
Like a stone the wave!

We walk in time, and these
Our dazzling bodies
Have steps ineffable
That mark in fable . . .

Translated by Vernon Watkins

LE RAMEUR

Penché contre un grand fleuve, infiniment mes rames
M'arrachent à regret aux riants environs;
Ame aux pesantes mains, pleines des avirons,
Il faut que le ciel cède au glas des lentes lames.

Le cœur dur, l'œil distrait des beautés que je bats,
Laissant autour de moi mûrir des cercles d'onde,
Je veux à larges coups rompre l'illustre monde
De feuilles et de feu que je chante tout bas.

Arbres sur qui je passe, ample et naïve moire,
Eau de ramages peinte, et paix de l'accompli,
Déchire-les, ma barque, impose-leur un pli
Qui coure du grand calme abolir la mémoire.

Jamais, charmes du jour, jamais vos grâces n'ont
Tant souffert d'un rebelle essayant sa défense:
Mais, comme les soleils m'ont tiré de l'enfance,
Je remonte à la source où cesse même un nom.

En vain toute la nymphe énorme et continue
Empêche de bras purs mes membres harassés;
Je romprai lentement mille liens glacés
Et les barbes d'argent de sa puissance nue.

Ce bruit secret des eaux, ce fleuve étrangement
Place mes jours dorés sous un bandeau de soie;
Rien plus aveuglément n'use l'antique joie
Qu'un bruit de fuite égale et de nul changement.

THE ROWER

Back bent to a great river slowly I pull
Plucking myself away from the smiling shores;
Soul with heavy hands, burdened with these oars
The sky must give way to the slow waters' knell.

Hard in heart, eyes turned from the beauty I beat,
While the rings around me widening swirled,
My long strokes shall shatter your famous world
Of leaves and of fire that I would celebrate.

Ample iridescence, trees whereon I glide,
Arabesqued water, and fulfilment's peace,
Cleave them, my boat, leave there your trace
So that of great calm no memory abide.

Never, charms of day, never your grace
Has suffered so much from a rebel's blow:
But, as the suns shone and made my childhood grow,
I row back to the source where even names cease.

In vain the vast nymph, embracing, infinite,
Restrains with pure arms my harassed hands;
I shall slowly break a thousand frozen bonds
And the silvery ripples of her naked might.

These discreet murmuring waters strangely place
Under a silken bandage my days of gold;
Nothing more blindly frays a joy that was of old
Than the sound of smooth flight, the untroubled pace.

Sous les ponts annelés, l'eau profonde me porte,
Voûtes pleines de vent, de murmure et de nuit,
Ils courent sur un front qu'ils écrasent d'ennui,
Mais dont l'os orgueilleux est plus dur que leur porte

Leur nuit passe longtemps. L'âme baisse sous eux
Ses sensibles soleils et ses promptes paupières,
Quand, par le mouvement qui me revêt de pierres,
Je m'enfonce au mépris de tant d'azur oiseux.

AU BOIS DORMANT

La princesse, dans un palais de rose pure,
Sous les murmures, sous la mobile ombre dort;
Et de corail ébauche une parole obscure
Quand les oiseaux perdus mordent ses bagues d'or.

Elle n'écoute ni les gouttes, dans leurs chutes,
Tinter d'un siècle vide au lointain le trésor,
Ni, sur la forêt vague, un vent fondu de flûtes
Déchirer la rumeur d'une phrase de cor.

Laisse, longue, l'écho rendormir la diane,
O toujours plus égale à la molle liane
Qui se balance et bat tes yeux ensevelis.

Si proche de ta joue et si lente la rose
Ne va pas dissiper ce délice de plis
Secrètement sensible au rayon qui s'y pose.

Beneath the ringed bridges, borne by waters in spate
I drift where the wind and night-whispers tease,
They straddle a brow they crush with weariness,
But whose arrogant bone is harder than their gate.

Their night is slow to pass. The soul lets through
Its responsive eyelids, its sensitive suns,
When, in the movement that covers me with stones,
I plunge in defiance of all this idle blue.

Translated by W. J. Strachan

THE SLEEPING BEAUTY

In a palace of pale-rose purity she sleeps,
The princess, in leaf-animated murmurings;
Sometimes a half-heard utterance in coral shapes
Itself, when random birds peck at her golden rings.

She listens neither to the tinkling water-sounds
Of treasure hidden in a wilderness of days,
Nor, on the far-off forests, to flute-blended winds
That tear these ruminations with a horn's clear phrase,

Let lingering echoes lull the dawn-stirred sleeper,
You who resemble more and more the soft creeper
That waves and gently beats upon your shrouded eyes.

The slow-petalled rose that hangs so close to your cheek
Will never squander those in-folded treasuries
That blush in secret when the sun's rays on them break.

Translated by James Kirkup

HÉLÈNE

Azur! c'est moi . . . Je viens des grottes de la mort
Entendre l'onde se rompre aux degrés sonores,
Et je revois les galères dans les aurores
Ressusciter de l'ombre au fil des rames d'or.

Mes solitaires mains appellent les monarques
Dont la barbe de sel amusait mes doigts purs;
Je pleurais. Ils chantaient leurs triomphes obscurs
Et les golfes enfouis aux poupes de leurs barques,

J'entends les conques profondes et les clairons
Militaires rythmer le vol des avirons;
Le chant clair des rameurs enchaîne le tumulte,

Et les Dieux, à la proue héroïque exaltés
Dans leur sourire antique et que l'écume insulte
Tendent vers moi leurs bras indulgents et sculptés.

INTÉRIEUR

Une esclave aux longs yeux chargés de molles chaînes
Change l'eau de mes fleurs, plonge aux glaces prochaines,
Au lit mystérieux prodigue ses doigts purs;
Elle met une femme au milieu de ces murs
Qui, dans ma rêverie errant avec décence,
Passe entre mes regards sans briser leur absence,
Comme passe le verre au travers du soleil,
Et de la raison pure épargne l'appareil.

HELEN, THE SAD QUEEN

Azure, 'tis I, come from Elysian shores,
To hear the waves break on sonorous steps,
And see again the sunrise full of ships,
Rising from darkness upon golden oars.

My solitary arms call on the kings
Whose salty beards amused my silver hands.
I wept; they sang of triumphs in far lands,
And gulfs fled backwards upon watery wings.

I hear the trumpet and martial horn
That wield the rhythm of the beating blade,
The song of rowers binding the tumult.

And the gods! exalting on the prow with scorn
Their ancient smile that the slow waves insult,
Hold out their sculptured arms to my sad shade.

Translated by Janet Lewis

INTERIOR

A slave with slant eyes weighed down by subtle fetters
Changes the water in the vases, in mirrors
Swims, lavishes on the mysterious bed her pure
Caress; brings a woman into this enclosure
Who, moving unobtrusively across my dream
Passes before my eyes yet does not break their calm
Withdrawal, as a glass will move across the sun
Simply, without the mechanicals of reason.

Translated by James Kirkup

LES VAINES DANSEUSES

Celles qui sont des fleurs légères sont venues,
Figurines d'or et beautés toutes menues
Où s'irise une faible lune . . . Les voici
Mélodieuses fuir dans le bois éclairci.
De mauves et d'iris et de nocturnes roses
Sont les grâces de nuit sous leurs danses écloses.
Que de parfums voilés dispensent leurs doigts d'or!
Mais l'azur doux s'effeuille en ce bocage mort
Et de l'eau mince luit à peine, reposée
Comme un pâle trésor d'une antique rosée
D'où le silence en fleur monte . . . Encor les voici
Mélodieuses fuir dans le bois éclairci.
Aux calices aimés leurs mains sont gracieuses;
Un peu de lune dort sur leurs lèvres pieuses
Et leurs bras merveilleux aux gestes endormis
Aiment à dénouer sous les myrtes amis
Leurs liens fauves et leurs caresses . . . Mais certaines,
Moins captives du rythme et des harpes lointaines,
S'en vont d'un pas subtil au lac enseveli
Boire des lys l'eau frêle où dort le pur oubli.

THE EXQUISITE DANCERS

They who are delicate as flowers are come,
Figures of golden loveliness, minute and slim.
The frail moon throws its rainbows round them . . . Here they come,
Melodious and fleet through the wood's lighted gloom.
Mallow and iris and the deep nocturnal rose
In the dark at their dancing like graces arise.
What scented mists trail from their golden fingertips!
The azure sky is bare above this barren copse
And scarcely gleams the shallow lake, reposing now
Like some vague treasure fallen with a long-lost dew,
Wearing a flowered stillness . . . Once again, they come
Melodious and fleet through the wood's lighted gloom.
Their hands are gracious to the cherished flower-cups,
A thread of moonlight sleeps on their devoted lips,
And their enchanting arms that move with dreamy grace
Unravel lovingly, beneath the myrtle's boughs
Their tawny tresses and the trees' caress . . . But some,
Less bound by the remoteness of the harps' strange rhythm,
Steal on pointed feet towards the lake's shrouded fan,
To drink the lily-dew of pure oblivion.

Translated by James Kirkup

LA CEINTURE

Quand le ciel couleur d'une joue
Laisse enfin les yeux le chérir
Et qu'au point doré de périr
Dans les roses le temps se joue,

Devant le muet de plaisir
Qu'enchaîne une telle peinture,
Danse une Ombre à libre ceinture
Que le soir est près de saisir.

Cette ceinture vagabonde
Fait dans le souffle aérien
Frémir le suprême lien
De mon silence avec ce monde . . .

Absent, présent . . . Je suis bien seul,
Et sombre, ô suave linceul!

THE CINCTURE

When the sky, color of a cheek,
at last lets my eyes enjoy it,
and turning gold at the moment of dying,
time plays among the roses,

before the dumb contemplative
whom such a painting ravishes,
there dances a free-cinctured Shadow
which evening is waiting to seize.

This wandering cincture sets trembling
in the light breath of the air
the ultimate tie that is holding
my silence to the world . . .

Absent and present . . . I am alone
and somber, O soft cerement!

Translated by C. F. MacIntyre and J. Laughlin

LE SYLPHE

Ni vu ni connu
Je suis le parfum
Vivant et défunt
Dans le vent venu!

Ni vu ni connu,
Hasard ou génie?
A peine venu
La tâche est finie!

Ni lu ni compris?
Aux meilleurs esprits
Que d'erreurs promises!

Ni vu ni connu,
Le temps d'un sein nu
Entre deux chemises!

THE SYLPH

Unseen unknown
I am the perfume
Living and dead
Come in the wind!

Unseen unknown,
Luck or genius?
Barely come
The task is done!

Neither read nor understood?
How many errors promised
To the best spirits!

Unseen unknown,
The moment of a naked breast
Between two robes!

Translated by Lloyd Alexander

LES PAS

Tes pas, enfants de mon silence,
Saintement, lentement placés,
Vers le lit de ma vigilance
Procèdent muets et glacés.

Personne pure, ombre divine,
Qu'ils sont doux, tes pas retenus!
Dieux! . . . tous les dons que je devine
Viennent à moi sur ces pieds nus!

Si, de tes lèvres avancées,
Tu prépares pour l'apaiser,
A l'habitant de mes pensées
La nourriture d'un baiser,

Ne hâte pas cet acte tendre,
Douceur d'être et de n'être pas,
Car j'ai vécu de vous attendre,
Et mon cœur n'était que vos pas.

THE FOOTSTEPS

Born of my voiceless time, your steps
Slowly, ecstatically advance:
Toward my expectation's bed
They move in a hushed, ice-clear trance.

Pure being, shadow-shape divine—
Your step deliberate, how sweet!
God!—every gift I have imagined
Comes to me on those naked feet.

If so it be your offered mouth
Is shaped already to appease
That which occupied my thought
With the live substance of a kiss,

Oh hasten not this loving act,
Rapture where self and not-self meet:
My life has been the awaiting you,
Your footfall was my own heart's beat.

Translated by C. Day Lewis

LA FAUSSE MORTE

Humblement, tendrement, sur le tombeau charmant,
    Sur l'insensible monument,
Que d'ombres, d'abandons, et d'amour prodiguée,
    Forme ta grâce fatiguée,
Je meurs, je meurs sur toi, je tombe et je m'abats,

Mais à peine abattu sur le sépulcre bas,
Dont la close étendue aux cendres me convie,
Cette morte apparente, en qui revient la vie,
Frémit, rouvre les yeux, m'illumine et me mord,
Et m'arrache toujours une nouvelle mort
    Plus précieuse que la vie.

LIFE IN DEATH

Humbly, tenderly, on the charming monument,
    The tomb that never will relent,
Where love's profusions, surrenderings and shadows
    Give fresh grace to your tired pose,
I die, I die upon you, fall, and rise no more.

But scarcely have I touched this dim, low sepulchre
Whose sheltered vastness invites to ashen death,
Look, in the body that was left for dead, the breath
Returns, she trembles, lifts her eyes, illuminates
With laughing teeth—but always with renewed death waits,
More precious to me now than life.

Translated by James Kirkup

THE YOUNG MOTHER

This afternoon of the sunniest season of the year, is ready to burst like a ripe orange.

The garden in the fullness of its vigour, the light, life, are slowly passing through the period of the perfection of their being. It is as though all things from the beginning had been engaged only in bringing to maturity this splendour of an instant. Happiness is visible like the sun.

The young mother, in the cheeks of the little child she is holding, breathes in her own purest substance. She presses him to her so that he shall remain always herself.

She embraces the being she has made. She forgets and rejoices at having given herself, since she has retrieved and found herself again in the tender contact of the intoxicating freshness of his flesh. And vainly those beautiful hands squeeze the fruit she has formed, she feels herself pure, through and through, and like a virgin fulfilled.

Her heedless eyes caress the leaves, the flowers, and all the splendour of the world.

She is like a Philosopher and a natural Sage who has found his idea and who has constructed what he required.

She is not sure whether the center of the universe is in her heart or in this little heart that is beating in her arms and that, in its turn, brings all things to life.

Translated by Louise Varèse

HOW CALM THE HOUR IS . . .

How calm the hour is, and the early end of the night, how delicately colored! Shutters pushed aside to the right and to the left with the vigorous
gesture of a swimmer, I plunge into the ecstasy of space. It is pure, it is
virgin, it is sweet and holy. I salute you, grandeur proffered to all the acts of
a look, beginning of perfect transparency! What an event for the spirit, such
an expanse! I should like, O all things, to bless you, if I only knew! . . .
On the balcony that tenders itself above the leaves, on the threshold of the
first hour, on the threshold of all that is possible, I sleep and I wake, I am
day and night, lingeringly I offer an infinite love, an immeasurable fear.
The soul quenches its thirst at time's spring, drinks a little dusk, a little
dawn, feels itself to be a sleeping woman, an angel made of light; com-
munes with itself, grows sad, and flees in the shape of a bird to the half-
naked height whose rock pierces, flesh and gold, right through the nocturnal blue. An orange tree is breathing there in the shadow. Very high,
only a few delicate stars still subsist at the ultimate treble. That fragment
of melting ice is the moon. I know only too well (all at once) that a gray-
haired child is contemplating old sadnesses, half dead, half deified, in
that celestial object made of a sparkling and dying substance, tender
and cold, which is going gradually to dissolve.

I look at it as though I were not really in my heart. My former youth
used to yearn and feel tears rising at the same hour and under the same
spell of the vanishing moon. My youth has seen the same morning, and I
see myself by the side of my youth . . . Divided, how can one pray?
How can one pray when another oneself would be listening to the prayer?
—That is why one should only pray in unknown words. Render enigma
to enigma, enigma for enigma. Lift what is mystery in yourself to what
is mystery in itself. There is something in you that is equal to what
surpasses you.

Translated by Louise Varèse

THE BATH

In the pure and shining sarcophagus, sweet water reposes, warm and perfect, bride of the body's form. Light and free, the nude settles down and is assuaged. Everything is easy in the fluid where the exempted legs are as alive as arms. Here man has laid his stature down; here he has glided his whole length into which his height has changed; he stretches out until he reaches the limit of his own extent; he feels commensurate with his feeling of his capacity to relax. Blissfully he changes his point of support; one finger holds him and lifts him; and his floating powers, half melted in the calm mass of the water, dream of algae and angels. The weight of the blessedly bathed flesh is almost imperceptible; the heat of the blood being hardly different from that of the contiguous water, the blood spreads out under every inch of skin. The living body is hardly distinguishable from that formless body whose substance is constantly taking its place. A person is mixed with the indefinite plenitude that surrounds him; someone feels himself being gently dissolved. The whole body is now only a pleasant dream that the mind vaguely dreams. The sweet moment looks at itself and through the window of the water sees limpid limbs. What is looking at and what is speaking to oneself is astonished at the size and the symmetry of the limbs over which it rises; and the thinking head is amused by a foot that has appeared far away and that obeys it as by magic. It observes a toe that bends, sticking out of the water, a knee emerging and disappearing into the transparency, like an oceanic island that a whim of the sea bottom intermittently unwaves and hides again. The will itself and the general freedom of the being are calmed in the comfort of the water. Perhaps in the vapid and vaporous air there is a perfume whose complex flower stirs memories, caresses or colors the indistinct desires of the naked being. Eyes waver and close. Without contacts, duration disappears. The mind opens its veins in a dream.

Translated by Louise Varèse

AS ON THE SHORE OF THE OCEAN

As on the shore of the ocean
On the front of separation,
On the pendulous frontier of motion
Time gives, takes back,
Strikes, deploys,
Vomits, gulps back,
Gives and regrets,
Fingers, falls, kisses and moans,
Returns to the mass,
Returns to the ocean . . .

I plunge into the interval of two waves.—
Time regretfully
Finite, infinite . . .
What does this time enclose?
What shrinks, what bridles?
What measures, refuses and snatches time away from me again?
Imposing impotence to go beyond, O wave!
The very sequence of your act is to take back,
To flow back so as not to break
The integrity of the water's body!

To remain sea and not to cede
The power of motion!
Fated to flow back
Rasping, regretfully,
To be reduced, to be restored,
To be transformed into immutable number.

As idea to the body returns,
As thought from the point falls
Where its secret cause,
Having dared and lifted it,
It cannot but return
To the pure and simple presence,
To all things less itself,
Even though not itself,
Itself never for long,
Never long enough
Either to be done with all things,
Or to begin other times . . .
It will always be for another time!
For the next and for the other time,
An infinity of times!
Disorder of times!

Listen endlessly, hear
The song of waiting and the shock of time,
The constant rocking of the reckoning,
Identity and quantity,
And the voice of the ocean
Reiterating: I win and lose,
I lose and win . . .
Oh! fling a little time outside of time!

More than alone on the shore of the ocean,
I give myself like a wave
To the monotonous transmutation
Of water into water,
Myself into myself . . .

Translated by Louise Varèse

PSALM ON A VOICE

Half whispering,
In a soft voice and a faint voice saying great things:
Important, astonishing, profound and true things,
In a soft voice and a faint voice.
The menace of thunder, the presence of absolutes.
In the voice of a robin-red-breast,
In the delicate defining of a flute and the fineness of pure sound.
The whole sun suggested
By means of a half smile,
(O whisper)
And a sort of murmur
In infinitely pure French

Anyone not catching the words, anyone hearing them at a distance,
Would have thought he was saying light nothings.
And they were nothings for the ear
Reassured . . .
But that contrast and that music,
That voice scarcely wrinkling the air,
That power in a whisper,
Those perspectives, those discoveries,
Those abysses and those guessed-at maneuvers,

That smile dismissing the universe! . . .

I think too in the end
Of the sound of silk alone and discreet
Of a fire creating the whole room as it burns itself out,
And that talks to itself
Or that talks to me
Almost for itself . . .

Translated by Louise Varèse

SONG OF THE MASTER-IDEA

Up! To your feet! Leap! Listen!
Listen! Awake! Break your chains! Be!
Come out of the shades, out of limbus, regions eternal, O, remote in com-
plete immobility,
Tear yourself from the night, from peace, emerge,
Spread your elbows, fingers, and hands, stretch! yawn!
Up! Up! Steel yourself that your strength may appear! Grit your teeth,
Refashion a statue, a stature, be ready! legs your support!
And let your eyes be a crown of clearest eyes.
Crown yourself. Order your glance. Feel yourself
Wholly the instrument of this day that begins and the act
That demands you.
I who call you, I am nothing without you.
I, the Idea,
Who with you am all powerful,
I was in your shade and in your formation.
I was scattered, near and far (like a drop of wine in a keg of clear water)
In your substance.
Come to my aid! Be the flesh and the frame,
Be my form, eyes, tongue and hams,
Be so that I may be! Be in order to be!
Obey so that I may be the command that you speak.
My voice is your voice and you recognize
My will. But you want . . . ME! The Idea!

II

At first I was not. Later I was born among your thoughts,
Only one among many. Innate, vague.

But now you are not yourself altogether,
Yourself, your life, your blood, your fears, your hours, your voice,
Only the slave of the favorable occasion, my chance!
I am the only idea conformable to your being, and you
Are the man for me.
You are my chance, I am your ruin, unique and immortal
I came to you in the agitation of your mind, haphazard,
But other hazards and another face of things
Made you, as it were, for me.
Be off! Give chase! Run after the one who quickens you!
You are going to mistake me for yourself, you will think I am yourself.
You will fall only over an object that is hidden . . .
Your eyes will see what I want to see.
Your ordinary intelligence will amaze itself;
It will discover such ways that to yourself you will seem mad.
You will say what surprises you. You will find yourself, having done
Your utmost.
You will not understand your own perspicacity.
You will find excuses for your clairvoyance and your strength.
You will be ashamed to have gained such gains,
And humbly you will murmur miracles! . . .

III

And yet, Oh! what a miracle for me,
This decrepit body, this sickly individual,
This failing health,
These nerves forever irritated with themselves, these are exactly what I
    needed!
What a miracle that caused me to be! O circumstance, Human,
Only chance!
So many other men have not possessed me.
I have found in your structure and in your substance
The hour, the being, the hour of being and the being of the hour!
The coincidence of your memories, of the kind of day it was,
Of the nature of your sleep, of your leisure and of your manias,

I have found
My nourishment in your weaknesses,
My possibilities in your ignorances,
An opportunity in your disgusts . . .
Now we belong to each other. We are indistinguishable.
This is love!
You are my *Mad-One-because-of-me:* YOUR IDEA.

Translated by Louise Varèse

PROSE

FRAGMENTS FROM "INTRODUCTION TO THE METHOD OF LEONARDO DA VINCI"

Since mind has found no limit to its activity, and since no idea marks the end of the business of consciousness, it must most likely perish in some incomprehensible climax foreshadowed and prepared by those terrors and odd sensations of which I have spoken; they give us glimpses of worlds that are unstable and incompatible with fullness of life: inhuman worlds, feeble worlds, worlds comparable to those that the mathematician calls forth when he plays with axioms, the physicist when he postulates *constants,* other than those admitted. Between the clarity of life and the simplicity of death, dreams, anxieties, ecstasies, all the semi-impossible values and transcendental or irrational solutions into the equation of knowledge, all these form curious stages, variations, phases that it is beyond words to describe—for there are no names for those things amongst which one is completely alone.

As the elusive art of music unites the liberties of sleep with the development and consistency of extreme attention and makes a synthesis of intimate things which last only a moment, so the fluctuations of the psychic equilibrium give one a glimpse of deviating modes of existence. We have in us forms of sensibility which, though they may be born, may not develop. They are instants snatched from the implacable criticism of the passage of time; they cannot survive if our being is to function fully: either we perish or they disperse. But they are monsters full of lessons for us, these monsters of the intelligence, these transitory stages, these spaces in which the continuity, the relation, the mobility we know, are altered; empires in which illumination is associated with sorrow; powerhouses where the orientation of fears and desires sends us on strange circuits; matter which consists of time; abysses literally of sorrow, or love, or quietude; regions curiously attached to themselves; non-Archimedean realms which defy movement; perpetuities in a flash of lightning; surfaces that shape themselves to our nausea, bend under our lightest decisions. . . . One cannot say that they are real; one cannot say that they are not real. Who has not experience of them does not know the value of natural intelligence and of even the most ordinary environment; he does not understand the true fragility of the world—which has no relation to so simple a thing as our alternative of being or not being. The wonder is not that things should be; it is that there should be such things and not such other things. *The image of this world* is part of a family of images, an infinite group, all the elements of which we possess—but unconsciously—consciousness of possession is the secret of the inventors.

*

The consciousness as it emerges from these gaps, these personal deviations in which weakness and the presence of poisons in the nervous system, but also the power as well as the subtlety of the attention and a most exquisite logic, a cultivated mysticism, all, severally, direct it, the consciousness, then, comes to suspect all accustomed reality of being only one solution amongst many others of universal problems. It tells itself that things should be somewhat different from what they are without its being very different from itself. It dares to consider its body and its world as almost arbitrary restrictions imposed on the range of its functions. It sees itself as corresponding, or as responding, not to a world, but to some system of a higher order the elements of which may themselves be worlds. It is capable of more interior combinations than are necessary for living; it judges itself deeper than the abyss of physical life and death. And this attitude to its own position cannot react back on itself, so far is it withdrawn, placed beyond all things, so much has it applied itself to the task *of never figuring in anything that it might imagine or agree to*. It has become no more than a dark body which absorbs everything and gives out nothing.

Drawing from these exact observations and from these inevitable pretensions a dangerous boldness; strong in this type of independence and unchangingness that it has to admit it possesses, it postulates itself in the end as the direct heir and image of that being that has no form, no origin, on which devolves, to which is related, the whole effort of the cosmos. A little more and it will admit as necessary existences only two entities, both of them essentially unknown: itself and *X;* both of them abstracted from everything, implicated in everything, implicating everything; equal and consubstantial.

The man who has been led by a mind that works tirelessly to this contact with living shadows, to this point of pure being, sees himself naked and destitute, reduced to the supreme poverty of power without a purpose, victim, masterpiece, perfection of simplification and dialectic order; his state comparable to that reached by the richest mind when it has become assimilated to itself, when it has recognized itself and consummated itself in a little group of characters and symbols. The work which we devote to the object of our reflections he has expended on the subject which reflects.

He is no longer concerned to choose or to create, to maintain or to develop himself. There is nothing to conquer. There cannot even be question of destroying himself. Genius is now entirely consumed, cannot be used to any further purpose. It was no more than a means to attain to the last simplicity. There is no act of genius which would not be *less* than the act of being. An imbecile is created and informed by a magnificent law; the most powerful mind finds nothing better than itself.

To sum up, being constrained to define itself by the sum of things and excess of knowledge over the sum of things, this perfected consciousness, which, to establish itself, has to begin by denying an infinite number of faiths, an infinite number of elements, and by exhausting the objects of its force without exhausting the force itself, this perfected consciousness differs as little as could be wished from nothingness. It reminds one absurdly of an audience invisible in the darkness of a theater which cannot see itself, which can see only the spectacle before it, and which, yet, all the time, invincibly feels itself the center of a breathlessly interesting evening. It is complete, impenetrable, absolute night; but filled with things, eager, secretly organized, made up of organisms which limit and compress themselves; a compact night, its shadows packed with organisms which live, breathe, warm themselves and which defend, each according to its nature, their places and functions. Before this intense, mysterious assembly, are all the things of sensibility, intelligibility, possibility, glittering and moving in an enclosed framework. Nothing can be born, die, or exist in any degree, or have time, place, form or meaning, except on this stage which the fates have circumscribed, and having separated which, from nobody knows what primordial confusion, as on the first day darkness was separated from light, they have opposed and subordinated to the condition of *being seen*. . . .

If I have brought the reader to this solitude and to this desperate clarity, it is because it was very necessary to carry the idea that I have formed of intellectual power to its ultimate consequences. The human characteristic is consciousness; the characteristic of consciousness is a process of perpetual exhaustion, of detachment without rest or exclusion from everything that comes before it, whatever that thing may be—an inexhaustible activity, independent of the quality as of the quantity of the things which appear and by means of which the man of intellect must at last bring himself deliberately to an unqualified refusal to be anything whatsoever.

All phenomena being thus regarded with a sort of equal repulsion and as rejected successively by an identical gesture, appear to be, in a certain sense, equivalent to each other. Feelings and thoughts are included in the uniform condemnation extended to all that can be perceived. It must be quite understood that nothing is exempted from the rigor of this exhaustion, that our attention should suffice to put our most intimate feelings on the same plane as exterior objects and events; from the moment that they become observable they go to join the rest of observed things.

Color, grief, memories; surprises and things expected; the tree outside, the rustling of its leaves, its yearly change, its shadow as well as its substance, its accidents of shape and position, the far-off thoughts that it brings back to my wandering attention—*all these things are equal.* . . . All things are replaceable by all things—may not this be the definition of *things?*

It is impossible that the activity of the mind should not in the end force it to this ultimate, elementary consideration. Its multiplied movements, its intimate struggles, its perturbations, its analytic returns on itself—do these leave anything unchanged? Is there anything that resists the lure of the senses, the dissipation of ideas, the fading of memories, the slow variation of the organism, the incessant and multiform activities of the universe? There is only this consciousness, and this consciousness only at its most abstract.

Our *personality* itself, which, stupidly, we take to be our most intimate and deepest *possession,* our sovereign good, is only a thing, and mutable and accidental in comparison with this other most naked ego; since we can think about it, calculate its interests, even lose sight of them a little, it is therefore no more than a secondary psychological divinity that lives in our looking-glass and answers to our name. It belongs to the order of Penates. It is subject to pain, greedy for incense like false gods; and, like them, it is food for worms. It expands when praised. It does not resist the power of wine, the charm of words, the sorcery of music. It admires itself, and through self-admiration becomes docile and easily led. It is lost in the masquerade and yields itself strangely to the anamorphosis of sleep. And further, it is painfully obliged to recognize that it has equals, to admit that it is *inferior* to some—a bitter and inexplicable experience for it, this.

Besides, everything convinces it that it is a mere phenomenon; that it must figure with all the accidental facts of the world amongst statistics and tables; that it had its beginning in a seminal chance, a microscopic incident; that it has run thousands of millions of risks; that it has been shaped by a number of happenings and that, however much it may be admirable, free, acknowledged, brilliant, it is, in sum, the effect of an incalculable disorder.

Each person being a sport of nature, a *jeu de l'amour et du hasard,* the most beautiful purpose and even the most learned thought of this recreated creature inevitably recall his origin. His activities are always relative, his masterpieces are fortuitous. He thinks mortally, individually, by fits and starts; and he finds the best of his ideas in casual and secret circumstances which he refrains from making public. Besides, he is not sure of being positively *some one,* he disguises and denies, more easily than he affirms, himself. Drawing from his own inconsistency some strength and much vanity, he puts his most cherished moments into fictions. He lives by romance, sees himself in a thousand roles. . . . His hero is never himself. . . .

And finally he passes nine-tenths of his time in what has yet to happen, in that which no longer is, in what cannot possibly be; to such an extent that our true *present* has nine chances out of ten of never being.

But all the time each private life possesses, deep down as a treasure, the fundamental permanence of consciousness which depends on nothing. And as the ear catches and loses and catches again, and loses again through all the varying movement of a symphony some grave and persistent *motif* which ceases to be heard from moment to moment, but which never ceases to be there—so the pure *ego,* the unique and continuous element in each being in the world, rediscovering itself and then losing itself again, inhabits our intelligence eternally; this deep *note* of existence itself dominates the whole complication of circumstance and change in existence from the moment that it is heard.

Is it not the chief and secret achievement of the greatest mind to isolate this substantial permanence from the strife of everyday truths? Is it not essential that in spite of everything he shall arrive at self-definition by means of this pure relationship, changeless amongst the most diverse objects, which will give him an almost inconceivable universality, give him, in a sense, the power of a corresponding universe? It is not his cherished self that he elevates to so high a degree, since by thinking about it he has renounced it, and has substituted for it in the place of subject this *ego* which is unqualified, which has no name, no history, which is no more sensitive, no less real than the center of gravity of a planetary system or ring, but which is a result of the whole—whatever that whole may be . . .

A moment since, and the obvious purpose of this wonderful intellectual life was still to astonish itself. Its preoccupation was to produce offspring that it could admire; it limited itself to what is most beautiful, most sweet, most bright, most substantial; and it was untroubled—save for its resemblance to other existing organisms, the strangest problem that one can propound to oneself; which is put to us by the existence of those who resemble us, and which consists simply in the possible existence of other intelligences, in the plurality of the singular, in the contradictory coexistence of lives independent amongst themselves *tot capita, tot tempora* —a problem comparable to the physical problems of *relativity* but infinitely more difficult.

But now, carried away by his anxiety to be unique and guided by his ardor for omnipotence, this same being has passed beyond all creations, all works, beyond even his greatest designs at the same time that he has put away from him all tenderness for himself and all preference for his own desires. He immolates, in one instant, his individuality. He feels himself pure consciousness; and two of that cannot exist. He is the *I,* the pronoun of universality, the name of *that* which has no relation to appearance. Oh, to what a point has pride been transformed! How it has arrived at a position that it did not even know it was seeking! How temperate the reward of its triumphs! A life so firmly directed, and which has treated as obstacles to be avoided or to be mastered all the objects it could propose to itself, must, after all, have attained an unassailable end, not an end to its duration, but an end within itself. Its pride has brought it as far as this. And here its pride is consumed. Pride, which conducted it, leaves it, astonished, naked, infinitely simple at the pole of its treasures.

II

I propose to imagine a man whose activities seem so distinct from each other that if I can find a unifying idea of them it may well seem more comprehensive than all other ideas. I wish him to have an abnormally lively perception of the difference between things—the adventures of such a perception could well be described as analysis. Everything interests him. It is of the universe that he thinks always. And he thinks of rigor.[1] He is so made that he misses nothing of all that enters into the tangle of what exists—not a single shrub. He goes down into the depth of that which is for all men to see, but there he wanders away and studies himself. He learns the habits and organizations of nature, works on them from every angle. And he comes to be the only man who constructs, calculates, sets in motion. He leaves behind him churches and fortresses; he fashions ornaments—full of sweetness and strength—and a thousand machines; and he makes rigorous calculation along many unsurveyed lines. He leaves the remains of no one knows what great playthings. In these pastimes mixed up with his scientific studies—themselves constituting something not distinguishable from passion—he has the charm of always seeming to be thinking of something else. I shall follow him through the rude unity and density of the world, where he will become so familiar with nature that, in order to keep in contact with it he will imitate it, and will finish by finding it difficult to conceive an object which is not in nature.

It remains to give a name to this creature of thought in order to set a limit to the elaboration of terms ordinarily too far apart and likely to escape from any attempt to associate them. No name seems to me more suitable than that of Leonardo da Vinci. Whoever imagines a tree to himself must also imagine a sky or a background against which to see

[1] *Hostinato rigore*, obstinate rigor. Leonardo's motto.

it standing. That is logic of a kind that is almost self-evident and almost unrealized. The figure I imagine reduces himself to an inference of this nature. Little of what I say of him must be considered as applicable to the man who has made the name illustrious: I am not following up a coincidence that seems to me impossible to make clear. I am trying to express a point of view with regard to the detail of an intellectual life, to make one suggestion as to the methods which every discovery implies, one chosen amongst the multitude of things that may be imagined, a model, that may well be thought a rough one but in every way preferable to strings of doubtful anecdotes, to commentaries in the catalogues of art collections, to dates—erudition of that sort would only falsify the purely hypothetical aim of this essay. I am not altogether ignorant of such matters, but them, above all, I must refrain from discussing, in order not to cause confusion between a surmise as to conditions that are quite general and the outward fragments of a personality which has vanished to a point where we are given—by the fragments—the certitude that we can never know it better.

Many an error which distorts the judgements made on human achievements is due to a singular forgetfulness of their genesis. One forgets often that they have not always been in existence. From which has arisen a kind of reciprocal coquetry of silence on the part of artists as to the origins of their work—to the extent of too carefully hiding them even. We fear that they are humble, these origins, even that they are mere nature. And though very few artists have the courage to say how they produced their work, I believe that there are not many more who take the risk of understanding it themselves. Such understanding commences with the very difficult abandonment of the notion of glory, of the laudatory epithet; it tolerates no idea of superiority, no delusion of greatness. It leads to the discovery of the relative beneath the apparent perfection. And it is necessary if we are not to believe that minds are as profoundly different as their products make them appear. For example, certain works of science, and mathematical works in particular, show such clarity in their construction that one would say that they were not the work of any person at all. There is something *unhuman* about them. And this quality has had the effect of making people suppose so great a difference between certain studies, as, for instance, between the sciences and the arts, that, owing to it, opinion has also assumed a separation between the minds devoted to

96

each, as complete as that which seems to exist between the results of their labors. These labors, however, only differ as variations from a common basis, differ in what of it they include and what of it they leave out in forming their languages and their symbols. One must, therefore, have some distrust of books and explanations that seem too clear. We are deceived by what is definite; and then what is made specially to be looked at changes its aspect in our eyes and takes on a nobler air. It is when working on movements which are still irresolute, unstilled, which may not either be called diversions or laws, works of art or theorems, movements which, when completed, lose their likeness to each other, that the operations of the mind can be of use to us.

Interiorly there is a drama. 'Drama,' 'adventure,' 'agitation,' all words of this kind may be used, provided that they be numerous and that one is corrected by the other. This drama, like the plays of Menander, is often lost. Nevertheless we have the manuscripts of Leonardo, the celebrated notes of Pascal. These fragments command attention. They help us to divine through what intellectual somersaults, what odd intrusion of human affairs, what repeated sensations, after what immense passages of languor, the shadows, the specters that presage their future works, show themselves to men. It suffices, without resorting to such outstanding examples as might imply the possibility of making the mistakes that attach to the study of exceptions, to study someone who believes himself alone and abandons himself to himself, who *recoils* before an idea; grasps it; denies, smiles or shrinks back—acting, as it were, the curious character of his own variety. It is the way madmen behave before the world.

Such examples relate definite, measurable, physical movements immediately to the personal comedy of which I spoke. The actors in this drama are mental images, and it is easy to understand that if the peculiarities of these images be eliminated, and if only their succession, frequency, periodicity, their diverse capacities for association, and, finally, their duration, be studied, one is at once tempted to find analogies in what is called the material world, to compare them with scientific analyses, to give them an environment, a continuity, properties of displacement, of speed, and then mass and energy. One comes to the conclusion that many such systems are possible, that no one of them is worth more than another, and that the use of them—which is important since it always throws light on something—ought to be at every instant under supervision and its purely verbal role kept in mind. For, in reality, analogy is only the faculty of varying the images, of combining them, of making part of one coexist with part of another and perceiving, voluntarily or otherwise, the similarities in their construction. And that renders it impossible to describe the mind which is their world. Here words lose their virtue. It is here that they are formed and spring to the mind's eye—it is the mind that describes words to us.

In this way man comes to have *visions* whose power is his power. He relates his history to them. They bind it geometrically. And from that come those decisions which surprise, the perspectives, the blinding divinations, precisions of judgement, illuminations, and also the incomprehensible anxieties, the stupidities. In certain outstanding cases one invokes abstract gods, genius and inspiration and a thousand others, and asks oneself with stupefaction how these accidents arise. And once more one believes that something has created itself—for man adores mystery and the marvelous precisely as he likes to shut his eyes to what is going on behind the scenes at the theater. One treats what is logical as if it were a miracle. But the 'inspired' author has been ready to perform his task a year before it was done, had been ripe, had been thinking of it always, perhaps without being conscious of the fact, and while others could not yet see, he had studied, arranged, and now had only read what was already in his mind. The secret—Leonardo's and Buonaparte's, as that which all highest intelligences possess once—is, and can only be, in the relationship that they can find—that they were forced to find—*between things whose laws of continuity escape us*. It is certain that at the decisive moment they had only to perform some definite acts. And the achievement that impressed the world, the supreme achievement, was quite a simple affair—like comparing two lengths.

This attitude makes it possible to grasp the unity of method with which we are so concerned. Here it is natural, elementary. It is life and the explanation of life. And thinkers as powerful as he of whom I think as I write these words, having mastered the resources implicit in this method, may well write at this clearer and more conscious point: *Facil cosa e farsi universale*—it is easy to make oneself universal! They can for a moment admire the prodigious instruments that they are, though the next moment they must deny anything in the nature of prodigy.

This final clarity, however, is only found after long wanderings, inevitable idolatries. The consciousness of the operations of thought, the unrecognized logic of which I have spoken, exists but rarely, even in the most powerful minds. The number of conceptions, the power to extend them, and the abundance of discoveries made, are another thing and are produced independently of any judgement that one may make as to their nature. This judgement is, notwithstanding, of easily realized importance. A flower, a proposition, a noise, can be imagined almost simultaneously: one can make them follow each other at what distance one pleases; any of these subjects of thought can also be changed, distorted, made to lose its initial aspect following the will of the mind that holds it; but it is the knowledge of this power of the mind alone that gives the thing its value. This alone permits one to criticize such *formations,* to interpret them, to find in them only what they contain, and not to stretch them to the point of confusing their various stages with those of reality. With this knowledge commences the analysis of all intellectual phases, of all that itself will have the power to classify as folly, idolatry, discovery— hitherto mere nuances, not to be distinguished from each other. They were equivalent variations from a common substance, comparable one to the other, carelessly, as it were, finding indefinite levels, sometimes name-able but all belonging to the same category. Consciousness of the thoughts that one has, to the extent to which they are thoughts, is awareness of this equality or homogeneity: the feeling that all combinations of the kind are legitimate, natural, and that the method consists in exciting them, in seeing them with precision, in searching for their implications.

At a point in this awareness or double mental life which reduces ordinary thought to something like the illusions of a waking sleeper, it seems that the sequence of these illusions, the cloud of combinations, of contrasts, of perceptions, which group themselves about some study or which float on indeterminately, at pleasure, develop with a regularity that is *perceptible,* with the evident continuity of a machine. Then emerges the idea or the wish to precipitate the movement of this progress, to carry its terms to their *limit,* the limit of their imaginable expression—*after which all shall be changed.* And if this mode of being conscious becomes habitual, one will come to consider at once all the possible results of a contemplated act, all the implications of a conceived object, and in this way to achieve their annihilation, to achieve the faculty of divining always a thing more intense or more exact than the thing allowed, to attain the power of shaking oneself free of any thought that has lasted too long. No matter what it be, a thought that has become fixed takes on the characteristics of hypnosis and becomes, in the language of logic, an idol; in the domain of poetic construction and art, a sterile monotony. The sense of which I speak, which leads the mind to foresee its own activities, to imagine the structure of what has to be imagined in detail as a whole, and the effect of the sequence thus calculated, this sense is the condition of all generalization. It is that which in certain individuals appears as a veritable passion, and with an energy that is remarkable; which, in the arts, permits of progress and explains the more and more frequent employment of concentrated terms, abridgements and violent contrasts; and it exists implicitly in its rational form as the basis of all mathematical conceptions. It is an operation very similar to it which under the name of reasoning by recurrence,[2] extends the range of these analyses, and which, from simple addition to infinitesimal, achieves something more than merely to spare the necessity for an indefinite number of useless experiments; achieves existences more complex—for the conscious imitation of an act is a new act which comprehends all possible modifications of the first.

This picture, drama, whirl, clarity, opposes itself naturally to other movements and other stages which we call 'nature' or 'the world,' things that we do not know what to do with, except distinguish ourselves from them—and then we immediately reincorporate ourselves in them.

Philosophers have generally ended by implicating our existence in this notion and it inversely in our notion of ourselves; yet they rarely go farther; we know that their business is to contend against the thought of their predecessors rather than to look into it for themselves. Scientists and artists have used the notion of nature variously: scientists finishing by measuring and then constructing themselves; artists by constructing as if they had already measured. Everything that they have made takes its place of itself in the sum of things and plays its part there, continuing things through the new shapes it gives to the materials that constitute them. But, before considering and building, one observes; the characters of the sense, their different ways of accommodation, distinguish and choose, amongst the qualities offered in the aggregate, those which are

---

[2] The philosophic importance of this method of reasoning was demonstrated for the first time in a recent article of M. Poincaré. The distinguished mathematician confirmed the priority attributed to him when consulted by the author.

to be retained and developed by the individual. The process is at first submitted to, almost without thinking, with a feeling of letting oneself be filled, of slow circulation, as of happiness; then one begins to be interested and to give different values to things that had seemed settled, simple; one adds to them, takes more pleasure in isolated details, explains them to oneself, and what happens is as the re-emergence of an energy that the senses had absorbed; soon this distorts the aspect of things in its turn, using for the purpose the considered thought of a human being.

The universal man begins also by simple contemplation, but he always returns to be impregnated by what he sees, returns to the intoxication of the particular instinct and to the emotion which the least of things real arouses if one keeps in mind the two, thing and instinct, in every way separate from each other and yet combining, in so many ways, so many different qualities.

III

He who has never completed—be it but in dream—the sketch for some project that he is free to abandon; who has never felt the sense of adventure in working on some composition which he knows finished when others only see it commencing; who has not known the enthusiasm that burns away a minute of his very self; or the poison of conception, the scruple, the cold breath of objection coming from within; and the struggle with alternative ideas when the strongest and most universal should naturally triumph over both what is normal and what is novel; he who has not seen the image on the whiteness of his paper distorted by other possible images, by his regret for all the images that will not be chosen; or seen in limpid air a building that is not there; he who is not haunted by fear of the giddiness caused by the receding of the goal before him; by anxiety as to means; by foreknowledge of delays and despairs, calculation of progressive phases, reasoning about the future—even about things that should not, when the time comes, be reasoned about—that man does not know either—and it does not matter how much he knows besides—the riches and resources, the domains of the spirit, that are illuminated by the conscious act of *construction*. The gods have received from the human mind the gift of the power to create because that mind, being cyclical and abstract, may aggrandize what it has imagined to such a point that it is no longer capable of imagining it.

Construction exists between a project or an image deliberated on and the materials that one has chosen. One order is substituted for some other that was the initial one, whatever the objects arranged may be. Be they stones, colors, words, concepts, men or anything else, their particular nature does not change the general conditions of that species of music in which—if one may pursue the metaphor—it does no more than determine the timbre. The surprising thing is that one sometimes gets an impression of poise and consistency in human constructions made with an agglomeration of apparently irreconcilable materials, as if he who had arranged them had known that they had secret affinities. But astonishment passes all bounds when one realizes that the author himself, in the vast majority of cases, is unable to give any account of the lines he has followed, that he is the wielder of a power the nature of which he does not understand. He can never make sure of success beforehand. By what calculations do the parts of an edifice, the elements of a play, the factors in a victory, fall into their places with regard to each other? Through what series of dark analyses is the production of a work brought about?

In such cases it is usual to explain everything by reference to instinct. But it is not too clear what instinct itself is, and besides, in this case, one would have to have recourse to rigorously personal and exceptional instincts, that is to say to a contradictory notion of 'hereditary habit'—which would no more be habitual than it is hereditary.

Construction, from the moment that the effort involved attains to some comprehensible result, ought to set us thinking of a common measure of the terms used, an element or principle, however, that the simple fact of consciousness already supposes and which could have none but an abstract or imaginary existence. We cannot represent to ourselves a whole that is made of changes, a single edifice of multiple qualities, except as common ground between different forms of some single material or law, the hidden continuity of which we affirm at the same instant that we recognize the edifice as a unity, as the enclosed domain of our investigations. Here again is that psychical postulate which in our consciousness resembles the principle of inertia in mechanics. Purely abstract, purely differential combinations alone, those of numbers, for instance, may be constructed by means of fixed unities; we should note that these are in the same relationship to other possible constructions as measured parts of the world to those which are not measured.

In art there is a word which applies to all styles and all fancies, and at one stroke dismisses all the pretended difficulties with regard to the opposition or the relationship between art and that 'nature' which, for good reasons, is never defined: the word is *ornament*. Let us recall the series of curves, the coinciding divisions with which the most antique objects known are covered: the profiles on vases and temples; the lozenges, spirals, ovals, striae of the ancients; the crystalline forms and the sensuous beauty of Arab wall-decoration; the bony shapes and the symmetry of Gothic art; the waves, the fires, the flowers on Japanese bronze and lacquer; and, in each of these schools, the introduction of representations of plants, beasts and men, and the perfection of these representations of plants, beasts and men, in painting and sculpture. Let us, considering language, recall its primitive melody, the separation of words from music, the flowering of each, the invention of verbs, of writing, the dawning possibility of the *figurative* complexity of phrases, the strange introduction of abstract words; and on the other hand, the system of sounds becoming more flexible, extending beyond the voice to include the resonance of materials, deepening with the discovery of harmonies, varying with the utilization of different pitches. And let us finally, then, observe the parallel progress of the formations of thought across the species of psychical onomatopœia of the primitives, and elementary symmetries and contrasts, to the ideas of substances, to metaphors, the faltering beginnings of logic, formalisms, entities, metaphysical existences.

All this multiform activity may be appreciated from the point of view of ornament. The instances enumerated may be considered as finite parts of space and time containing different variations, which are sometimes known, and characterized objects, but of which the ordinary and significant uses are neglected, so that only their order and mutual reactions may subsist. On the order depends the effect. The effect is the ornamental aim, and the work thus takes on the character of a mechanism created to impress a public, to arouse emotions and their corresponding images.

Regarded thus, the ornamental conception is to the individual arts what mathematics is to the other sciences. In the same way that the physical notions of time, length, density, mass, are only homogeneous quantities in calculations, and recover their individuality only in the interpretation of results, so the objects chosen and arranged with a view to a particular effect seem as if disengaged from most of their properties and only reassume them in the effect, in, that is to say, the mind of the detached spectator. It is thus by means of an abstraction that the work of art can be constructed, and this abstraction is more or less active, and is more or less easy to define according as the elements borrowed from reality for it are more or less complex. Inversely it is by a sort of induction, by the production of mental images, that all works of art are appreciated, and this production must equally be more or less active, more or less tiring, according as it is set in motion by a simple interlacing on a vase or a broken phrase by Pascal.

The painter disposes colored pigments on a plane and he must use their lines of separation, thicknesses, harmonies and contrasts to express himself. The spectator only sees a more or less faithful representation of flesh, gesture, landscape, things he might see through the window of a museum. The picture is judged in the same way as reality. One person will complain of the ugliness of the face, others will fall in love with it; some indulge in the most verbose kind of psychological analysis; others only look at the hands, which they always think look 'unfinished.' The truth is that it is taken for granted that the picture should reproduce the physical and natural conditions of our environment. Volume must be weighty and light must shine in the way we know, and gradually anatomy and perspective take a supreme place in pictorial aesthetic. I believe, notwithstanding, that the surest method of judging a picture is to begin by identifying nothing and then to proceed step by step to make the series of inductions that is necessitated by the presence at the same moment of a number of colored spots within a given area in order to rise from metaphor to metaphor, from supposition to supposition, to a knowledge of the subject—sometimes only to a consciousness of pleasure—that one has not always had to begin with.

I do not think that one could give a more amusing example of the general attitude with regard to painting than the fame of that 'La Gioconda smile,' to which the epithet 'mysterious' seems to be irrevocably attached. That line on a face has had the fortune to produce the sort of phrase-making that 'sensations' or 'impressions' with regard to art have legitimized in all languages. It is shrouded behind a mass of words and disappears amongst the many paragraphs that begin by calling it 'disturbing' and finish with a description of *soul*—generally vague. It would justify less intoxicating studies. They were no inaccurate observations or arbitrary symbols that Leonardo utilized, or *La Gioconda* would never have been painted. He was guided by a perpetual sagacity.

In the background of *The Last Supper* there are three windows. The one in the middle, which opens behind Jesus, is distinguished from the others by a cornice that describes an arc of a circle. If we continue this curve we get a circumference of which Christ is the center. All the main lines of the fresco converge at this point, the symmetry of the composition is relative to this center and to the long line of the supper-table. The mystery, if there be one, is to learn why we consider such combinations mysterious. And it can, I fear, be explained.

It is not from painting, nevertheless, that we shall choose the salient example we need in order to study the intercommunications between different activities of the mind. The host of suggestions emanating from the necessity to give diversity to, to people, a surface, the resemblance between the first efforts of this order and certain natural phenomena, the evolution of sensibility in the retina, these will be disregarded here so as not to lead the reader toward too arid speculation. A vaster art, the ancestor, as it might be, of painting, will serve our purpose better.

The word *construction*, which I employed deliberately to indicate more definitely the problem of human intervention in the things of the world and to give the mind of the reader an orientation, a material suggestion, in the direction of the logic of the subject, is now to be used in its more restricted sense. We shall consider architecture.

The building which composes the city—which is practically the whole of civilization—is a thing so complex that our understanding of it discerns, successively, first a changing decorative scheme that blends with the sky; then a rich texture of motives following the vertical, horizontal, and receding lines and varying infinitely with different perspectives; then a thing that is solid, bold, resisting, that has the characteristics of an animal; subordination of the parts to the whole; and finally it is a machine, the operating principle of which is gravity, which takes us from notions of geometry to ideas on dynamics and to the most delicate speculations on the subject of molecular physics—of which science it suggests the theories and the models made by physicists to represent molecular structure. It is through the building—or rather amongst imaginary scaffoldings set up in order to harmonize its qualities with each other—the purpose it is to serve with its stability; its proportions with its situation; its form with its material; and the harmonizing of each of these qualities with itself, of its thousands of aspects amongst themselves, of its balances amongst themselves, of its three dimensions amongst themselves—that we can best realize the clarity of a Leonardesque intelligence. The intelligence can play with the conception of the future sensations of the man who will make the circuit of the edifice, draw near to it, appear at a window; following the weight of the coping along the walls and down the arches to the foundation it can imagine what he will see; it can feel the thrust and counterthrust of the beams and the vibrating wind that assails them; can note the forms of the play of free light over tile and cornice, and the diffusion of the light caught in a room where the sun merely shines on part of the floor. It will experiment with and judge the weight of the lintel on its supports, the fitness of the arches, the difficulties of the vaulting, the thrust of the steps thrown upward from their landings; and all the invention that realizes itself in this durable, decorated, defended mass, limpid with glass, made for our use, which will contain our words, from which our smoke will escape.

Architecture is not, as a rule, comprehended. We regard it variously, now thinking of the decoration of a theater, now of a tenement house. I suggest that one should relate it to the idea of the city in order to appreciate it more generally, and that to grasp its complex charm one should try to recall the infinity of its aspects—a motionless building is the exception—the pleasure is in changing one's position until the building moves, and in the enjoyment of all the combinations of its varying members—the column turns, the depths recede, the galleries glide—a thousand visions emerge from the building, a thousand harmonies.

(Many designs for a church that was never built are to be met with in the manuscripts of Leonardo. It is generally imagined that they were for a St. Peter's, Rome. They make one regret the St. Peter's of Michelangelo. Leonardo, at the end of the ogival period, at a time when antique works of art were beginning to come to light, rediscovered, between antique and Gothic, the grandeur of Byzantine design—of the raising of a cupola on other cupolas, of a roof of swelling domes clustering about a higher dome—but with a boldness and a purity of ornamentation that the architects of Justinian never knew.)

The stone being exists in space—what we call space is relative to the conception of any buildings we choose to take; the architectural edifice interprets space and leads us to hypotheses on the nature of space in a very particular manner, for it is at one and the same time an equilibrium, molecular and ill-understood. He who designs a building imagines first the mass and then penetrates into the obscure realm of atoms. He tackles the problem of construction: of learning what combinations must be imagined to satisfy the conditions of resistance, elasticity, and so on, worked out in a given space. We see the logical extension of the subject; how from the purely architectural domain, which is so generally left to the professional architects, one passes to the most profound questions of mechanics and of physics in general.

Translated by Thomas McGreevy

LEONARDO AND THE PHILOSOPHERS

(*Extracts*)

One must admit that Esthetics is a great, even an irresistible, temptation. Almost all people who have a strong feeling for the arts do a little more than feel them; they cannot escape the necessity of closely examining their appreciation.

How can we endure to be mysteriously enchanted by certain aspects of the world or by certain works of man and not to explain to ourselves this accidental or calculated pleasure, which seems on the one hand independent of the intelligence,—of which it is, however, perhaps the hidden guiding principle—and on the other quite distinct from our ordinary tastes—the variety and depth of which it, nevertheless, sums up and deifies?

Philosophers could not fail to feel concerned about this strange type of emotion. Moreover they have a less naive and more methodical reason for giving it their attention, and for seeking out its causes, mechanism, significance and its core.

The vast undertaking of philosophy, when contemplated in the very heart of the philosopher, consists, after all, of an attempt to transmute all that we know and all that we would like to know, and that undertaking demands to be carried out, or at least presented, or at least to be made capable of presentation, in a definite order.

Philosophies are characterized by the system of their speculations, for in the philosophic mind there are not, and there cannot be, entirely independent and substantially isolated questions. On the contrary one finds in it, like an incessant bass accompaniment, the consciousness, the fundamental sound of a latent though quite proximate interdependance between all the thoughts it contains, or could ever contain. The realization of this profound liaison suggests and imposes the order and the order of questions leads of necessity to a supreme question, which is that of knowledge.

But once a philosophy has admitted or established, justified or discredited, knowledge—whether it has exalted it and developed it *ultra vires* by an effective combination of logic and intuition, or whether it has measured it as if it were reduced to its component parts by the science of criticism—it is invariably forced to explain,—that is to express within its system, its personal system of comprehension—human activity in general, the intellectual understanding of which is, in short, only one of the modalities, although it represents the whole.

*

We are now at a critical point in the whole of philosophy.

Thoughts which are very exact and very pertinent, which, in reality, seek (whatever the content and the conclusions may be) the ideal of a uniform distribution of concepts around a certain attitude or singular and characteristic aspect of mind of the thinker, must nowadays try to recapture the diversity, the irregularity and the unexpectedness of bygone thoughts; and their order must set in order their apparent disorder.

They must re-establish the plurality and the autonomy of the mind as a result of their own unity and sovereignty. They must legitimize the existence of what they have convicted of error and destroyed as such, they must recognize the vitality of the absurd, and fecundity of the contradictory, and sometimes even feel themselves inspired as they are by the universality from which they believe themselves to spring, restricted to the particular state of mind or individual characteristics of a certain person. And this is the beginning of wisdom and, at the same time, the twilight of philosophy.

*

It is true that the existence of others is always disturbing to the magnificent egotism of a thinker. He cannot fail to be confronted by the great problem posed by the arbitrariness of others. The feelings, thoughts and actions of others almost always seem arbitrary to us. Every preference we give our own thoughts we justify by a necessity of which we believe ourselves the agent. But after all the other person does exist and the problem does confront us. It besets us in two forms, one of which consists in the difference in behavior and character, in the diversity of decisions and attitudes toward everything that has to do with the preservation of the body and its possessions; the other of which is manifested in the variety of tastes, expressions and creations of the sensibilities.

*

The philosopher cannot decide not to absorb into his own intelligence all these realities which he wants to make similar to his own or reduce to potentialities within his scope. He wants to understand; he wants to understand them in every sense of the word. He then proceeds to meditate framing a science of the meaning of action, and a science of the meaning of the expressions and the creations of the emotions,—an *ethic* and an *esthetic*—as if the Palace of his Thoughts must seem to him imperfect without those two symmetrical wings in which his all-powerful and abstract Ego could hold passion, action, emotion and invention captive.

Every philosopher, when he has finished with God, with the Self, with Time, Space, Matter, with Categories and with Essences returns to man and his works.

*

Then as he had invented Truth, the Philosopher invented the Good and the Beautiful; and as he had invented the rules of agreement between an isolated thought and itself, he likewise undertook to prescribe rules for conformity of action and expression for the precepts and patterns which, through the contemplation of a unique and universal Principle, escaped the caprices and the doubts of the individual,—a Principle which must therefore, above all and independently of all personal experience, be defined and designated.

There are few more remarkable events in the history of the mind than this introduction of Ideals, in which one can see a completely European event. Their debasement in the mind coincides with that of the virtues typical of Europe.

However, in the same way that we are still quite attached to the conception of pure science, developed strictly according to tangible evidence which can be stretched indefinitely from identity to identity—so we are still half convinced of the existence of Ethics and Beauty independent of time, place, race, or people.

*

Nevertheless each day reveals a little more the ruin of this noble structure. We are watching this extraordinary phenomenon; the very development of the sciences is tending to diminish the idea of knowledge. I mean that that part of science which seemed unshakeable and which was common to it and to philosophy (that is to say to faith in the comprehensible and to belief in the real value of the attainments of the mind) is little by little giving way to a new mode of understanding or evaluating knowledge. The efforts of the intellect can no longer be regarded as converging toward a spiritual limit, toward the Truth. One only has to examine oneself to recognize this contemporary conviction: that to *know* everything, which indicates no corresponding effective *power*, has only a conventional or arbitrary importance. To know everything is only worth while if it is the prescription or the receipt for real power. From now on all metaphysics and even any theory of knowledge, whatever they may be, will find themselves violently divided and removed from what is held to be, more or less consciously by everyone, the only real knowledge—payable in gold.

In the same way ethics and esthetics are themselves being distorted into problems of legislation, statistics, history and physiology—and into lost illusions.

*

Moreover on what grounds can one form or specify a plan for "creating an Esthetics"— A science of the Beautiful? But do the moderns still use this word? It seems to me that they only still use it lightly. Or perhaps . . . in thinking of the past. Beauty is a kind of corpse. Novelty, intensity, strangeness,—in a word all the values of surprise have supplanted it. Crude excitement is the ruling mistress of contemporary minds; and the actual purpose of any work is to tear us from the contemplative state, from the static happiness whose image was formerly part of the general conception of Beauty. People are more and more occupied with the most unstable and immediate characteristics of the psychic and sensitive life. The unconscious, the irrational, the temporary which are, and their names proclaim the fact, denials or negations of the intentional and sustained forms of mental activity, have been substituted for the patterns natural to the mind. One hardly ever sees any more a product of the desire for perfection. Let us note in passing that this superannuated desire must necessarily fade before the fixed idea and the insatiable thirst for originality. The ambition to reach perfection is confused with the idea of making a work independent of any particular time; but the desire to be new insists on making of it an event remarkable by its contrast to the present moment. The former admits of, and even demands, heredity, imitation or tradition, which are steps in its climb toward the absolute object it wishes to attain. The latter rejects them, and in so doing implies them still more strongly,—for its essence is to be different.

In our time a definition of 'Beauty' can only be considered as a historical or philological document. Taken in the former fullness of its meaning, this illustrious word is on its way to join many other kinds of verbal coinage, which are no longer in circulation, in the drawers of the numismatists of language.

*

What most obviously separates philosophical esthetics from the thoughts of the artist, is that it springs from a way of thinking which believes itself foreign to the arts and which feels itself to be of quite another species than that of a poet or a musician,—in which I shall say in a moment that it is deceived. Works of art are to it accidents, particular cases, the results of an active and industrious intelligence going blindly toward a principle of which Philosophy alone can possess the vision or the absolute and immediate understanding. This activity seems unnecessary to it, since its supreme object should be in the immediate realm of philosophic thought, and should be directly accessible only by attention applied to the knowledge of knowledge, or to a system of the perceptible world and the intelligible world combined. The philosopher does not recognize any particular necessity for it; he does not think much of the importance of the material means, of the ways and of the values of the execution, for he tends inevitably to distinguish them from the general conception. It is repugnant to him to think of an intimate, perpetual, equal interchange between what one wants and what one can do, between what he considers accidental and what he considers substantial, between 'form' and 'essence,' between consciousness and automatism, between the circumstances and the design, between 'matter' and the 'mind.' Now it is precisely this wonderful ability, the freedom acquired in these exchanges, the existence in the artist of a sort of common standard concealed beneath the extremely divergent elements of his temperament, it is the inevitable and indivisible collaboration, the coordination, at every moment and in every one of his acts, of the arbitrary and the necessary, of the expected and the unexpected, of his body, of his material, of his wishes, even of his absences—which finally allows him to endow nature (considered as a practically infinite source of subjects, models, means and pretexts) with some object which cannot be simplified and reduced to a simple and abstract thought in that it has its origin and its effect in a system which cannot be separated from independent conditions. One cannot summarize a poem as one summarizes . . . a universe. To summarize a thesis is to retain the essence of it. To summarize (or replace by a scheme) a work of art, is to lose its essence. One can see to what extent this fact (if one can understand its scope) makes an illusion of the analysis of the esthetic.

In fact one can only extract from an object or from a natural or artificial work certain esthetic characteristics, which could be found elsewhere, for use as a general formula for beautiful things. It is not that this method has not often been used; it is that one does not remember that this sort of research is only applied to an 'old discovery,' and moreover that the work under consideration cannot be reduced to any of its component properties without losing its intrinsic emotional value.

The philosopher cannot easily comprehend that the artist passes, almost with indifference, from form to content and from content to form; that form comes to the artist with the meaning that he wishes to give it, nor that the idea of form is the same thing to him as the idea which demands a form.

In a word, if esthetics could exist the arts would fade before it—that is to say before their essence.

What I am now saying should not be applied to technical studies which are only concerned with means and with particular solutions, and which have as their more or less direct object the production or the classification of works of art, but do not aim at reaching Beauty by a road that does not lie in their domain.

Perhaps one only really understands what one has created. Pascal tells us that he would not have invented painting. He could not see the reason for laboriously reproducing the most insignificant objects. However sometimes this great artist of language did apply himself to drawing, to painting the portrait of his thoughts in words. . . . It is true that he seems to have finished by rejecting all activities, save one, and by considering everything, with the exception of death, as something painted.

*

The philosopher took to the field to overcome the artist, to 'explain' what the artist feels and what he does; but quite the contrary took place and was discovered. Far from Philosophy enveloping and assimilating, in the name of the conception of Beauty, the whole domain of creative sensibility and making itself the mother and the mistress of esthetics, it so happens that it can no longer find its justification, the appeasement of its conscience or its real 'depth' except in its creative powers and in its abstract poetic freedom. Only an esthetic interpretation can save the venerable monuments of metaphysics from ruin by their more or less hidden postulates, or from the destructive effects of the analysis of language and of thought.

Perhaps it will seem very difficult at first to consider as artists certain philosophers whom up to now we have considered as seekers after truth, to transform into lies—into self-deceptions—the products of the deepest sincerity. . . . "What a state of affairs," one will say! Philosophers should set their minds at rest about this change, which is after all only a change of habit. I can only see in it a reform demanded by the course of events, of which I see a counterpart in the history of the ancient plastic arts. Once upon a time the likeness of a man or of an animal, even though it had been seen to come from the hands of the artist, was considered not only as a living thing, immobile and crude though it was, but also endowed with supernatural powers. Stones and pieces of wood which did not even resemble human beings were worshipped as gods. Images which were only very approximate likenesses were given food and were honored; and here is an extraordinary fact—the cruder they were the more they were worshipped—something that can also be observed in children playing with their dolls and lovers with their loved ones, and which is a profoundly significant fact. (Perhaps this is because we believe that the more we are obliged to give life to an object the more we receive from it in return). But as this communicated life became gradually weaker and weaker, and was little by little refused to such crude images, *the idol became beautiful*. Compelled to this by criticism, it lost its imaginary powers

114

over events and persons in order to gain real power over the eyes. Sculpture became free and became itself.

Can I without shocking, without cruelly hurting philosophic feelings, compare its so idolized truths, its principles, its Ideas, its Entity, its Essence, its Categories, these Noumena, this Universe, this mass of conceptions which became successively necessary, to the idols of which I was speaking?— If one asks oneself how philosophy nowadays would compare to traditional philosophy the answer would be that it is as a fifth-century statue compared to the featureless gods of ancient times.

I sometimes think that as arrangements of ideas and abstract constructions without illusions—without recourse to the power of hypostasis—gradually become possible and acceptable, it will perhaps come about that this kind of untrammeled philosophy will prove itself more fruitful and more true than philosophy which was bound to primitive beliefs in explanations, more human and more seductive than that which demands a rigorous critical attitude. Perhaps it will allow us to begin again in a new spirit, with quite different aims, the great work undertaken by metaphysics in directing thought toward ends which criticism has greatly attenuated. For a long time mathematics has been independent of any aim foreign to the concept of itself found in the pure development of its technique, and in the value it has given to the value inherent in this development; and everyone knows to what extent this freedom in its practice, which seemed bound to lead it very far from reality into a world of make-believe, of difficulties and of useless elegances, has made it flexible and equipped it to aid the physicist.

Is an art of ideas, an art of the order of ideas, or of the plurality of the orders of ideas a vain conception? I allow myself to believe that all architecture is not concrete, that all music cannot be heard. There is a certain consciousness of ideas and of their analogies which seems to me to be able to act and to be developed in the same way as the consciousness of sound or of color; I should even be inclined, if I had to propose a definition of a philosopher, to base it on the predominance in his character of this type of sensibility.

I believe that one is born a philosopher, in the way that one is born a sculptor or a musician; and that this gift, if it takes the pursuit of any truth or reality as its justification and as its object, can nowadays be proud of itself and need no longer so much seek out as create. The philosopher should use freely the powers that he has acquired through discipline; and in an infinity of ways, and in an infinity of forms he should dispense the strength and the ability—which are his characteristics—to give life and movement to abstract things.

That is what will allow the Noumena to be saved by the simple understanding of their intrinsic harmonies.

Finally I say that there exists an excellent demonstration of what I have just proposed in the form of a question. Once it was only a possibility, but now it suffices to consider the fate of the great systems to find it already realized. In what way do we read the philosophers, and who ever consults them with the real hope of finding anything but a pleasure or an exercise for the mind? When we set out to read them, do we not have the feeling that we are submitting for a short time to the rules of an enjoyable game? What would become of these masterpieces of pointless discipline, if it were not for this convention which we accept for love of an exacting pleasure? If one refutes a Plato or a Spinoza would nothing remain of their astonishing works? Absolutely nothing—if there did not remain a work of art.

*

However in the field of philosophy, and on certain strategic points of the domain of the pursuit of intelligence, a few remarkable figures have appeared of whom one knows that their abstract thoughts, though extremely expert and capable of every variety of subtlety and depth, never wandered from their preoccupation with figurative creations, with applications and tangible proofs of their attentive abilities. They seem to have possessed an indefinable and intimate knowledge of the continual interchanges between the arbitrary and the necessary.

Leonardo da Vinci is the supreme example of these superior individuals.

Translated by Anthony Bower

TWO FRAGMENTS FROM "THE INTELLECTUAL CRISIS"

(1919)

Today, on an immense platform which might be that of Elsinore, but runs instead from Basle to Cologne, touching the sands of Nieuport, the marshes of the Somme, the granites of Alsace, and the chalky plateaus of Champagne—the European Hamlet stares at millions of ghosts.

But he is an intellectual Hamlet. He meditates on the life and death of truths. For phantoms he has all the subjects of our controversies; for regrets he has all our titles to glory; he bows under the weight of discoveries and learning, unable to renounce and unable to resume this limitless activity. He reflects on the boredom of recommencing the past, on the folly of always striving to be original. He wavers between one abyss and the other, for two dangers still threaten the world: order and disorder.

If he takes a skull in his hands, the skull is illustrious.—"Whose was it?"—That was *Leonardo*. He invented the flying man, but the flying man has hardly fulfilled the purpose of the inventor; we know that the flying man mounted on his great swan (*il grande uccello sopra del dosso del suo magno cecero*) has other uses in our days than to go fetch snow from the mountain-tops and sprinkle it over city streets in the heat of summer. . . . And this other skull is that of *Leibnitz*, who dreamed of universal peace. And this was *Kant, Kant who begat Hegel, who begat Marx, who begat* . . .

Hamlet hardly knows what to do with all these skulls. But if he throws them away! . . . Will he then cease to be himself? His fearfully lucid mind surveys the passage from war to peace. This transition is more dangerous, more obscure than the passage from peace to war; all nations are convulsed by it. "And I, the European intellect, what will become of me? . . . And what is peace?" he asks. *"Peace is perhaps the state of things in which the natural hostility of man toward man is manifested by creation, in place of the destruction which marks a war. It is the period* of creative competition and the struggle of inventions. But as for me, am I not weary of inventing? Have I not exhausted the desire for extreme attempts and made a vice of my skillful fabrications? Must I abandon my difficult duties and my transcendent ambitions? Should I follow the movement like Polonius, who has become the editor of a great newspaper? like Laertes, who is somewhere in the aviation? like Rosenkrantz, who does I don't know what under a Russian name?

"Phantoms, farewell! The world has no more need of you. Nor of me. The world, which has given the name of 'progress' to its tendency toward a fatal precision, is seeking to unite the blessings of life with the advantages of death. A certain confusion still reigns, but yet a little while and all will be made clear; at last we shall behold the miracle of a strictly animal society, a perfect and final ant-hill."

II

Now, the present situation permits of this capital question: Will Europe retain its leadership in all activities?

Will Europe become *what she is in reality:* that is, a little cape of the Asiatic continent?

Or will Europe remain *what she seems to be:* that is, the most precious part of the terrestrial universe, the pearl of the globe, the brain of a vast body?

In order to set forth this alternative in all its rigor, I will take the liberty of developing a sort of fundamental theorem.

Consider a map which shows the whole of the habitable world. This whole is divided into regions, and in each of these regions there is a certain density of population, a certain quality of men. To each of these regions also corresponds a natural wealth—a more or less fertile soil, a more or less precious subsoil, a more or less watered territory, more or less adapted to transportation, etc. These characteristics enable us to classify these regions at any epoch, in such a way that at any epoch *the state of the living world can be defined by a system of inequalities between the inhabited regions of its surface.*

At any moment the *history* of the following moment depends on this given inequality.

Let us now examine, not this theoretical classification, but the classification which existed in reality, and still existed yesterday. We perceive a fact which is both remarkable in itself and extremely familiar to us: The little region of Europe stands at the head of the classification, and so has stood for centuries. In spite of its small area, and although the wealth of the soil is not extraordinary, it dominates the picture. By what miracle? Certainly the miracle must reside in the quality of its population. This quality must compensate for the smaller number of men, square miles, and tons of ore assigned to Europe. Put the Empire of India in one scale of a balance; put the United Kingdom in the other. See: the balance inclines toward the scale with the lighter weight!

Here is an extraordinary upset of equilibrium. But its consequences are more extraordinary still: *they lead us to foresee a progressive change in the opposite direction.*

We suggested a moment ago that the quality of its men must determine the pre-eminence of Europe. I cannot analyze this quality in detail, but I find by rapid examination that burning desire, ardent and disinterested curiosity, a happy blend of imagination and logical precision, a scepticism that is not pessimistic and a mysticism that is not resigned . . . are the more specifically active qualities of the European psyche.

A single example of this European spirit—it is an example of the first rank and of paramount importance. Greece—for all the shores of the Mediterranean belong in Europe, Smyrna and Alexandria being as European as Athens or Marseilles—Greece invented geometry. It was a foolhardy enterprise; we are still disputing over the *possibility* of such folly.

In order to achieve this fantastic creation, what had to be done? Remember that neither the Egyptians nor the Chinese, the Chaldeans nor the Hindus ventured so far. Reflect that it was an enthralling adventure, a conquest a thousand times more precious and positively more poetic than that of the Golden Fleece. No mere sheepskin is worth the proposition of Pythagoras.

Geometry was an enterprise demanding gifts which are generally incompatible. It required Argonauts of the mind, hardy pilots who would let themselves neither be lost in their thoughts, nor distracted by their impressions. Neither the fragility of the premises which bore them on, nor the sublety or infinity of the inferences which they were exploring, could divert them from their course. They were equidistant from the variable Negroes and the indefinite yogis. They adjusted common speech to precise reasoning, an extraordinarily delicate and improbable achievement. They analyzed motor and visual operations of great complexity. They made these operations correspond to grammatical and linguistic properties. Blind seers, they trusted in speech to guide them through space. . . . And space itself, as the centuries passed, became an always richer and more surprising creation; it developed along with thought, which was acquiring more mastery over itself and placing more confidence both in the power of reason and in the initial subtlety which had provided it with such incomparable tools: definitions, axioms, lemmata, theorems, problems, porisms, and the rest.

I should need a whole book to discuss the subject. I only wished to specify, in a few words, one of the characteristic acts of the European genius. This very example carries me back to my original thesis.

I was arguing that the inequality which has so long been observed to favor Europe might, *by its own effects,* be changed progressively into an opposite sort of inequality. This is what I called by the ambitious name of a fundamental theorem.

How can we demonstrate this proposition?—I will take the same example, that of Greek geometry, and ask the reader to consider the effects of this discipline through the ages. Little by little, very slowly but very surely, one can see it assuming such authority that all researches and all acquired experience tend irresistibly to borrow its rigorous manner, its scrupulous economy of 'matter,' its automatic generalization, its subtle methods, and that infinite prudence which permits it the wildest daring. . . . Modern science was born from this education in the grand style.

But once it was born, once tried and rewarded by its practical applications, our science, becoming a means of power, a means of concrete domination, a stimulant of wealth, a device for exploiting the capital of the planet, ceased to be an artistic activity, and an end in itself; instead it has become an exchange value. The utility of knowledge makes it a *commodity,* desired no longer by a few distinguished enthusiasts, but by Everyman.

This commodity, as a result, will be prepared in more and more convenient or comestible forms; it will be distributed to a larger and larger circle of buyers; it will be transformed into something commercial, something which is imitated and produced almost everywhere.

Result: the inequality which used to exist between the different regions of the world, in respect to the mechanical arts, applied sciences, and scientific methods of war or peace—the inequality on which European predominance was based—tends gradually to disappear.

Hence, *the classification of the habitable regions of the world tends to become such that brute size, numbers, and statistical elements—population, area, raw materials—will at last exclusively determine this classification of the compartments of the world.*

And hence, the balance which inclined to our side, although we *seemed* lighter, is slowly beginning to change its direction—as if we had stupidly taken the invisible weight which bore us down and cast it into the other scale. *We have been fools enough to make forces proportional to masses.*

This phenomenon of our times might be compared with another, which can be observed in the heart of every nation; it consists in the diffusion of culture, and in the accession to culture of larger and larger categories of individuals.

To predict the consequences of this diffusion, and determine whether it will necessarily produce a degradation, would be attempting a delightfully complicated problem of intellectual physics.

For the speculative mind the charm of this problem arises first from its resemblance to the physical fact of diffusion, and thence from the sudden change of this resemblance into a profound difference, as soon as the thinker returns to his first subject, which was *men* and not *molecules.*

A drop of wine will fall into water and hardly color it; after a rosy mist the wine tends to disappear. This is the physical fact. But now suppose that some time after this disappearance and this return to limpidity, we saw drops of *pure wine* being formed here and there in this vessel which seemed once more to contain only *pure water*—our wonder would have no bounds. . . .

This miracle of Cana is not impossible in the field of intellectual and social physics. We then speak of *genius* and oppose it to diffusion.

A short time ago we were considering a curious balance, which moved contrary to weight. Now we are watching a liquid system which passes, as if spontaneously, from homogeneous to heterogeneous, from a thorough mixture to complete separation. . . . These paradoxical images give the simplest and most practical representation of the rôle played in the world by what has been called—for five or ten thousand years—the Mind.

"But can the European mind, or at least its most precious elements, be totally diffused? The exploitation of the globe, the equalization of techniques, democracy—these phenomena point to a *deminutio capitis,* a loss of rights, by Europe; should they be taken as irrevocable decisions of destiny? Or have we some liberty *against* this menacing conspiracy of things?"

It is perhaps by seeking this liberty that one creates it. However, for such a research, we must temporarily abandon the consideration of groups, and study the struggle of personal life against social life in the thinking individual.

Translated by Malcolm Cowley

FRAGMENT FROM "ON POE'S *EUREKA*"

The Cosmogony is one of the oldest of all literary forms. It belongs to a department of literature remarkable for its persistence and astonishing in its variety.

One might say that the world is hardly more ancient than the art of making the world. With a little more knowledge and much more intelligence, we might employ these Books of Genesis, whether taken from India, China, or Chaldea, whether belonging to Greece, Moses, or Svante Arrhenius, as standards to measure the spiritual simplicity of their own epochs. We should find, beyond doubt, that the naïvety of their aim is constant, but we should have to confess that its manifestations are exceedingly diverse.

Just as tragedy borders on history and psychology, the cosmogonic form verges sometimes on religion, with which it is confused at many points, and sometimes on science, from which it is necessarily distinguished by the absence of experimental proof. It includes sacred books, admirable poems, outlandish narratives full of beauties and absurdities, and physico-mathematical researches often so profound as to be worthy of a less insignificant subject than the universe. But it is the glory of man, and something more than his glory, to waste his powers on the void. Often these crack-brained researches are the cause of unexpected discoveries. The rôle of the non-existent exists; the function of the imaginary is real; and we learn from strict logic that *the false implies the true*. Thus it would seem that the history of thought can be summarized in these words: *It is absurd by what it seeks; great by what it finds*.

Both the problem of the totality of things and that of the origin of this totality arise from a very simple state of mind. We want to know what came before light; or perhaps we test some particular combination of ideas, to see whether it might not be placed before all others—whether it might not be considered as giving birth to the system which is the source of all our ideas—this system being the world; and to the author of all our ideas —this author being ourselves.

Whether we dream of an infinitely imperious Voice breaking, as it were, eternity; its first cry announcing Space, like tidings which grow ever more pregnant with consequence as they are carried toward the furthermost limits of the creative will; and the divine Word giving a place to essences, to life, to liberty, to the fatal contest between law and intelligence, between law and chance—or whether (if we hesitate to launch ourselves from pure nothingness toward any imaginable state) we find that the first epoch of the world is a little easier to consider in the vague idea of a mixture of matter and energy, composing a sort of substantial, but neutral and powerless mud, which patiently awaits the act of a demiurge—or finally whether, more profound, better equipped, but no less thirsty for marvels, we invoke the aid of all the sciences to reconstruct the earliest possible condition of the system which is the object of every science—in any case our idea of the origin of things is never more than a reverie based on their present disposition; it is in some sort a degeneration of the real, a variation on what is.

What do we actually need before we can think of this origin?

If we need the idea of nothingness, the idea of nothingness is nothing; or rather, it is already something; it is a pretence of the mind, which plays a comedy of silence and perfect shadows; in the midst of these shadows I am sure that I lie hidden and am ready to create, simply by relaxing my attention; I feel myself to be present, and indispensable, and endowed with will, so that I may preserve, by a conscious act, this ephemeral absence of all images and this apparent nullity. . . . But it is an image and it is an act; I call myself *Nothingness* by a momentary convention.

Or, if the idea which I place at the origin of all things is that of an extreme disorder, extending to the smallest particles of existence, I can easily perceive that this inconceivable chaos is ordered by my purpose of conception. I jumbled the cards myself, for the joy of arranging them later. And besides, to define a disorder so confused that one could neither discover the slightest trace of order nor substitute another chaos more thorough and more advanced, would be a masterpiece of art and logic. A confusion which truly lies at the beginning of things must be an infinite confusion. But in this case we cannot derive the world from it, and the very perfection of this chaos renders its use forever impossible.

124

As for the idea of a beginning—I mean an absolute beginning—it is necessarily a myth. Every beginning is a coincidence: we must imagine it as some sort of contact between all and nothing. In trying to think of it, we find that every beginning is a consequence—every beginning *ends* something.

But principally we need the idea of this Whole we call the *universe*, the beginning of which we desire to know. Even before we commence to puzzle over the problem of its origin, let us see whether the very notion of a universe, which seems to impose itself on our minds, and which we find so simple and inevitable, will not disintegrate under our eyes.

We imagine vaguely that the *Whole* is *something*, and imagining *something*, we called it the *Whole*. We believe that it began as all things begin, and that this beginning of the Whole, which must have been far more strange and impressive than that of the parts, must also be infinitely more important to know. We form an idol of totality, and an idol of its origin, and are drawn to conclude the reality of a certain body of nature, whose unity corresponds to another unity of which we are firmly convinced—that of ourselves.

Such is the primitive, almost the childish, form of our idea of the universe. It is very natural; in other words very impure. We must examine it more closely, and ask ourselves whether this notion can form a part of any but a fallacious chain of reason.

I shall observe in myself what I think under this head.

A rudimentary universe is offered by all the things I see, considered as a whole. My eyes conduct my vision from place to place, and everywhere find impressions. My vision, by stimulating the mobility of my eyes, is increased, broadened, and deepened continually. There is no movement of the eyes which encounters a region of invisibility; there is none which does not give rise to effects of color. By these movements, which are prolonged and mutually connected, which absorb or correspond to one another, I am as if enclosed in my power of vision. All my different perceptions are harmonized and arranged in the unity of my directing consciousness.

I acquire the general and constant impression that a sphere of simultaneity is attached to my presence. It moves along with me, and its contents are infinitely variable; but through all the substitutions it may undergo, it preserves its fullness. I may change my place, or the bodies which surround me may be modified, but the unity of my total representation, and the property it has of surrounding me, are in no wise altered. It is vain to flee or attempt in any manner to escape; I am always enveloped by all the *seeing-movements* of my body, which are transformed one into another, and inevitably carry me back to the same central situation.

Thus I see a *whole*. I regard it as a Whole, because it might be said to exhaust my capacity for seeing. My vision is confined to this closed circle, and to the juxtaposition which surrounds me. All my other sensations have reference to some spot within this circle, of which the center thinks and speaks.

Such is my first Universe. I do not know whether a man blind from birth could have so clear and immediate notion of a sum of all things, for I am convinced that the particular properties of vision are essential to the formation, *by myself,* of an entire and complete domain. Sight in some sort assumes the function of simultaneity—in other words, of unity as such.

But the unity which is necessarily formed of everything I can see in an instant—this mass of figures or blotches reciprocally joined, from which I later disentangle matter, depth, movement, and events, giving a place to each—this whole which I observe in order to discover what attracts and what alarms me—it is this which inspires me with the first idea, the model and, as it were, the germ of the total universe which I believe to exist around my sensation, masked and revealed by it. Inevitably I imagine that an immense and hidden system supports, penetrates, nourishes, and reabsorbs every actual and sensible element of my duration, forcing it to exist and to be resolved; and that hence every moment is formed of an infinite number of roots that plunge to an unknown depth in an *implicit space*—in the past—in the secret structure of this our machine for perceiving and combining, which returns incessantly to the *present*. The present, considered as a permanent relationship of all the changes which touch me, suggests the image of a solid to which all my perceptive life is attached, like a sea anemone to its bit of shingle. On this stone, this pebble, how can I build an edifice outside of which nothing could exist? How can I pass from a limited and instantaneous universe to one which is complete and absolute?

It would now be a question of conceiving and constructing, around a real germ, a figure which must satisfy two essential conditions: first, that it should admit all things, be capable of all things, and represent all things to us; secondly, that it serve our intelligence, lend itself to our reasonings, and render us, to a little higher degree, the lords of knowledge and masters of ourselves.

But merely to specify these two necessities of the intellect, merely to set them side by side, is enough to waken sharply all the insurmountable difficulties which reside in the slightest attempt to give a workable definition of the Universe.

Universe, therefore, is only a mythological expression. The thoughts suggested by this word are perfectly irregular and entirely independent. As soon as we leave the bounds of the moment, as soon as we attempt to enlarge and extend our presence outside of itself, our forces are exhausted in our liberty. We are surrounded by all the disorder of our knowledge, of our faculties. We are beseiged by all that is memory, all that is possible, all that is imaginable, all that is calculable, all the combinations of our spirit in all degrees of probability, in all states of precision. How can we form a concept of something which is opposed to nothing, rejects nothing, resembles nothing? If it resembled something, it would no longer be the whole. If it resembles nothing. . . . And, if this totality is equivalent in power to our mind, our mind has no hold over it. All the objections which are raised against an active infinity, all the difficulties which arise when one attempts to draw order out of multiplicity, are here involved. No proposition can be advanced about this *subject* so disordered in its richness that all *attributes* apply to it. Just as the universe escapes our intuition, in the same way it is transcendent to our logic.

And as for its origin—*in the beginning was fable.* There it will always remain.

Translated by Malcolm Cowley

METHODICAL CONQUEST

(1896)

. . . Present day Germany displays a superiority in practical results and in the sum total of its actions. But it seems that the individual qualities of its agents are mediocre, static, and, moreover, perfectly suited to general developments. The heroic age is passed: it has been deliberately put aside. Sometimes it is used for purposes of self-advertisement and appears in certain useful phrases, but that puts it back even further into the past. The great philosophers are dead, the great speculative scholars no longer have a place.[1] They give way to an anonymous, immediate form of knowledge, without any general criticism, without any new theories, and fertile only in patents. And only what can be imitated is retained of all that these outstanding individuals have discovered—imitated in order to add to the resources of their mediocre successors.

However here is the novelty. An entire national body acts as one. Its competitive energies are reconciled and are directed abroad. National enterprises are successively undertaken, and in each one everyone gives of his best. All classes of society assume, in turn, supreme importance. Moreover in the history of this century, Germany seems to be committed to a carefully studied plan. Each step she takes increases her stature. She realizes ambition after ambition, and the symmetry of this progress gives an artificial appearance to all of her endeavors. For example she extends her domain by calculated attacks. Then she imposes on Europe an armed peace which all the other countries imagine to be abnormal. Then she puts her industry and her commerce on a war basis. Then she simultaneously builds a merchant and a military marine. Then she suddenly starts looking for colonies. . . . The famous affair of the Carolinas appeared, like so many other German undertakings, like a thunderbolt. It was a detail of some master plan. Of the same nature was the famous

---

[1] This sentence should be removed; many like Einstein, Planck, etc., make it inexact —or rather unjust (1925).

telegram from the Kaiser to President Kruger. England and the world were aroused. Then it becomes apparent that the Transvaal is already profoundly germanized: one recalls the views of Baron von Marshall about Delagoa Bay and Beira: a whole scheme is revealed.[1] And recent books have, in the same way, abruptly disclosed the intensive development of the whole empire, first fruits of the premeditated war waged on the riches of the whole world.

One must not ignore the fact that, for the older leading nations, the struggle will become more and more difficult. It has assumed such an aspect that the very qualities in them which were considered most favorable to their survival and the principle reasons for their greatness, have now become handicaps. Thus the practice of striving for perfection in manufactured goods, the encouragement given to internal competition, the improvement of living conditions for the working classes, are so many obstacles in the struggle . . . But the question is much broader than that.

Germany owes everything to a quality which is the most antipathetic in the world to certain temperaments—particularly to an Englishman or a Frenchman. That quality is discipline. It should not be despised. Moreover it has another name, it is called method—and I have often called it by that name. An Englishman or a Frenchman can invent a method. They have proved it. They can submit to discipline; they have proved that also. But they will always prefer something else. For them it is a last resort, a temporary means or a sacrifice. For a German it is life itself. Moreover it so happens that Germany is a recent entity as a nation. Now, all peoples who become great nations, or who regain this position at a period already provided with great nations both older and more complete—are inclined suddenly to start imitating things which have taken centuries of experience for the older nations—and completely organize themselves according to a deliberate plan—in the same way that all planned cities are always built on a geometrical plan. Germany, Italy and Japan are such nations embarked very late on as perfect a scientific plan as the analysis of neighboring prosperity and contemporary progress can provide. Russia would

[1] In January 1896, they were singing on the Cape:

> "Strange German faces passing to and fro
> What have you come for, we should love to know?
> Looking mysterious as you join the train
> Say, now, you Uhlans, shall we meet again?"

offer a similar example if the immensity of its territory were not a handicap to the rapid execution of a concerted plan.

In Germany one finds a national character naturally suited to organization and to the division of labor, and at the same time a new State which wants to equal and then surpass the oldest states. It must be recognized that, altogether, she has shown uncommon energy and application in this undertaking.

I have tried to demonstrate the mechanism of this ambitious plan by comparing its military to its economic form; but the same conclusions could be reached by taking examples in other fields. German science would have served just as well. In that, there also reigns the principle of segmentation, of classification, and of discipline imposed on the objects of knowledge. In that too marvellous instruments increase the results: laboratories, each more specialized than the last, interminable bibliographies, men lost all their lives in solving imperceptible problems, compose a national science completely dedicated to the country which generously maintains them.

Thus we can consider in an abstract way this question of method. Everyone imagines, the moment that this word is pronounced, a sort of receipt or practical set of rules for passing from a given condition to another predetermined condition. Everyone sees in it the exclusion of certain experiments and the strict observance of certain prescriptions assimilated once and for all into a primordial way of thinking which is considered more than adequate. And everyone must understand the full force of such a thing. It is easy to demonstrate that, with the help of mental processes of this kind, the hazards of any enterprise are reduced to a minimum. Surprises are foreseen. A good method has an answer for any possible occurrence, and an answer that is influenced as little as possible by the unexpectedness of the event or of the problem. But of all its attributes, the following are the most interesting: a well-constructed method greatly reduces the effort of invention. It allows research to play a part. An example: a manufacturer wants to furnish a designated article to a certain country. Instead of having to invent the form of the object, he makes inquiries. Its form is given him by the taste of the future consumer. Then he turns to the scientist whom he pays to reduce, scientifically, the net cost, etc. When finally the object has been manufactured, transported and sold, one notices that this object has successively required the use of almost every form of human knowledge, and that it has borrowed from each everything it needed to satisfy the customer relatively, and the manufacturer absolutely. Nothing more simple than this operation, and yet it is only in Germany that it is completely and vigorously carried out. As one can see it is a question of strictly conforming to the nature of things and of neglecting nothing. It is a question of logic. One must do what is necessary; and while the manufacturer without a method will make a bad syllogism and a bad bargain while affirming, I suppose, that every good product must sell . . . and so on . . . a wiser one will reconcile logic and fortune by not leaving the definition of a good product in the air and to chance. He will go and look for it in the readable mind of his client.

Moreover it is easier to carry out these very exact procedures in Germany than in any other country. I mentioned discipline. In Germany it is native, and the strength of discipline lies in determining the place of man and the complete compass of his actions. In the army as elsewhere, it is a question of each one being able to do his best. That is only achieved by constraint, and the limitations imposed *a priori* on each individual are justly based on his best performance. If a soldier has to remain in ranks it is because, on his own, his personal actions are less effective. A crowd of a thousand men is more powerful than a batallion of five hundred. The most striking detail about the German army, which is so carefully regulated, so exact in its smallest components, is the artificial encouragement of limited initiative. An ordinary soldier, as well as a captain, *must* do what seems the right thing to him from one moment to the next in combat: something like a conscious cashiering of freedom of action is successively permitted to every rank. The results of discipline resemble those of method. Through it individual efforts increase. It gives to each particular case a simple and definite solution. It absolutely necessitates finding anything that can be found. It only demands obediences, and *never anything out of the ordinary*. It diminishes the role of chance.

Translated by Anthony Bower

EXTRANEOUS REMARKS

(1927)

In modern times, not one great power, not one empire in Europe has been able to remain at the top, to extend its influence, or even to hold on to its conquests for longer than fifty years. The greatest men have failed in that direction; even the most successful have led their countries to ruin. Charles V, Louis XIV, Napoleon, Metternich, Bismarck—average duration: forty years. No exceptions.

*

Europe had the ability to submit, to govern and to regulate the rest of the world to European ends. It had invincible means and the men who had created them. Far inferior to these were the men who disposed of her fortunes. They fed on the past: they only knew how to recreate the past. Also the opportunity has gone. European history and political traditions; its petty, short-sighted, shop-worn quarrels; its jealousies and envy of its neighbors; and in short the lack of insight, the narrow-mindedness inherited from the period when Europe was as ignorant and as weak as other parts of the globe, made it miss this great opportunity, the existence of which it did not even suspect at the right time. Napoleon seems to be the only man who had any inkling of what could happen and of what should be undertaken. He thought on the scale of the world as it was, was not understood, and admitted it. But he came too soon; the time was not ripe; his means were far less than ours. After him people again started surveying their neighbors' acres and thinking in terms of the immediate present.

The wretched Europeans preferred to play at being Normans or Burgundians to taking over, throughout the world, the great role that the Romans had known how to play, and to maintain for centuries, in the world of their time. Their numbers and their means were nothing in comparison to ours; but they found in the entrails of their chickens more correct and consequential ideas than all our political science contains.

*

Europe will be punished for its politics; it will be deprived of its wines, and its beer and its liqueurs. And of other things. . . .

*

Europe visibly aspires to be governed by an American commission. Its entire policy is directed to that end.

Not knowing how to rid ourselves of our history, we will be relieved of it by a fortunate people who have almost none. They are a happy people and they will force their happiness on us.

*

Europe was clearly set apart from all the other parts of the world. Not by its politics, but despite, or rather against, its politics, it had developed to the extreme its freedom of mind, combined its passion for understanding with its desire for discipline, created an active curiosity, and accumulated by dint of obstinate research into results *which could be compared and summed up* a capital of very valuable laws and procedures. Its politics, however, remained what they were; borrowing nothing from the singular riches and resources of which I have just been speaking but what was needed to bolster its primitive policies and give them more formidable and barbarous equipment.

Thus a contrast, a difference, an astonishing discrepancy could be seen between the state of the same mind when it was applied to disinterested work, to disciplined critical perceptions, or to consciously explored profundities, and its state when applied to political interests. It seemed to reserve its most neglected, most negligible and most vile products for politics: instincts, idols, memories, regrets, envies, sounds without meaning, and meanings to make the head swim . . . everything that science and the arts no longer wanted or could tolerate.

*

All political systems imply (and are generally not aware that they do imply) a certain conception of man, and even an opinion about the destiny

133

of the species, an entire metaphysic which embraces the crudest sensuality and the most daring mysticism.

*

About nations.

It is never very easy to picture to oneself clearly what is called a *nation*. Its simplest and most marked characteristics are overlooked by its inhabitants who are insensible to what they have always known. The foreigner who perceives these things, perceives them too clearly, and does not understand all the intimate connections and invisible interchanges by which the mystery of the deep union of millions of men is brought about.

Thus there are two ways of being deceived about any given nation.

Moreover even the idea of a *nation-in-general* cannot easily be apprehended. The mind wanders amongst the very diverse aspects of this conception, and hesitates between the very different modes of definition. Hardly has it come to the conclusion that it has found a satisfactory formula, than the formula itself immediately suggests some particular case which it has overlooked.

This conception is as familiar to us in practice and as present in our consciousness as it is complex and indeterminate when under consideration . . . But so it is with all words of great importance. We speak glibly of *rights,* and *race* and *property*. But what are rights, and race and property? We know and we do not know.

Thus all these potent ideas, which are both abstract and vital and on occasion so intensely and imperiously alive in us,—all these terms which constitute, in the minds of the people and of statesmen, the thoughts, projects, reasonings and decisions on which hang the destiny, the prosperity or the ruin and the life or death of human beings, are but vague and corrupt symbols when they are carefully considered. . . . However when men use these indefinable terms among themselves, they understand each other very well. Thus these ideas are quite clear and satisfactory when communicated; obscure and seemingly completely divergent when isolated.

*

Nations are strangers to one another, as are people of different characters, ages, beliefs, customs and requirements. They contemplate one an-

134

other with curiosity and with anxiety; they smile, pout, admire a detail and imitate it; despise the general effect; are smitten with jealousy or inflated with contempt. No matter how sincere their desire to agree and understand each other may sometimes be, the understanding always becomes obscured and stops at a certain point. There are certain insurmountable barriers to its depth and its duration.

More than one nation is deeply convinced that it is intrinsically the leading nation, the nation elect of the limitless future, and the only one able to claim, whatever may be its present condition, its poverty or its weakness, the supreme development of the virtues it attributes to itself. Each one finds its arguments in the past or in future possibilities; not one likes to consider its misfortunes as its legitimate offspring.

In that they compare themselves to other nations in relation to the extent, or the amount, or the material progress of the customs and freedoms of either the social order, or of culture and of intellectual achievements—or even of memories and expectations—it necessarily follows that nations find motives for liking themselves best. In the perpetual game that they play each holds all the cards. But some of the cards are real and others are imaginary. There are some nations who only hold the *trumps* of the middle ages, or of antiquity—dead and venerable values; others rely on their fine arts, their buildings, their local music, their graces and their distinguished history which they throw on the table in the midst of real *clubs* and real *spades*.

All nations have present, or past, or future reasons for thinking themselves incomparable. And moreover so they are. Not one of the least difficulties of speculative politics is the impossibility of comparing these large entities *which only meet and affect each other in their exterior characteristics and methods*. But the essential fact which is the core and the principle of their existence, the internal bond which binds together the individuals and the generations of a nation, is not, in the various nations, of the same nature. Sometimes the race, sometimes the memories, sometimes the interests, diversely comprise the national unity of an organized human agglomeration. The basic cause of one such grouping can be quite different to that of another.

*

Growing nations should remember that there is no tree in all of nature that, though it is planted in the very best conditions of light and sun and terrain, can grow and spread indefinitely.

*

History is the most dangerous product that the chemistry of the intellect has invented. Its properties are well known. It engenders dreams, it intoxicates the people, it begets false memories, it exaggerates their reactions, keeps their old wounds open, disturbs their sleep, leads them to delusions of grandeur or of persecution, and makes nations bitter, arrogant, insufferable and vain.

History can justify anything. It can teach nothing with restraint, for it contains everything and gives examples of everything.

How many books have been written called: *Lessons in This, Instructions in That!* . . . And there is nothing more ridiculous to reread after the events which followed the events that these books attempt to interpret in the light of the future.

In the present state of the world, the danger of allowing oneself to be seduced by history is greater than ever it was.

The political phenomena of our time are accompanied and complicated by a change in scale without parallel, or rather by a change in the *order of things*. The world to which we are beginning to belong, both as men and as nations, is not a *replica* of the world with which we were familiar. The system of causes which governs the fate of us all, extending from now on over the whole globe, makes all of it resound with each concussion: there are no more local problems, no more finite questions to be dealt with on the spot.

History, as it was formerly understood, was presented as a series of parallel chronological tables with accidental transversals indicated here and there between them. A few attempts at synchronization gave no results other than a sort of demonstration of their futility. What was going on in Peking in Caesar's time, or in Zambesi in Napoleon's, was going on on another planet. But *melodic* history is no longer possible. All political themes are entangled and every event that takes place immediately assumes a multitude of simultaneous and inseparable meanings.

The politics of a Richelieu or a Bismarck are lost and lose their meaning in this new environment. The ideas that they made use of in their schemes, the aims that they could advance to satisfy the ambitions of their people, the forces which figured in their calculations, all become of no import. The main object of politics was, and still is for some, *to acquire territory*. Coercion was used, this coveted territory was taken from someone, and all was over. But who cannot see that those enterprises which consisted of a conference, followed by a duel, followed by a pact, will have such inevitable general consequences in the future that *nothing is more likely to happen than that the whole world becomes involved,* and that one can never foresee nor limit the *almost immediate results* of what one has begun.

All the genius of the great governments of the past is exhausted, made impotent and even *worthless* by the enlargement and increase in the interdependence of political phenomena; for it is certainly not genius, not strength of character or intellect, not tradition (even British) which can now boast of being able to counteract or modify at will the conditions and the reactions of a human world to which the old *political geometry* and the old *political mechanics* are not at all suited.

Europe makes me think of an object that finds itself suddenly transplanted into a more complex sphere, where its known characteristics remain the same in appearance but are subject to quite different *interpretations*. In particular the predictions and the traditional forecasts that once could be made become more futile than ever.

The consequences of the war demonstrate that events which, formerly, would have determined for a long time to come, and *in the sense of their results,* the aspect and the trend of politics in general, have in a few years and in consequence of the number of participants, of the enlargement of the stage, and of the complication of divergent interests, been as though drained of their energy, amortized or contradicted by their immediate consequences.

One must wait until such transformations become the rule. The further we go, the less simple and the less predictable will be the results, and the less will political undertakings and even interventions by force, in other words direct and obvious actions, be what one expected them to be. Their extent, their superficialities, their aggregate effect, their interconnections, the impossibility of localizing them, the promptitude of their repercussions will increasingly impose a very different kind of politics than that of the present.

With effects so rapidly becoming independent of their causes, and even antagonistic to their causes, perhaps it will now be considered puerile, dangerous and insane to *seek out events*—a habit essentially due to history and sustained by it. It is not that, in the meanwhile, there will no longer be events and *monumental moments;* there will be prodigious ones! But those whose function it is to await them, or prepare them, or to ward them off, will of necessity learn more and more to beware of their results. It will no longer suffice to combine the will with the ability in order to undertake some enterprise. Nothing has been more destroyed by the last war than the pretention to foresight. But it seems to me that historical knowledge was not lacking?

Translated by Anthony Bower

WITH REFERENCE TO ADONIS [1]

The exigencies of a strict prosody are the artifice which endows our natural speech with the qualities of a refractory material, foreign to the soul and, as it were, deaf to our desires. If they were not quite mad, and if they did not goad us to revolt they would be thoroughly absurd. Once they have been accepted we cannot do everything we please; we cannot say everything, and to say anything whatsoever it is no longer enough to conceive an idea strongly, to be saturated and intoxicated with it, nor merely to release from the magic moment a figure that has been practically finished in our absence. The ineffable *indistinction* between act and thought is the prerogative of a god alone. As for us, we must toil, painfully learn to know the difference. We have to pursue words that do not always exist; chimerical coincidences; we must keep on in our impotence trying to unite sound and sense, creating in broad daylight one of those nightmares that exhaust the dreamer as he tries endlessly to align two phantoms whose outlines are as unstable as himself. We must then wait with passionate patience, try another hour, another day, as we would try another tool—and wish and wish—and not wish too hard either.

Today, free of all compulsion and false necessity, the old, inflexible laws have no other virtue than that of defining, quite simply, an absolute world of expression. That, at least, is the new meaning I find in them. We have resolved to submit nature—I mean language—to other laws than its own, laws which are not necessary, but which are ours; and we even carry this resolution to the point of no longer deigning to invent them: we accept them as they are.

They sharply separate that which exists of itself from that which exists through outselves alone. How strictly human this is: a decree. But, in submitting to it our pleasures do not perish, nor our emotions languish:

[1] Fragment of a preface for the *Adonis* of La Fontaine, (1920).

they are multiplied, are also generated by conventional disciplines. Consider the case of chess players—all the pains their curious pacts cause them, the ardor afforded them by all the imaginary restrictions: they behold their little ivory horse invincibly held to a certain definite jump on the chess board; they feel magnetic fields and invisible forces unknown to physics. This magnetism vanishes with the game, and the excessive concentration that has so long sustained it is transformed and dissipated like a dream. . . . The reality of a game is in the player alone.

*

You must not misunderstand me. I do not say that "pathless delight" is not the principle, and very aim of the poet's art. I do not disparage the dazzling gift that our life offers our consciousness when, all at once, it flings a thousand memories onto the flames. But, up until now, never has one windfall, nor a whole collection of windfalls, appeared to constitute a work of art.

*

I only wanted to point out that all these arbitrary rules, the prescribed measures, the rhymes, the fixed forms, once they have been adopted, and at complete variance with ourselves, have a sort of philosophic beauty of their own. Chains, tightening with every movement of our genius, instantly remind us of all the contempt that is without a doubt the just portion of this familiar chaos which the average person calls *thought,* ignoring the fact that its *natural* conditions are no less fortuitous and futile than those of a charade.

This skillfully contrived poetry is an art of the profound skeptic. It presupposes an extraordinary freedom with regard to the totality of our ideas and sensations. Graciously the gods give us the first line *for nothing,* but it is up to us to furnish a second that will harmonize with it and not be unworthy of its supernatural elder brother. All the resources of experience and of intelligence are hardly enough to make it comparable to the verse which came to us as a gift.

*

Only a singularly observant mind could have authored *Adonis,* made up entirely of grace and subtleties. The La Fontaine who a little later was to write such admirably varied verse, was able to do so only after twenty years devoted to regular verse; *Adonis* is the finest of all these exercises. Meanwhile he afforded the observers of his day a spectacle of simplicity and indolence, and this tradition, simply and indolently, he hands down to us.

Literary history, like all history, is woven of variously gilded legends. The most fallacious are necessarily due to the most faithful witnesses. Who could be more misleading than the scrupulously truthful man who confines himself to telling what he saw as we would have seen it ourselves? But what do I care for what can be seen? One of the most serious and level-headed men I have ever known generally appeared to be the very personification of frivolity. A second nature clothed him with nonsense. Our minds resemble our bodies in that they envelope in mystery what they feel to be most important, hide it even from themselves; they distinguish and defend it by burying it deep. Everything that counts is veiled; it is obscured by witnesses and documents; acts and works are specially designed to disguise it. Did Racine know where that inimitable voice of his came from, that delicate tracery of the inflection, that transparency of the dialogue, all the things that make him Racine, and without which he would be reduced to that not very considerable personage about whom the biographies tell us a great many things which he had in common with ten thousand other Frenchmen? The so-called lessons of literary history have little bearing on the arcana of the making of poems. Everything happens in the artist's inner sanctuary, as though the visible events of his life had only a superficial influence on his work. The thing that is most important—the very act of the Muses—is independent of adventures, the poet's way of life, incidents, and everything that might figure in a biography. Everything that history is able to observe is insignificant.

What is essential to the work is all the indefinable circumstances, the occult encounters, the facts that are apparent to one person alone, or so familiar to that one person that he is not even aware of them. One knows from one's own experience that these incessant and impalpable events are the solid matter of one's personality.

All these people who create, half certain, half uncertain of their powers, feel two beings in them, one known and the other unknown, whose incessant intercourse and unexpected exchanges give birth in the end to a certain product. I do not know what I am going to do; yet my mind believes it knows itself; and I build on the knowledge, I count on it, it is what I call *Myself*. But I shall surprise myself; if I doubted it I should be nothing. I know that I shall be astonished by a certain thought that is going to come to me before long—and yet I ask myself for this surprise, I build on it and count on it as I count on my certainty. I hope for something unexpected which I designate. I need both my known and my unknown.

How then are we to conceive the creator of a great work? But he is absolutely *no one*. How define the *Self* if it changes opinion and sides so often in the course of my work that the work is distorted under my hands; if each correction can bring about immense modifications; and if a thousand accidents of memory, attention, sensation that cross my mind appear, finally, in my finished work to be the essential ideas and original objects of my efforts? And yet it is all certainly a part of me, since my weaknesses, my strength, my lazy repetitions, my manias, my darkness and my light, can always be recognized in everything that falls from my hands.

And so, let us give up all hope of ever seeing clearly in these matters, and comfort ourselves with an image. I imagine this poet with a mind full of resource and ruse, dissembling sleep in the imaginary center of his still uncreated work, waiting to seize the moment of his power which is his prey. In the vague depths of his eyes, all the forces of his desire and the springs of his instinct are stretched taut. There, intent on the hazards from which she chooses her nourishment; very shadowy there, in the midst of the webs and secret harps that she has made out of language— those interweaving threads, those vaguely and endlessly vibrating strings —a mysterious Arachne, huntress muse, keeps watch.

Translated by Louise Varèse

KNOWLEDGE OF THE GODDESS [1]

Absolute poetry can only proceed from one exceptional marvel to another; the works made up entirely of absolute poetry constitute what is most rare and most improbable among the imponderable treasures of any literature. But just as the perfect void, and in the same way that the lowest degree of temperature cannot be attained, cannot even be approached except at the price of an exhausting succession of efforts, so the ultimate purity of our art, for those who have such a conception of it, demands such endless and rude restraints that they absorb all the natural joy in being a poet and, in the end, leave him nothing but the pride of never being satisfied. Such severity is almost unbearable to most young men endowed with the poetic instinct. Our successors have not envied us our torments; they have not adopted our scruples; they have sometimes mistaken for liberties what we had taken on as new problems; and sometimes they have torn to pieces what we had meant only to dissect. They have also fixed their eyes on the accidents of being, whereas we had closed ours to make ourselves more like its substance. . . . All this was to be foreseen. But it was not impossible to guess the sequel too. Wouldn't it be well to try one of these days to join our inner past and that past which follows after, by borrowing from each of them all that is compatible in their teachings? I see this natural travail going on in a few minds, here and there. In no other way does life proceed; and this same process to be seen in human succession, and in which continuity and atavism are combined, literary life reproduces in its concatenations. . . .

Translated by Louise Varèse

[1] Fragment from a preface to *Knowledge of the Goddess* by Lucien Fabre, (1920).

FRAGMENT FROM AN INAUGURAL ADDRESS BEFORE THE FRENCH ACADEMY

(1927)

. . . I have just been thinking of the singularity of that art which is called classic; I have noticed that it begins to make its appearance as soon as acquired experience begins to intervene in the composition and criticism of works of art. It is inseparable from the notion of precepts, rules, and models. . . .

Soon I began to ask myself how it was that this art had manifested itself and taken root especially in France. Of all the countries in the world, I thought, it is in France that the consideration of form, the exigency of form, and preoccupation with form prevail. Neither the force of the ideas, nor the interest provoked by the passions described, nor the marvelous generation of images, nor even a burst of genius, suffice to satisfy a nation so difficult as never fully to enjoy anything that cannot be enjoyed after reflection. France does not willingly separate the spontaneous from that which will be weighed. She never wholly admires until she has discovered solid and universal reasons for her pleasure; and the search for these reasons has led her in the past, just as it had the ancients, carefully to distinguish the art of speech from speech itself.

It is not astonishing (my reverie again whispered) that in an anything but credulous country such discrimination should have triumphed. The feeling for form and the worship of form seemed to me passions which spring only from intellectual resistance. In short, I said to myself, doubt leads to form.

Then, thinking of the man I had just left,[1] who is known for his love of art better than for anything else, unless it be for the extreme skepticism he professed (for he was doubt personified), I began to suspect that there is some connection, rather obscure perhaps but extremely seductive, between the worship of form and that critical and skeptical turn of mind.

[1] Anatole France.

Credulity, I thought, is not exigent. It consists in not being. It is content to be ravished. It is carried away by impressions, enchantments; and, completely absorbed in the moment, it hails the surprising, the prodigious, the excessive, the marvelous and the novel. But the time comes, although not for everybody, when a warier state of mind suggests a more exacting attitude. Just as doctrines and philosophies which are offered without proofs find in the course of time greater difficulty in getting themselves believed and stir up greater objections, until in the end one holds as true only what can be verified, so it is in the realm of the arts. There is a sort of literary doubt which corresponds to philosophic and scientific doubt.

But how insure works against the back-fire of scrutiny and how strengthen them against the impression of arbitrariness? By arbitrariness itself, by arbitrariness organized and decreed. The system of conventions has been instituted by skeptical creators—creators in their way—against personal excursions, against overabundance and confusion—in short against unbridled fancy. The conventions are arbitrary, or so considered at least; but skepticism is hardly possible in regard to the rules of a game.

Such a remark may seem scandalous. To suggest that classical art is an art oriented toward the ideals of games, being as it is so self-conscious and preserving both the same rigor and the same freedom, is without doubt shocking; but shocking, we hope, only for a moment, only long enough for you to remember that human perfection consists in nothing more than the strict fulfillment of a certain expectation that we have held out to ourselves.

Classical art says to the poet: Thou shalt not sacrifice to graven images which are the beauties of detail; nor make use of all possible words, for among them are rare and baroque words which will attract all the attention to themselves and, in their vanity, shine at the expense of your thought; nor yet try to dazzle at small expense to yourself, nor speculate on novelty; nor deal in thunderbolts, for in spite of what you may think, you are not a god; but rather, if you can, simply give men the idea of a perfection that belongs to man.

Classical art says a great many other things but there are more accomplished voices than mine to speak for it. I shall content myself with repeating after everybody else what classical art has been, summing it up in a few words: it seems to me admirable, and true particularly in France, that under the empire of conscious intelligence an art which is the *summum* of grace should have been created; and that a greater ease of style, a constant union of form and thought, a delicious modesty should have been the astonishing fruits of such extraordinary constraints.

Let us consider a little how this was brought about.

The Muses' shackles were cruelly multiplied. Formidable restrictions were imposed on the number of their steps and on their natural movements. The poet was loaded with chains. He was overwhelmed by odd interdictions, his vocabulary was decimated. And the laws of prosody were atrocious.

And so, strict rules, and sometimes absurd, having been promulgated, and wholly artificial conventions having been established, what happened, gentlemen, and what still fills us with wonder, was that through the agency of half a dozen men of the highest order and thanks to a few *salons,* there were born and flourished miracles of purity, of precise force and of life, those incorruptible works which make us bow, in spite of ourselves, before their divine perfection: Goddesses, they attain a degree of naturalness that is supernatural. . . .

Translated by Louise Varèse

LITERATURE

A poem must be a holiday of Mind. It can be nothing else.

Holiday: it is a game, but solemn, ordered and significant; image of what one ordinarily is not, partaking of a state where efforts are rhythms—are redeemed.

One celebrates something in accomplishing it, or representing it in its purest and fairest state.

Here we have the power of language and its inverse phenomenon, understanding, identity of the things it separates. One discards its poverty, its weaknesses, it everydayness. One organizes all the possibilities of language.

The holiday over, nothing must remain. Ashes, trampled garlands.

*

In the poet:
The ear speaks,
The mouth listens;
It is intelligence, vigilance, that gives birth to dream;
It is sleep that sees clearly;
It is the image and the phantom that look;
It is the lack and the blank that create.

*

Most people have such a vague idea about poetry that this vague feeling itself is their definition of poetry.

*

POETRY

It is the attempt to represent, or to restore, by means of articulated language those things, or that thing, which cries, tears, caresses, kisses, sighs, etc., try obscurely to express, and which objects seem to want to express in all that is lifelike in them or appears to have design.

147

In no other way can that thing be defined. It is of the nature of that energy which spends itself in responding to what is. . . .

*

Thought is hidden in verse like the nutritive virtue in fruit. A fruit is nourishment but it seems to be nothing but pure delight. One perceives only pleasure but one receives a substance. Enchantment veils this imperceptible nourishment it brings with it.

*

Poetry is only literature reduced to the essence of its active principle. It has been purged of idols of every sort and realistic illusions: of any possible ambiguity between the language of 'truth' and the language of 'creation' etc. . . .

And this half-creative, half-fictive role of language (itself of such a practical and veracious origin) is made perfectly evident by the fragility or arbitrary character of the subject.

*

The subject of a poem is as foreign to it and as important, as his name is to a man.

*

Some people, even poets and good poets, see in poetry an arbitrary luxury occupation, a special industry that can exist or not exist, flourish or perish—perfumers could very well be suppressed, liquor dealers, etc.

Others see in it a phenomenon whose nature and activity are altogether essential, profoundly related to the situation of the inner being in relation to knowledge, duration, hidden conflicts and endowments, memory, dream, etc.

*

While the interest in prose writings is, as it were, apart from the writings themselves and born of the consumption of the text,—the interest in poems is an integral part of the poems and can never be separated from them.

*

Poetry is a survival.

Poetry, in a period of language simplification, of changing forms and insensibility in regard to them, of specialization—is a *thing preserved.* I mean that today verse would not be invented. Nor, indeed, rites of any kind.

*

The poet is also the one who looks for the comprehensible and conceivable system that would have a place in its expression for a beautiful accident of language: a certain word, a certain chord of words, a certain syntactic progression—a certain opening—that he has encountered, awakened, stumbled on by chance—thanks to his poet's nature.

*

Lyric poetry is the development of an exclamation.

*

Lyric poetry is the kind of poetry that thinks of the *voice in action*— the voice as direct issue of, or provoked by,—things that one sees or that one feels as *present.*

*

It sometimes happens that the mind seeks poetry or the continuation of poetry in some source or hidden divinity.

But the ear demands a certain sound when the mind demands a certain word whose sound does not conform to the ear's desire.

*

For a long, long time the *human voice* was the foundation and condition of *literature.* The presence of the voice explains the earliest literature from which classical literature derived its form and its admirable *temperament.* The whole human body present *beneath the voice,* as a support and necessary balance for the idea . . .

Then came the day when people knew how to read with their eyes, without spelling out the words, without hearing, and literature was thereby entirely altered. . . .

Evolution from the articulated to the glanced-at—from the flowing and progressive to the instantaneous—from that which is demanded by an audience to that which is demanded and snatched by a quick and avid eye running freely over the page.

*

CLASSICAL

To the ancients the celestial world seemed more orderly than it seems to us and, consequently, totally distinct from our terrestrial world; reciprocity between the two worlds did not occur to them.

The terrestrial world seemed very badly regulated.

Chance, liberty, caprice were the things that struck them (for chance is the liberty of things, the impression we have of the plurality and indifferent importance of solutions).

Their *Fatum* was something vague which undoubtedly won in the long run and as a whole (like the law of large numbers) but prayers, sacrifices, rites were feasible. Man still had some power over circumstances where his direct action is inapplicable.

And, therefore, to *set in order* seemed to him *divine*.

What differentiates Greek art and Oriental art is that the latter is concerned only with giving pleasure, Greek art with attaining *beauty,* that is, giving to things a form which will make us think of universal order, divine wisdom, the domination of mind, things that do not exist in close, tangible, existing nature, all made up of *accidents*.

*

VARIATIONS ON THE CLASSICAL

A classical writer is a writer who dissimulates or reabsorbs associations of ideas.

*

CLASSICS

Thanks to the curious rules of French classical poetry the distance between the initial thought and the final expression is the greatest possible. This is important. A work is accomplished between the emotion received, or intention conceived, and the completion of the instrument which will restore it or an analogous *impression*. Everything is retraced, the thought is re-examined, etc.

Add to this the fact that the men who have raised poetry to its highest point were all translators. Skilled in transposing the ancients into our language.

Their poetry bears the mark of this practice. It is a translation, a *faithless beauty*—faithless to what is not in accord with the exigencies of a pure language.

*

Another and no more arbitrary definition of classical.

An art is classical if it is adapted not so much to individuals as to an organized society and one which is stable (as to customs).

Marriage in France was classical; and still is to some extent. It followed the same lines as stock comedy. There were stereotype roles. The drama began with an accidental and concerted meeting. *"Est-toi, chère Elise?"* . . . The parents conversed with each other through the intermediary of their attorneys.

*

Under the heading of classical, people placidly and indiscriminately include writers who say very little in endless sentences; writers who have simply propounded old wives' verities; others who show a crude vigor, or a defense counsel's verbosity, or an exquisite affected elegance; others who observe an obvious and very pronounced regularity, or the rules of the game.

*

Classical and cultivation—in the true sense of the word—trimming, grafting, selecting, pruning.

Thus Greek grafted on French, Tacitus on Jesuit, Euripedes on Jansenist.

Abrupt returns of the fruit to the wild state.

*

Since the advent of romanticism *singularity* has been imitated instead of, as in the past, *mastery*.

The instinct of imitation has remained the same. But to it the modern adds a contradiction.

Mastery, as the word indicates, is to appear to have command over the technical resources of an art—instead of being visibly commanded by them.

The acquisition of mastery then presupposes the acquired habit of always thinking, or combining, with the technical means as *point of departure,* and of never thinking of a work except in terms of its *means:* of never beginning a work with a subject or an effect which has not been imagined in relation to the technical means.

But it sometimes happens that mastery is taken off its guard and overcome by some innovator who by chance, or by gift, creates *new technical means* and seems at first to have given the world a new world. But it is never more than a question of technique.

*

The classical theatre deprived of description. But is it *natural* for a *character* to be always picturesquely expatiating?

A character should see only what is necessary and sufficient for him to see to further the action—and indeed that is all most men *see*. In that the classics are justified and confirmed by observation. The ordinary man is abstract, that is he is limited (in his own eyes and in those of his fellows) to his preoccupation of the moment. He sees only what is connected with it. . . .

Between classical and romantic the difference is very simple: it is the difference that separates the one who is ignorant of his technique and the one who has learned his.

A romantic who has learned his art becomes a classic. That is why romanticism ended in *Parnasse.*

Translated by Louise Varèse

A POET'S LETTER

Dear Friend,

Thank you for all the beautiful things you have written me about my verse and the just things you say about poetry. My verse has had no direct interest for me except as it has suggested a great many reflections on the poet. How often I have lost myself in the analysis of those operations, so difficult to define, to disentangle, to render clear and distinct! Perhaps it is true, as most people think, that they can only occur, in all their confusion and conflicts, by means of spiritual surprises and accidents; or in a sort of oblivion and frenzy, or in a truly admirable outburst.

The idea of inspiration, if one still clings to that naive conception of an extraneous force, or an all-powerful soul, suddenly taking the place, for a moment, of our own, may be sufficient for the ordinary mythology of the mind. It satisfies most poets. Indeed they will not hear of any other. But I have never been able to understand why one should not delve as profoundly as possible into oneself.

It would seem that one risks losing one's talent in attempting to explore its infernos. But what of it? Would we not discover something else?

What things I have discovered about myself while I was working on my verse!—I undertook the Pythie and several other pieces in a country planted with the most beautiful trees I have ever seen; in the neighborhood of Avranche; watered by a little river where the tide coming up drove a single wave, and often very high, far, far up from the sea. The little river made a thousand twists and turns through the rich pale soil; and the flood would arrive at its appointed hour, could be heard coming long before it could be seen. Under my windows were purple clumps of extremely tall red beeches, enormous linden trees in groups of four emerging from high square mounds of earth that were entirely hidden by the leaves falling to the ground. . . .

Mornings, I would go down into the park before dawn. I walked barefoot in the icy grass. The very first moment of the day has a strange and potent effect upon my nerves. Sadness is mixed with enchantment, emotion, and a sort of almost painful lucidity. The sky would be barely tinted when I went indoors again quite drunk with freshness and determination.

You can't imagine what mornings I spent during those two or three summer months, in that fertile region where giant trees grow like grass, where grass grows with incredible force and facility, and where the vigor of vegetable life is inexhaustible. My work was what it was. But I felt my mind possessed of a vitality that today seems to me the most enviable of possessions. My body, however, was not without discomfort. I would feel myself succumbing toward the middle of the day.

Now, this work, these researches, these struggles of the poet against the stringent conditions I had set myself—and whose indirect importance so few people grasp—were never, I must say, wasted efforts. I made those hours of labor and tension yield everything they could possibly contain. The art of poetry is, happily, not an exact one. At every instant insurmountable problems confront one. A nothing—and a beautiful poem is shipwrecked, achievement compromised, the charm broken. The poet's brain is a sea-bottom on which many hulls repose.

But these desperate plights that all poets know, are not always without their uses; it is a question of intelligence. After all, hasn't the observer in us learned something from this defeat? What is done easily is done without us.

Think this over. We'll discuss it on the beach in a little while. I am horribly weary. Sleep, always light and brief. Worries of three or four sorts, always present. No consecutive work. But letters, letters—and mostly useless. I have lingered over this one.—It's absurd. You may tell your wife that her protégé is without talent. Consequently, I suppose one should concede him genius. One must never despair in a magic age when anything whatsoever can be disseminated and acquire a value.

Goodbye, dear you. It seems to me I have not said what I thought I was going to say to you.

Write me as soon as possible. There is nothing definite in my plans except my desire to spend a few days with you. The date oscillates but the intention remains fixed.

Translated by Louise Varèse

EXTRACTS FROM "A DISCOURSE ON THE DECLAMATION OF VERSE"

How Should Verse Be Recited?

This is a ticklish subject.

Everything connected with poetry is difficult. All those who are mixed up with it are of an exquisite irritability. The inextricable mixture of individual views and common exigencies gives rise to infinite differences of opinion. Nothing more natural than not to agree; the contrary is always surprising. I believe that it is only by mistake that people ever agree on anything, and that all harmony is the fruit of a happy error.

Considering only this question of the recitation of verse, it is easy to realize how little chance there is of agreeing on the right way to go about it. First of all, you must bear in mind that there are, necessarily, as many different styles of elocution as there are, or have been, poets, for each poet writes his verse according to his own particular ear.

There are, moreover, as many ways of reciting verse as there are kinds, and as there are different types, or different metres. There is still another source of variation: there are as many styles of declamation as there are interpreters, each having his own means, timbre of voice, his reflexes, his habits, his aptitudes, his impediments and physiological aversions.

The sum of all these factors is an admirable number of possible sides and of possible misunderstandings, and I have not even mentioned differences of exegesis. . . .

You know very well how easy it is, by a very plausible use of the variables of declamation, to change a verse that seems beautiful into a verse that seems atrocious, or, on the other hand, to save a verse which is a calamity by spacing or slightly softening the syllables in speaking them.

In a word, the interpreter according to his intelligence, according to his intentions—and sometimes contrary to them—can bring about astonishing transmutations of euphony into cacophony, or cacophony into euphony. A poem in itself, like a piece of music, offers only a text which is, strictly speaking, nothing but a recipe; the cook who executes it plays an essential role. To speak of a poem in itself, judge a poem in itself, has no real and precise meaning. It is to speak only of a possibility. The poem is an abstraction, a piece of writing that is waiting, a law that only obtains on some human lips, and those lips are what they are.

However, as every poet for his own work necessarily believes in some ideal reader who will serve him to perfection, and who, indeed, resembles him rather more closely than a brother, so I, too, had conceived for my own personal use, a certain kind of declamation I desired, and this altogether private idea, in the form of advice, might be thus summarized:

That in studying a piece of poetry one intends to recite, one should not take as source or point of departure ordinary conversation and common parlance, in order to rise from this level of prose to the desired poetic tone: but, on the contrary, I thought one should take song as a base, and should put oneself in the state of a singer; adjust one's voice to the plenitude of musical sound, and from there descend to the somewhat less resonant state suitable to verse. This, it seemed to me, was the only way to preserve the musical essence of poems. Above all, the voice must be placed quite away from prose and the text studied from the point of view of necessary attack, modulation, sustained tone, little by little, lowering this musical disposition, which in the beginning one has exaggerated, to bring it down to the proportions of poetry.

These very delicate proportions that distinguish it from true song are the result of the relative importance of sound and sense in the two cases where the human voice is used.

The idea of associating poetry and song seems to me correct in principle and consistent with the origins, as with the essence, of our art. It was in this spirit that two years ago I made the experiment of asking a singer to study the poems of Ronsard with me, and to recite them in public.

The first condition for reciting verse well is to know exactly what it is not, and what an enormous difference separates it from ordinary speech.

Current, level language, the language that is used for a purpose, flies to its meaning, to its purely mental translation, and is lost in it like the fertilizing germ in the egg. Its form, its auditive aspect, is only a stage that the mind runs past without stopping. If pitch, if rhythm are present, they are only there for the sake of the sense, they occur only for the moment as immediate necessities, as auxiliaries of the meaning they convey and which at once absorbs them without resonance, for meaning is its final aim.

But the aim of poetry is continuous delight, and it exacts, under pain of being reduced to a queerly and uselessly measured dissertation, a certain very close union between the physical reality of the sound and the virtual quickening of the sense. It demands a sort of equality between the two powers of speech. Poetry is a policy that makes use of two 'major parties.'

And to sum up, let us say, that in song the words tend to lose their significance, do often lose it, while at the other extreme, in current prose it is the musical value that tends to disappear—so that verse stands symmetrically, as it were, between song, on the one hand, and prose on the other—and is thus admirably and delicately balanced between the sensual and the intellectual power of language.

.   .   .   .

And thus I laid before the interpreters of *Bajazet* these sentiments on the declamation of verse I have just reviewed, and I begged them to abandon that tradition I find detestable which consists in sacrificing to immediate theatrical effect all the musical side of a work. This sorry tradition destroys the continuity, the infinite melody always so deliciously present in Racine. The result is that the actor seems to be struggling against the verses, seems hardly able to endure them, and to find them quite out of place in a play that could get along very well without them. They are hashed and hidden and seem to retain of other times only the constraints; the framework, the props of the alexandrine are exaggerated, its purely conventional signs which, to my mind, are very useful things but become clumsy devices unless elocution envelopes them and clothes them with its grace.

And so I said to our Racinian *Jeunes Turcs:* "First of all you must familiarize yourselves with the melody of the verse; study closely the formation of those phrases with their double construction whose syntax on the one hand, prosody on the other, compose a sonorous and spiritual substance and artfully create a form full of life. And be sure you don't let a slavish respect for rhymes and caesuras hamper you. True, this admirable author observed them; but a musical creation cannot be confined by rules as too many people have thought, with such barren results that

157

they have rendered the rules ridiculous and aroused terrible reactions in return. You must take time to feel. Listen to Racine's timbres, listen for the overtones, the nuances, the reciprocal reflections of the vowels, the clean pure acts, the supple links of his consonants and their adjustments.

"And therefore, and above all, do not be in a hurry to arrive at the meaning. Approach it without effort and, as it were, insensibly. And only in and by means of the music attain to tenderness or to violence. Keep yourselves for a long time from emphasizing the words. There are as yet no words, there are only syllables and rhythms. Remain in this pure musical state until such time as the meaning, appearing little by little, can no longer mar the musical form. You will introduce it at the very end as the supreme nuance that will transfigure the passage without altering it. But first of all you must have learned the passage.

"This moment will finally come. At last you will discover what your role is, and you will devote yourself to bringing your personnage to life. You will mix with this music, profoundly learned and felt, whatever accents and accidents are necessary to make it seem to spring direct from the emotions and passions of a human being. Now is the time for you to exert discrimination and display intelligence. For a moment put yourself in the author's place. Understand his aims, his difficulties, his lucky strokes and his struggles. You will soon see that a distinction must be made between different kinds of verses. Some help to forward the play itself, are an indispensible part of it; they serve to explain, develop, unravel the plot; they answer logical questions; they permit a recapitulation of the drama and are, in a way, on the same level as prose. To speak these verses is an art; much greater the art of fashioning them. But other verses, that constitute all the poetry of the work, sing, and contain all that is most profound in the poet's nature. I hardly need to commend to you these divine portions."

Such, I dare say, was my little exhortation.

Translated by Louise Varèse

FRAGMENT OF "THE MEMORIES OF A POEM"

It is a singular sensation that of an irresistible return, but by such small degrees, such divers ramifications that one remains long unconscious of it, toward a former phase of oneself one had thought forever dissipated.

One day I felt that I had been insensibly led back, by the most fortuitous and unrelated circumstances, to a mental region I had long ago abandoned, had, as a matter of fact, fled from. It was as though, fleeing a certain place —but because of the shape of space the most distant point of that place was the same place—one should suddenly find oneself there again and be very much surprised to recognize oneself as both the same and totally different.

I had fled poetry's ingenuous state, and I had energetically developed in myself what is considered, by general consent, quite opposed to the existence and to the productions of that state.

But, perhaps, the universe of mind too has its curve of which, if it exists, we can know nothing, of which we know nothing. I have observed in other mental things that although sometimes we are able to reach our antipodes, later we cannot help returning. It is only a 'matter of time'; for every fresh change can only invariably bring us nearer to the beginning. I am inclined to think that a man who lived long enough would, at the completion of his circumnavigation, on condition that his mind remained sufficiently active, have made the complete round of his emotions and, having in the end adored and burned, burned and adored all that was worth while in the sphere of knowledge, would die completed. From this I conclude that, in general, we see that we ourselves are only fragments of existence, and that our lived life does not fill the whole of our capacity to feel and to conceive. And consequently, when we impute tastes, opinions, beliefs or negations to a person, are we not emphasizing only some aspect of himself, only the one that has so far been revealed by circumstances and which, in spite of everything, is and must even necessarily be, subject to modification for the sole reason that it has been? This 'good and sufficient' reason is essential: the mind, in that which is most strictly mind, *cannot possibly repeat itself*. What repeats itself in the mind is no longer mind: it is, as it were, its flesh; it has become what our first essays at writing have become. Whatever, little by little, is confused with our functions and our native powers, ceases to make any impression on us in ceasing to be *without a past*. That is why every conscious resumption of an idea reconditions it; modifies, enriches, simplifies, or destroys what has been reappropriated; and even if in this return we find nothing to change in our former thought, this very judgement, which approves and conserves a certain acquired thing, forms with it a fact that has not yet existed, a novel event.

*

And so, here I was once more playing with syllables and images, with similarities and contrasts. Once more, my mind was filled with the forms and the words suitable to poetry and I would forget myself, waiting for it to give me those remarkable groupings of terms that offer us all at once such a happy combination, appearing spontaneously in the impure current of the things of the mind. Just as a definite combination is precipitated in a mixture, so some interesting *form* is detached from the disorder, or instability, or ordinary state, of our interior morass.

It is a pure sound that resounds in the midst of noise. It is a perfectly executed fragment of an edifice. It is the suspicion of a diamond in a mass of 'blue ground': a moment infinitely more precious than all the others and than the circumstances that gave it birth! It provokes an incomparable contentment and an instantaneous temptation; it arouses our hope of finding *in its vicinity* a whole treasure-trove of which it is the sign and the proof; and this hope often starts a man on a boundless labor.

Many people think that a certain heaven opens at this instant, and that out of it comes an extraordinary ray by which certain ideas, until now detached from each other and, as it were, unknown to each other, are lighted up together; and there they are, miraculously united all at once and seemingly made for each other through all eternity; and all this without any direct preparation, without toil through the happy effect of light and certainty. . . .

But the trouble is that too often what is revealed to us turns out to be a piece of childishness, an error, simple nonsense. One must not count on lucky strokes alone; this miraculous way of producing does not by any means assure us of the value of what is produced. Spirit blows where it wills; enters into fools and inspires them to do—what they can.

Translated by Louise Varèse

FOUR FRAGMENTS FROM *"EUPALINOS, OR THE ARCHITECT"*

SOCRATES

O co-eternal with me in death, faultless friend, and diamond of sincerity, hear then:

It served no purpose, I fear, to seek this God, whom I have tried all my life to discover, by pursuing him through the realm of thought alone; by demanding of him that most variable and most ignoble sense of the just and the unjust, and by urging him to surrender to the solicitings of the most refined dialectic. The God that one so finds is but a word born of words, and returns to the word. For the reply we make to ourselves is assuredly never anything other than the question itself; and every question put by the mind to the mind is only, and can only be, a piece of simplicity. But on the contrary, it is in acts, and in the combination of acts that we ought to find the most immediate feeling of the presence of the divine, and the best use for the part of our strength that is unnecessary for living, and seems to be reserved for the pursuits of an indefinable object that infinitely transcends us.

If, then, the universe is the effect of some act; that act itself, the effect of a Being, and of a need, a thought, a knowledge and a power which belongs to that Being, it is then only by an act that you can rejoin the grand design, and undertake the imitation of that which has made all things. And that is to put oneself in the most natural way in the very place of the God.

Now, of all acts the most complete is that of constructing. A work demands love, meditation, obedience to your finest thought, the invention of laws by your soul, and many other things that it draws miraculously from your own self, which did not suspect that it possessed them. This work proceeds from the most intimate center of your existence, and yet it is distinct from your self. If it were endowed with thought, it would

162

divine your existence, which yet it would never succeed in probing, nor in conceiving clearly. You would be for it a God. . . .

Let us now consider this great act of constructing. Note, Phaedrus, that when the Demiurge set about making the world he grappled with the confusion of Chaos. All formlessness spread before him. Nor could he find a single handful of matter in all this waste, that was not infinitely impure and composed of an infinity of substances.

He valiantly came to grips with this frightful mixture of dry and wet, of hard and soft, of light and gloom, that made up this chaos, whose disorder penetrated into his smallest parts. He disentangled that faintly luminous mud, of which not a single particle was pure, and wherein all energies were diluted, so that the past and the future, accident and substance, the lasting and the fleeting, propinquity and remoteness, motion and rest, the light and the heavy, were as completely mingled as wine and water when poured into one cup. Our men of science are always trying to bring their minds close to this state. . . . But the great Shaper acted in contrary wise. He was the enemy of similitudes and of those hidden identities that we delight to come upon. He organized inequality. Setting his hand to the rough matter of the world, he sorted out its atoms. He divided the hot from the cold, and the evening from the morning; he drove back almost all the fire into the subterranean hollows, and hung clusters of ice on the very trellises of dawn, beneath the vaultings of the eternal Ether. By him extension was distinguished from movement, night from day; and in his rage to disunite everything, he clove asunder the first animals, which he had just disassociated from the plants, into male and female. After he had finally disentangled even that which was most mixed up in the original confusion—matter and mind—he hoisted to the loftiest empyrean, to the inaccessible peak of history, those mysterious masses, whose silent irresistible descent into the uttermost depth of the abyss begets and measures time. He squeezed out from the mud the sparkling seas and pure waters, lifting the mountains out of the waves, and portioning out in fair islands what remained of concrete. Thus he made all things and from a remnant of mud, human kind.

But the Constructor whom I am now bringing to the fore finds before him, as his chaos and as primitive matter, precisely that world-order which the Demiurge wrung from the disorder of the beginning. Nature is formed, and the elements are separated; but something enjoins him to

163

consider this work as unfinished, and as requiring to be rehandled and set in motion again for the more special satisfaction of man. He takes as the starting point of his act the very point where the god had left off.—In the beginning, he says to himself, there was what is: the mountains and forests; the deposits and veins; red clay, yellow sand and the white stone which will give us lime. There were also the muscular arms of men, and the massive strength of buffaloes and oxen. But there were in addition the coffers and store-rooms of intelligent tyrants and citizens grown over-rich by trade. And lastly there were priests who wished to house their god; and kings so puissant that they had nothing more to desire but a matchless tomb; and republics that dreamed of inexpugnable walls; and refined archons, who had such partiality for actors and fair musicians, that they were all afire to build for them, out of the state treasuries, the most resonant theaters. Now the gods must not remain without a roof, nor souls without drama. The masses of marble should not remain lifeless within the earth, constituting a solid night; nor the cedars and cypresses rest content to come to their end by flame or by rot, when they can be changed into fragrant beams and dazzling furniture. But still less should the gold of rich men lazily sleep its heavy sleep in the urns and gloom of treasuries. This so-weighty metal, when it becomes the associate of a fancy, assumes the most active virtues of the mind. It has her restless nature. Its essence is to vanish. It changes into all things, without being itself changed. It raises blocks of stone, pierces mountains, diverts rivers, opens the gate of fortresses and the most secret hearts; it enchains men; it dresses, it undresses women with an almost miraculous promptitude. It is truly the most abstract agent that exists next to thought. But indeed thought exchanges and envelopes images only, whereas gold incites and promotes the transmutations of all real things into one another; itself remaining incorruptible, and passing untainted through all hands.

Gold, limbs, projects, various substances, all are present; yet nothing results.

Here I am, says the Constructor, I am the act. You are the matter, you are the force, you are the desire; but you are separate. An unknown industry has isolated and prepared you according to its means. The Demiurge was pursuing his own designs, which do not concern his creatures. The converse of this must come to pass. He was not concerned about the troubles that were bound to spring from that very separation which he diverted or perhaps bored himself with making. He has given you the means of living, and even of enjoying many things, but not generally those which you particularly want.

But I come after him. I am he who conceives what you desire a trifle more exactly than you do yourselves; I shall consume your treasures with a little more consistency and genius than you consume them; and without a doubt I shall cost you very dear; but in the end everyone will have gained. I shall make mistakes sometimes, and we shall have some ruins; but one can always very profitably look upon a work that has failed as a step which brings us nearer to the most beautiful.

PHAEDRUS

It is fortunate for them that you are a dead architect!

SOCRATES

Must I be silent, Phaedrus?—So you will never know what temples, what theaters, I should have conceived in the pure Socrates style! . . . I was going to give you an idea how I should have carried out my work. I should first have set out all the problems, envolving a flawless method. Where?—For what?—For whom?—To what end?—Of what size?— And exercising an ever stricter control over my mind, at the highest point I should have realized the operation of the transforming a quarry and a forest into an edifice, into splendid equilibriums! . . . And I was drawing up my plan with an eye to the purpose of the humans who pay me; taking into account loyalties, lights, shadows and winds; choosing the site according to its size, its aspect, its approaches, the adjacent lands and the true nature of the subsoil. . . .

Then out of raw materials I was going to put together my structures entirely ordained for the life and joy of the rosy race of men. . . . Objects most precious for the body, delightful to the soul, and such as Time itself must find so hard and so difficult to digest, that he will be able to subdue them only by the assaults of centuries; and that only after having clothed them in a second beauty: a mellow gold upon them, a sacred majesty upon them, and, wrought by the flight of time, a charm which comes of comparisons growing up about them and of a secret tenderness that wraps them all about. . . . But you shall learn no more. You can only conceive the old Socrates, and your stubborn shade . . .

Call it rather faithful, Socrates, faithful.

In that case it must follow me; and change if I change!

But do you mean to revoke in eternity all those sayings that made you immortal?

Immortal there—relatively to mortals! . . . But here . . . But there is no *here,* and all that we have been saying is as much a natural sport of the silence of these nether regions, as the fantasy of some rhetorician of the other world who has used us as puppets!

It is in this that immortality rigorously consists.

II

Well then, Phaedrus, this is how it was. I was walking on the very edge of the sea. I was following an endless shore. This is not a dream I am telling you. I was going I know not whither, overflowing with life, half-intoxicated by my youth. The air, deliciously rude and pure, pressing against my face and limbs, confronted me—an impalpable hero that I must vanquish in order to advance. And this resistance, ever overcome, made of me, too, at every step an imaginary hero, victorious over the wind, and rich in energies that were ever reborn, ever equal to the power of the invisible adversary. . . . That is just what youth is. I trod firmly the winding beach, beaten and hardened by the waves. All things around me were simple and pure: the sky, the sand, the water. I watched, as they came from the offing, those mighty shapes which seem to be running from the coasts of Libya, charioting their glistening summits, their hollow valleys, their relentless energy from Africa all the way to Attica across the immense liquid expanse. At last they come upon their obstacle, the very plinth of Hellas; they shatter themselves against those submarine foundations; they recoil in disorder toward the origin of their motion. When the waves at this point are destroyed and confounded, yet seized in turn by those that follow them, it is as though the forms of the deep were engaged in strife. The countless drops break their chains, a sparkling spray goes up. One sees white horsemen leaping beyond themselves, and all those envoys of the inexhaustible sea perishing and reappearing, with a monotonous tumult, on a gentle almost imperceptible slope, which all their vehemence, though it be come from the most remote horizon, will yet never be able to surmount. Here the foam, flung farthest by the highest wave, forms yellowish iridescent heaps which burst in the sunlight, or which the wind sweeps along and disperses in the drollest fashion, like beasts scared by the sudden bound of the sea. But as for me, I was revelling in the new-born virgin foam. Its contact is of a strange softness. It is a milk warm, airy—that comes in with a voluptuous violence, pours round one's bare feet, bathes them, passes beyond and flows down upon them again, moaning with a voice that forsakes the shore and withdraws into itself, while the human statue, a living presence, sinks a little deeper into the sand that draws it down, and whilst the soul gives itself up to that so puissant and so delicate music, is soothed by it, and follows it eternally.

PHAEDRUS

You make me live again. O language charged with salt! O words truly born of the sea.

SOCRATES

I have let my talk flow on. . . . We have all eternity during which to discourse upon time. We are here—Danaïd-like—to empty out our spirits.

PHAEDRUS

But the object?

SOCRATES

The object lay upon the beach where I was walking, where I have halted, where I have spoken to you at length of a sight with which you are as familiar as I, but which, when recalled in this place, acquires a kind of

167

novelty from the fact that it has forever disappeared. So wait, and in a few words I shall have found this thing that I was not looking for.

PHAEDRUS

We are still on the sea-shore?

SOCRATES

Necessarily. This frontier between Neptune and Earth, ever disputed by those rival divinities, is the scene of the most dismal and most incessant commerce. That which the sea rejects, that which the land cannot retain, the enigmatic bits of drift; the hideous limbs of dislocated ships, black as charcoal, and looking as those charred by the salt waters; carrion horribly pecked and washed sleek by the waves; elastic weeds torn by the tempests from the transparent pasture-grounds of Proteus' flocks; collapsed monsters, of cold deathly hues; all the things, in short, that fortune delivers over to the fury of the shore, and to the fruitless litigation between the wave and beach, are there carried to and fro; raised, lowered; seized, lost, seized again according to the hour and the day; sad witnesses to the indifference of the fates, ignoble treasures, playthings of an interchange as perpetual as it is stationary. . . .

PHAEDRUS

And it was there that you made your find?

SOCRATES

Yes, there. I found one of those things cast up by the sea; a white thing of the most pure whiteness; polished, and hard, and smooth, and light. It shone in the sun on the licked sand, that is somber and spark-bestrewn. I took it up; I blew upon it; I rubbed it against my cloak, and its singular shape suspended all my other thoughts. Who made thee? Pondered, thou resemblest nothing, and yet thou art not shapeless. Art thou a sport of nature, O nameless thing, that art come to me by the will of the gods, in the midst of the refuse that the sea this night has flung from her?

PHAEDRUS

How large was this object?

168

About as big as my fist.

And made of what matter?

As the same matter as its form: matter for doubt. It was perhaps some fish-bone weirdly worn by the rubbing of the fine sand under the water? Or a piece of ivory carved for I know not what purpose, by some crafts-man beyond the sea? . . . . A divinity, perhaps, that perished with the very vessel which it had been made to preserve from shipwreck? But who can have been the maker of this? Was it a mortal obedient to an idea, who, pursuing with his own hands an aim foreign to the sub-stance he is attacking, scratches, cuts off, or joins together again; pauses and considers; and finally takes leave of his work—something telling him that the work is finished? . . . . Or was it not rather the product of a living body, which, unwittingly, labors with its own substance, and blindly forms for itself its organs and its armor, its shell, its bones, its weapons; causing its nourishment, which it gathers from around it, to participate in the mysterious construction which ensures it a certain lastingness.

But perhaps it was but the fruit of an infinite lapse of time. . . . Through the eternal laboring of the sea-waves, a fragment of rock, by dint of being rolled and knocked to and fro, if its substance is of an un-equal hardness, and so is not liable in time to become rounded, may very well take on some striking semblance. It is not altogether impossible that, if a quite shapeless piece of marble or stone be given up to the permanent commotion of the waters, it should someday be thence recovered, by a chance of another kind, and should then bear the likeness of Apollo. I mean that the fisherman who has some notion of those divine features, might recognize them in this piece of marble drawn from the waters; but as for the thing itself, the sacred face is for it one fleeting form out of the family of forms that the action of the seas must impose upon it. Centuries cost nothing, and he who disposes of them changes what he will into what he will.

But then, dear Socrates, when an artist makes immediately, and by a consistent application of his will, such a bust (as that of Apollo), is not his work in some sort the contrary of indefinite time?

SOCRATES

Precisely. It is the exact contrary, as though acts illuminated by a thought abridged the course of nature; and so we may safely say that an artist is worth a thousand centuries, or a hundred thousand, or even many more! —In other words, that this almost inconceivable space of time would have been necessary for ignorance or chance blindly to bring to pass the self-same thing that our skilled man has accomplished in a few days. Here is a strange standard for measuring works by!

PHAEDRUS

Strange indeed. It is a great misfortune that we can hardly make use of it. . . . But tell me, what did you do with that thing in your hand?

SOCRATES

I stood still for some little time, examining it on all sides. I questioned it without stopping at an answer . . . I could not determine whether this singular object were the work of life, or of art, or rather of time—and so a freak of nature. . . . Then suddenly I flung it back into the sea.

PHAEDRUS

The water splashed up, and you had a feeling of relief.

SOCRATES

The mind does not reject a riddle so easily. The soul does not recover its calm again as simply as the sea. . . . This question that had just been born, finding in my spirit no lack either of sustenance or of resonance, of leisure or of space, began to grow, and busied me for hours. In vain I breathed in the delicious air and feasted my gaze on the resplendent beauties of the expanse. I felt myself still the prisoner of a thought. My memories nourished it with examples, which it endeavored to turn to its own advantage. I offered it a thousand things, for I was not yet, at that time, so expert in the art of reflecting, or of luring myself on, as to discern what one should and what one should not demand of truth still too young, and too delicate to withstand the full rigor of a lengthy cross examination.

PHAEDRUS

Let us have a view of this frail truth of yours.

SOCRATES

I hardly venture to proffer, even for your amusement . . .

PHAEDRUS

But you yourself suggested it!

SOCRATES

Yes. I thought it would bear exposition better. . . . But as I come closer to it and am almost on the point of telling it, diffidence overcomes me, and I feel some shame in acquainting you with this naive product of my golden age.

PHAEDRUS

What vanity! You forget that we are shades. . . .

SOCRATES

Well this was my ingenuous idea. Intrigued by this object the nature of which I could not get to know, and which was equally claimed and rejected by all the categories, I sought to escape from the perplexing image of my find. How was this to be managed, unless by proceeding indirectly and magnifying the difficulty itself? After all, I said to myself, the same embarrassment which this object I have found causes me can be conceived from an object that is known, but with this latter, since it is known, we are in possession of both the question and the answer; or rather more particularly in possession of the answer, and, feeling that we have it, we omit to ask the question. . . . Suppose now that I am looking at some very familiar thing such as a house, a table, a wine jar; and that I pretend for a brief space that I am a complete savage who has never seen such objects, I might well doubt whether those objects were of human fabrication. . . . Not knowing to what use they can be put, nor even if they are of use to anyone, and being moreover informed by nobody, I should needs have to imagine some means for setting my mind at rest concerning them.

And what did you imagine?

Seeking, finding, losing and re-discovering the means of discriminating between what is produced by nature and what is made by men, I remained standing for some time in the same place, my eye hesitating amid various lights; then I started walking very rapidly inland, like someone whose thoughts, after having long been tossed in all directions, seemed at last to have found their bearings; and to resolve themselves into a single idea, engendering at the same instant in his body a decision of clearly determined movement and a resolute bearing. . . .

I know that feeling. I have always marveled how an idea which comes to one, however abstract it may be, gives one wings and bears one any and everywhere. One stops, and then one is off again; that is what thinking is!

Well, half running I reasoned thus: a tree, with its leaves, is a product of nature. It is an edifice of which the parts are the leaves, the branches, the trunk and the roots. I assume that each of its parts gives me the idea of a certain complexity. I then say that the whole of this tree is more complex than any one of its parts.

That is evident.

I am very far from thinking so now. But then I was scarce eighteen, and all my knowledge was certitudes!—The tree then, which comprises such and such parts, comprises and includes all those various complexities;

and it is the same with an animal, whose whole body is a more complex thing than the foot. or the head, since the complexity of the whole comprises in some sort, as parts of itself, the complexities of its diverse parts.

The fact being, my dear Socrates, that we can scarce conceive a tree as part of a leaf, or the accessory of a root; nor a horse as an organ or part of its thigh. . . .

I forthwith inferred that, in all these beings, the degree or level of the whole is necessarily to be ranged higher than the level of the details; or rather that it can be equal to or higher than the latter, but never inferior to it.

Your thought seems to me clear enough; but it is difficult to conceive this degree of complication precisely.

I have told you more than once that I was eighteen! I was thinking as best I could, of degree in the order and distribution of the parts and in the elements brought together to form a being. . . . But all these beings of which I have spoken are of the class that nature produces. They increase in such wise that the matter they are made of, the forms they put on, the functions they are to fulfill, the means they possess for adapting themselves to places and seasons, are invisibly bound up with one another by secret relations; and that is perhaps the meaning of the words "produce by nature." But with the objects which are the work of man it is quite different. Their structure is . . . a disorder!

One day, dear Socrates, I spoke of this very thing with my friend Eupalinos.

"Phaedrus," he was saying to me, "the more I meditate on my art, the more I practice it; the more I think and act, the more I suffer and rejoice as an architect; and the more I feel my own being with an ever surer delight and clarity.

"I go astray with my long spells of waiting; I find myself again by the surprises I give myself; by means of these successive degrees of my silence, I advance in my own edification; and I draw near to such an exact correspondence between my aims and my powers, that I seem to myself to have made of the existence that was given me a sort of human handiwork. By dint of constructing," he put it with a smile, "I truly believe that I have constructed myself."

SOCRATES

To construct oneself, to know oneself—are these two distinct acts or not?

PHAEDRUS

. . . and he added: "I have sought accuracy in my thoughts, so that, being clearly engendered by the consideration of things, they might be changed as of their own accord into the acts of my art. I have apportioned my attentions; I have arranged the problems in another order; I begin where I finished off formerly, so as to go a little further. . . . I am niggardly of musings, I conceive as though I were executing. No more now, in the shapeless void of my soul, do I contemplate those imaginary edifices, which are to real edifices what chimeras and gorgons are to true animals. But what I think, is feasible, and what I do, is related to the intelligible. . . . And then . . . Listen, Phaedrus," he went on to say, "this little temple, which I built for Hermes, a few steps from here, if you could know what it means to me! There where the passer-by sees but an elegant chapel—'tis but a trifle: four columns, a very simple style—there I have enshrined the memory of a bright day in my life. O sweet metamorphosis! This delicate temple, none knows it, is the mathematical image of a girl of Corinth, whom I happily loved. It reproduces faithfully proportions that were peculiarly hers. It lives for me! It gives me back what I have given it. . . ."

"That then is why it is of inexplicable grace," I said to him. "One does indeed feel the presence of a person, the first flower of a woman, the harmony of a charming being. It vaguely awakens a memory which can not reach its goal; and this beginning of an image of which you possess the perfection does not fail to incite and confound the soul. Do you know, if I give myself up to my thought, I shall be comparing it to some nuptial song intermingled with flutes, which I feel coming to birth in me."

Eupalinos looked at me with a more definite and more tender friendliness.

"Oh!" said he, "how you seem made to understand me! None has come closer to you than my daemon. I would willingly confide all my secrets to you; but of some I myself could not speak adequately, for they defy language; the others would run a great chance of wearying you, for they are connected with the most special processes and the most detailed knowledge of my art. I can only tell you what truths, if not what mysteries, you are just now hinting at, when you spoke to me of concert, of songs and of flutes, in reference to my young temple. Tell me (since you are so sensible to the effects of architecture), have you not noticed, in walking about this city, that among the buildings with which it is peopled, certain are *mute;* others *speak* and others, finally—and they are the most rare— *sing?* It is not their purpose, nor even their general features, that give them such animation, or that reduce them to silence. These things depend upon the talent of their builder, or on the favor of the Muses."

"Now that you point it out to me, I recognize this for myself!"

"Good. Those among buildings that neither speak nor sing deserve only scorn; they are dead things, lower in the hierarchy than those heaps of rubble vomited by contractors' carts, which at least amuse the sagacious eye by the accidental order they borrow from their fall. . . . As for the monuments that limit themselves to speech, if they speak clearly, I esteem them. Here, say they, the tradesmen meet. Here the judges deliberate. Here captives groan. Here the lovers of debauchery . . . (I then told Eupalinos that I had seen very remarkable buildings in this last style. But he did not hear me.) These markets, these tribunals, and these prisons, when those that build them know their business, speak the most definite language. The one kind visibly draw in an active and ever changing crowd; they offer it peristyles and porticos; by means of their many doors and easy flights of steps they invite all to enter their vast, well-lighted halls, to form groups, to give themselves up to the seething ferment of business. But the habitations of justice should speak to the eye of the rigor and equity of our laws. Majesty befits them—masses, completely bare; and an awe-inspiring amplitude of wall. The silences of those bleak surfaces are scarce broken, at far intervals, by the threat of a mysterious door, or by the dismal outline of thick iron bars against the gloom of the narrow window they guard. All here pronounces sentence—everything is eloquent of penalties. The stone gravely declares that which it shuts in; the wall is implacable, and this work of stone, conforming so closely to the truth, strongly proclaims its stern purpose. . . ."

SOCRATES

My prison was not so terrible. . . . If I recollect, it was a drab and indifferent place in itself.

PHAEDRUS

How can you say so!

SOCRATES

I confess that I gave it little thought. I saw only my friends, immortality and death.

PHAEDRUS

And I was not with you!

SOCRATES

Plato was not either, nor Aristippus. . . . But the room was full, the walls were hidden from me. The evening light cast flesh tints on the stones of the vault. . . . In truth, dear Phaedrus, I never had a prison other than my body. But come back to what your friend said to you. I think he was going to speak of those most precious edifices, and I should like to hear about them.

PHAEDRUS

Well, I will continue.

Eupalinos went on to give a magnificent picture of those gigantic constructions which we admire in ports. They advance into the sea. Their arms, of a hard, absolute whiteness, circumscribe the lulled docks whose calm they defend. They keep them in security, peacefully gorged with galleys, sheltered by the bristling breakwaters and the resounding piers. High towers, where someone keeps watch, where during impenetrable

176

nights the flame of pine cones dances and rages, command the offing at the foaming extremities of the moles. . . . To venture upon such works is to brave Neptune himself. You must fling mountains in cart loads into the waters you wish to enclose. You must pit the coarse rubble drawn from the depths of the earth against the shifting depths of the sea, and against the monotonous onslaught of the horsemen, whom the wind urges on as it sweeps by. . . .

"Those ports, those vast ports," said my friend, "What a sudden brightness in the mind! How they spread wide their branches! How they descend to their task! But the wonders peculiar to the sea, and the accidental statuary of the shores are given to the architect by a grace of the gods. All noble, half-natural constructions: the presence of the pure horizon, the waxing and the waning of a sail, the emotion of perils, the sparkling threshold of lands unknown; and the very eagerness of the men, ready as it is to change into a superstitious dread the moment they give in to it and set foot aboard. . . . Admirable theaters they are, in truth; but let us place above them the edifices of art alone! It is necessary to abstract one's self from immediate enjoyment, even if for this purpose we must make a stern effort against ourselves. What is most beautiful is of necessity tyrannical. . . ."

But I said to Eupalinos that I did not see why this must be so. He replied that true beauty is precisely as rare as, among men, is the man capable of making an effort against himself, that is, choosing a certain self and imposing it upon himself. And then, taking up again the golden thread of his thought: "I now come," said he, "to the masterpieces entirely due to someone, of which I said, a moment ago, that they seem to sing of themselves.

"Was that a vain saying, O Phaedrus? Mere words negligently engendered by the discourse they adorn as it goes rapidly on its way, but which do not bear pondering over? No, Phaedrus, most assuredly no! . . . . And when, first of us two and without special intents, you spoke of music with reference to my temple, you were visited by a divine analogy. The hymen of thoughts which was consummated on your lips, as the unreflecting act of your voice; that seemingly fortuitous union of things so different, comes of an admirable necessity, which it is almost impossible to conceive in all its profundity, but whose persuasive presence you have obscurely felt. Just imagine strongly what would be the nature of a mortal pure enough, powerfully enough armed by Minerva to think out to the ultimate limits of his being, and therefore to ultimate reality, that strange parallel of visible forms with the ephemeral combinations of successive sounds; think toward what an intimate and universal origin he would advance; what a precious point of vantage he would reach; what a god he would find in his own flesh! And possessing himself finally in this state of divine ambiguity, if he then proposed to build I know not what monuments, whose gracious and venerable features should partake directly of the purity of musical sound, or were designed to communicate to the soul the emotion coming of an inexhaustible accord, think, Phaedrus, what a man! Imagine what edifices! And for us what delights!"

"And do you," I said to him, "conceive this?"

"Yes and no. Yes, as a dream. No as a science."

"Do you draw some help from these thoughts?"

"Yes, as an incentive. Yes, as a verdict. Yes, as a punishment. . . . But it is not in my power to link up, as I ought, an analysis with an ecstasy. Sometimes I come near to this precious power. . . . Once I was infinitely near to seizing it, but only in the way one possesses during sleep an object beloved. I can only speak to you of the approaches of so great a thing. When it makes its presence known, dear Phaedrus, I am already as different from myself as a tightened string differs from itself when loose and sinuous. I am quite other than what I am. All is clear and seems easy. Then my schemes follow their own course and are preserved in a light that is mine. I feel my need of beauty, proportionate to my unknown resources, engendering of itself alone forms that give it satisfaction. I desire with my whole being. . . . The powers assemble. The powers of the soul, as you know, behave strangely in the night. . . . By force of illusion they advance to the very borders of the real. I summon them, I adjure them by my silence. . . . Here they come, charged with clarity and with error. The true, the false, shine equally in their eyes, on their diadems. They crush me with their gifts, they besiege me with their wings . . . Phaedrus, here lies the peril! It is the most difficult thing in the world! . . . O moment most important of all, and chiefest rending! . . . These mysterious and over-bountiful favors, far from welcoming them as they are, solely derived from the great desire, naively formed of the extreme expectation of my soul, I must arrest them, O Phaedrus, and they must await my signal. And having obtained them by a sort

178

of interruption of my life (an adorable suspension of ordinary duration), I still force myself to divide the indivisible, and to temper and interrupt the birth of ideas itself. . . ."

"Poor mortal," I said to him, "what can you hope to do during a lightning flash?"

"Be free. There are many things," he resumed, "there are all things in that instant; and all that busies the philosophers takes place between the glance that falls on an object and the knowledge that results. . . . Always to end up prematurely!"

"I do not understand you. Do you strive then to delay these ideas?"

"I must. I prevent them from satisfying me. I postpone unmixed felicity."

"Why? Whence do you draw this cruel force?"

"What is important for me above all else is to obtain from *that which is going to be,* that it should with all the vigor of its newness satisfy the reasonable requirements of *that which has been.* How can one help being obscure?

". . . Listen: one day I saw a cluster of roses and modeled it in wax. When I had finished this model, I put it in sand. Hurrying Time reduces the roses to nothing; and fire promptly returns the wax to its natural formlessness. But the wax having fled its heated mould and now being lost, the dazzling bronze liquid comes to wed in the hardened sand the hardest similitude of the smallest petal. . . ."

"I understand! Eupalinos. The riddle is transparent to me; the myth is easy to translate.

"Do not those roses that were fresh and that perish before your eyes stand for all things about us and for moving life itself? As for the model of wax that you made, employing upon it your deft fingers, despoiling with your eye the corolas and returning laden with flowers to your work —is that not an image of your daily labors, enriched by the commerce between your acts and your latest observations? The fire is Time itself, which would entirely abolish or scatter abroad into the wide world both the real roses and your roses of wax, if your being did not in some way preserve, I know not how, the forms of your experience and the secret solidity of its own reason. . . . As for the liquid bronze, it surely stands for the exceptional powers of your soul and the tumultuous state of something that wills to be born. This incandescent bounty would be dissipated in vain heat and infinite reverberations, and would leave behind nothing but ingots or irregular streaks of run metal, if you were not able to lead it by mysterious conduits to cool down and to bestow itself in the pure matrices of your wisdom. Your being must therefore of necessity divide itself and become, at one and the same instant, hot and cold, fluid and solid, free and fast—roses, wax, and fire; matrix and Corinthian metal."

"Exactly! But I told you that I merely try my hand at it!"

"How do you set about it?"

"As best I can!"

"But tell me how you try!"

"Listen once more then, since you will it so. . . . I cannot very well make clear for you what is not clear for myself. . . . O Phaedrus, when I design a dwelling (whether it be for the gods, or for man), and when I lovingly seek its form, studying to create an object that shall delight the view, that shall hold converse with the mind, that shall accord with reason and the numerous properties . . . I confess, howsoever strange it may appear to you, *that it seems to me that my body is playing its part in the game.* . . . Let me explain. This body is an admirable instrument, of which I am sure that those who are alive and who all have it at their disposal do not make full use. They draw from it only pleasure, pain, and indispensable acts, such as living. Sometimes they become confused with it; sometimes again they forget its existence for a space; and, at one moment mere brutes, at another pure spirits, they know not what multitudinous bonds with all things they have in themselves, and of what a marvelous substance they are made. And yet it is through this substance that they participate in what they see and what they touch: they are stones, they are trees, they exchange contacts and breaths with matter that englobes them. They touch, they are touched; they have weight and lift weights; they move, and carry their virtues and vices about; and when they fall into reverie or into indefinite sleep, they reproduce the nature of waters, they turn into sand and clouds. . . . On other occasions they store up thunderbolts and hurl them abroad! . . .

"But their soul is unable to make exact use of that nature which is so close to it, and which it interpenetrates. It outstrips, it lags; it seems to flee the very instant. It receives shocks and jolts from this body, causing it to depart into itself, and to fade away into its own emptiness where it gives birth to mere smoke. But I, on the contrary, the wiser for my errors, say in the full light, I repeat to myself with every dawn: 'O body of mine, that recallest to me at every moment this tempering of my tendencies, this equilibrium of thy organs, these true proportions of thy parts, which make thee to *be* and to stabilize thyself ever anew in the very heart of moving things; keep watch over my work; teach me secretly the demands of nature, and impart to me that great art, with which thou art endowed, even as by it thou art made, of surviving the seasons, and of saving thee from the incidents of chance. Grant me to find in thy alliance the feeling of what is true; temper, strengthen and confirm my thoughts. Perishable as thou art, thou art far less so than my dreams. Thou endurest a little longer than a fancy; thou payest for my deeds, and dost expiate my errors. Instrument, thou, of life, thou art for each one of us the sole being which can be compared with the universe. The entire sphere always has thee for a center; O mutual object of the attention of all the starry heavens! Thou art indeed the measure of the world, of which my soul presents me with the shell alone. She knows it to be without depth and knows it to so little purpose, that she sometimes would class it among her dreams; she doubts the sun. . . . Doting on her ephemeral fabrications, she thinks herself capable of an infinity of indefinite realities; she imagines that other worlds exist, but thou recallest thou to thyself, as the anchor calls back the ship. . . .

" 'My intelligence, better inspired, will not, dear body, cease henceforth to call thee to herself; nor wilt thou cease, I trust, to furnish her with thy presences, with thy demands, with thy local ties. For we have at last come to find, thou and I, the means of joining ourselves, and the indissoluable knot of our differences: to wit, a work that is our child. We wrought each of us in his own sphere; thou by living, and I by dreaming. My vast reveries ended in a boundless impotence. But may this work, which now I wish to make, and which can not be made of itself, constrain us to answer one another, and may it spring solely from our alliance! But this body and this mind, this presence so invincibly real and this creative absence that strives for possession of our being, and which must finally be reconciled, this finite and this infinite which we bring with us, each in accordance with his nature, must now unite in a well-ordered structure; and if, thanks to the gods, they work in concert, if they interchange fitness and grace, beauty and lastingness, if they barter movements for lines, and numbers for thoughts, they will then have discovered their true relationship, their act. May they concert together, may they understand one another by means of the material of my art! Stones and forces, outlines and masses, lights and shadows, artificial groupings, the illusion of perspective and the realities of gravity, all these are the object of their commerce; and may the profit of this commerce finally be that incorruptible wealth which I name Perfection.' "

IV

PHAEDRUS

Eupalinos was the man of his precept. He neglected nothing. He ordered small laths to be cut following the grain of the wood, so that, when placed between the masonry and the beams which rested thereon, they should prevent the damp from rising into the fiber and rotting it when once absorbed. He gave a like care to all the sensitive points of the building. You would have thought that it was his own body he was tending. During the process of construction he scarcely left the works. I truly believe that he knew every stone in the place. He saw to the precision of their cutting; he minutely studied all the means that have been thought of for preventing the edges from being injured and the exactness of the joining from being impaired. He directed carvings to be contrived, toothings to be left, sloping edges to be made in the marble facings. He took the most exquisite pains with the coatings of polish which he ordered to be spread over the walls of plain stone.

But all these delicate devices making for the permanence of the edifice were as nothing to those which he bestowed when he elaborated the emotions and vibrations of the soul of the future beholder of his work.

For the light he prepared a matchless instrument, which was to redistribute it, endowed with intelligible forms and almost musical properties, into the space where mortals move. Like those orators and poets you had in mind just now, he knew, O Socrates, the mysterious virtue of imperceptible modulations. None perceived, when confronted by a mass so delicately lightened and so simple of aspect, that he was being held to a sort of bliss by insensible curves, by minute and all powerful inflections; and by those deep-wrought combinations of the regular and the irregular which he had introduced and concealed, and made as imperious as they were indefinable. They caused the ever shifting spectator, obedient to their invisible presence, to pass from vision to vision, and from

182

great spells of silence to mutterings of delight, according as he advanced, retreated, approached again, and as he moved within the radius of the work, impelled by its influence, and the plaything of admiration alone. *My temple,* this man from Megara would say, *must move men as they are moved by their beloved.*

SOCRATES

That is divine. I once heard, dear Phaedrus, an expression quite similar, and quite the contrary. One of our friends, whom it is useless to name, said of our Alcibiades who was so beautifully made: *Looking at him, one feels oneself becoming an architect!*

Translated by William McC. Stewart

FROM "DANCE AND THE SOUL"

ERYXIMACHUS

O Socrates, I am expiring! . . . Give me a helping of something spiritual! Pour me out a bumper of ideas! . . . Put to my nose some of your prickling riddles! This merciless meal surpasses all conceivable appetite and all believable thirst! . . . What a situation to be the successor of good things and the inheritor of a digestion! . . . My soul is nothing but a dream dreamt by matter struggling with itself! . . . O good things, too good things I bid you begone! . . . Alas! since nightfall we have been here a prey to the best in the world—that terrible best, multiplied by the passage of time, inflicts on us an unendurable presence. . . . I am perishing now of a mad longing for things that are dry and serious and wholly immaterial! . . . Let me come and sit beside you and Phaedrus; and, with my back resolutely turned to these perpetually recurring viands, to these inexhaustible urns, let me hold up my spirit's supreme cup to catch your words. What were you saying?

PHAEDRUS

Nothing so far. We were watching our fellows eat and drink. . . .

ERYXIMACHUS

But surely Socrates was not neglecting to meditate on something? . . . Can he ever stay alone with himself and silent to the depths of his soul? He was smiling tenderly at his daemon on the dark borderland of this banquet. What are your lips murmuring, dear Socrates?

SOCRATES

They are saying to me gently "The man who eats is of all men the most just. . . ."

Here come the riddle and the spirit's appetite, which it is meant to tickle. . . .

The man who eats, they say, feeds what is good in him and what is evil. Every mouthful he feels melt and dissipate within him carries fresh strength to his virtues as impartially as to his vices. It prolongs his anxieties just as it nourishes his hopes; and is divided somewhere between passions and reasons. Love needs it as well as hate. And my joy and my bitterness, my memories and my projects share like brothers the stuff of the same morsel. What do you think, son of Acumenes?

I think that I think as you do.

Oh, physician that you are, I was silently admiring the actions of all these feeding bodies. Each one of them unwittingly distributes its equitable due to each chance of life, to each germ of death within it. They know not what they do, but they do it like gods.

I have long observed it. Everything that enters into a man behaves in a very short time as the fates decree. One would think that the isthmus of the gullet was the threshold of capricious necessities and of organized mystery. There, the authority of will comes to an end and the certain rule of knowledge. That is why I, in the exercise of my art, have given up all those inconstant drugs which ordinary doctors prescribe to their diverse patients; and I keep strictly to the obvious remedies which are paired one with the other by their very nature.

What remedies?

There are eight of them—heat, cold; abstinence and its contrary; air and water; rest and movement. That is all.

But for the soul there are only two, Eryximachus.

What can they be?

Truth and falsehood.

How is that?

Are they not each to other as sleeping is to waking? Don't you seek waking and the clearness of light when a bad dream is disturbing you? Aren't we resuscitated by the sun in person and fortified by the presence of solid bodies?—But, on the other hand, do we not ask of sleep and dreams to dispel our troubles and to put an end to the pains that pursue us in the world of daylight? So that we fly from one to the other, invoking day in the middle of the night, imploring darkness, on the contrary, when we have the light; anxious to know, only too happy to be ignorant, we seek in what is, a remedy for what is not; and in what is not, a relief from what is. Now reality, and now illusion is our refuge; and the soul, in fine, has no other resource than truth, which is her arm—and falsehood, her armor.

Well, well . . . But aren't you afraid, dear Socrates, that that thought of yours may lead to a certain consequence?

What consequence?

This: Truth and falsehood tend to the same end. . . . It is one same thing, which, as we set about it differently, makes us liars or truthful; and, as at times heat, and at times cold, at times attack and at times defend us, so do truth and falsehood and the opposing forces that relate to them.

Nothing can be more certain. I cannot help it. Life itself wills it so; you know better than I do that it makes use of everything. Everything helps it, Eryximachus, never to come to a conclusion. That is to say, its only conclusion is itself. . . . Is it not that mysterious movement which, taking the devious way of all that happens, transforms me incessantly within myself and then returns me to the selfsame Socrates promptly enough for me to recover him, and necessarily imagining that I recognize him, I thereby come into being?—She is a dancing woman, who would divinely cease to be a woman, if she could pursue her leap up to the skies. But as we cannot go as far as infinity, either dreaming or waking, so she, likewise, returns always to being herself again; stops being a flake, a bird, an idea;—being, in a word, all that the flute has pleased her to be, for the same Earth that sent her out, calls her back and returns her, panting, to her woman's nature and to her lover. . . .

PHAEDRUS

Miracle! . . . Marvellous man! . . . Almost a real miracle! You have only to speak and you call into being what is wanted! . . . Your images cannot remain images! . . . Here, precisely,—as if your creative lips had given birth to a bee, and a bee, and a bee—here comes the winged choir of famous dancers! . . . The air resounds and hums with orchestral forebodings! . . . All the torches awake. . . . The murmur of the sleepers is transformed; and on the walls that waver in the flames, the huge shadows of drunkards bestir themselves in uneasy wonder. . . . Look at that troupe—half light, half solemn!—They are entering like souls!

II

SOCRATES

Eryximachus, what thoughts that little creature gives us! . . . She gathers to herself, she assumes singly a majesty which was inherent confusedly in us all, which dwelt imperceptibly in the partakers of this debauch. . . . A simple walk and behold—a goddess; and we almost gods!

. . . . A simple walk, the simplest linking of steps! . . . She seems to be paying space with lovely acts of pure and equal value, to be striking with her heel sounding effigies of movement. She seems to be numbering and counting in coins of pure gold what we squander carelessly in the vulgar change of steps when we walk about our common occasions.

ERYXIMACHUS

Dear Socrates, she is teaching us to understand what we do, showing our souls clearly what our bodies accomplish obscurely. By the light of her legs our immediate movements appear to us as miracles. They astonish us at last as much as they should do.

PHAEDRUS

So that according to you, this dancer has something socratic in her, teaching us, as far as walking goes, to know ourselves a little better.

ERYXIMACHUS

Precisely. Our steps are so easy and so familiar to us that they never have the honor of being considered in themselves and in their character of strange actions (unless, becoming infirm or paralyzed, we are induced by privation to admire them). . . . Knowing then what they do, they lead us, who in our simplicity are unaware of them; and, according to the ground, the end, the man's mood and state, or even the lighting of the road, they are what they are: we waste them without giving them a thought.

But consider Athikte's perfect progress on a floor with no unevenness, open, clear and barely elastic. On this mirror of her energies she symmetrically places the alternate pressure of her feet; her heel first sends her body flowing toward the tip of her toe, the other foot then passes in front, receives the weight of the body, sending it onward again in another forward flow; and so on and so on; while the lovely crown of her head traces in the eternal present the crest of an undulating wave.

As the floor here is in a certain sense absolute, having been carefully cleared of every impediment to rhythm and certainty, this monumental walk which has no object but itself, and from which all impurities and variations have been removed, becomes a universal model.

See what beauty, what full security for the soul results from the length of those noble strides. The amplitude of her steps is exactly matched with their number, which emanates directly from the music. But number and length are, on the other hand, in secret harmony with her stature . . .

SOCRATES

You speak of these things so well, learned Eryximachus, that I am obliged to see them in the light of your mind. I gaze at this woman walking and she gives me the sensation of immobility. I can attend only to the equality of these measures. . . .

PHAEDRUS

She is pausing now in the midst of these commensurable graces. . . .

ERYXIMACHUS

You will soon see!

PHAEDRUS

She has shut her eyes. . . .

SOCRATES

She is wholly in her shut eyes, alone with her soul, in the bosom of deepest attention. She is feeling herself become an event.

ERYXIMACHUS

Look out for . . . Silence, silence!

PHAEDRUS

Delicious moment . . . This silence is a contradiction . . . How can one help calling out. 'Silence!'

SOCRATES

Moment of absolute virginity. And then, moment when something is about to break in our souls, in our waiting, in our company . . . Something break . . . And yet it is like a welding too.

ERYXIMACHUS

O Athikte, how excellent you are upon the verge!

189

PHAEDRUS

The music seems to be gently taking hold of her in another way, to be lifting her . . .

ERYXIMACHUS

The music is changing her soul.

SOCRATES

In this moment which is about to die, you, O Muses, are all-powerful! Oh! Delicious catching of the heart and of the breath! . . . Weight drops at her feet, and we are made to understand it by the noiseless fall of that great veil. Her body must only be seen in motion.

ERYXIMACHUS

Her eyes have returned to the light . . .

PHAEDRUS

Let us enjoy the exquisitely delicate moment when she is in the act of making up her mind! . . . As the bird which has reached the very edge of the roof, breaks away from the beauty of the marble and falls into flight . . .

ERYXIMACHUS

I care for nothing so much as for what is on the point of occurring; and even in love, I know nothing which surpasses in pleasure the first earliest feelings. Daybreak is my favorite of all the hours of the day. That is why I watch with tender emotion the divine dawn of divine movement upon this living being. See! . . . It is born of that sliding look which irresistibly draws the head with its gentle nostrils toward the gleaming shoulder . . . And the whole lovely fiber of her well-cut, muscular body, from nape to heel, stretches and twists progressively; and a quiver runs through it . . . She slowly prefigures the birth of a leap . . . She forbids us to breathe until the very moment when she springs darting upward in a startling act of response to the expected—the unexpected clash of the ear-rending cymbals! . . .

Oh! now she is at last making her way into exception, entering the heart of impossibility! . . . O my friends, how much alike are our souls in presence of this marvel which, for each of them, is equal and entire! . . . How they drink together of beauty!

ERYXIMACHUS

She has become wholly dance and is wholly consecrated to total movement!

PHAEDRUS

Her steps are so full of wit that she seems at first to be wiping from the earth all fatigue and all foolishness . . . And now she is building herself an abode a little above things terrestrial, and seems to be arranging herself a nest in her white arms . . . But now one would think her feet were spinning her an indescribable carpet of sensations . . . She crosses, she uncrosses, she weaves the warp of earth with the woof of time . . . Oh what a charming fabric is made by this precious workmanship of her intelligent toes, as they attack and elude, knot and unknot, chase each other and fly off! How clever they are, how sprightly these pure artificers of the delights of lost time! . . . Her two feet chatter to each other and wrangle like doves! . . . They quarrel for the same spot of ground as if it were a grain of corn! . . . Off they both fly in a temper and go on still squabbling in the air! . . . By the Muses, no feet have ever made my lips so envious!

SOCRATES

So then, your lips envy the volubility of these amazing feet! You would like to feel their wings on your words, and adorn your speech with figures as lively as their leaps!

PHAEDRUS

I? . . .

ERYXIMACHUS

He was only wanting to bill and coo with the pedestrian turtle-doves! . . . A result of the passionate attention he bestows on the spectacle of dancing. What can be more natural, Socrates, more ingenuously mysterious? . . . Our Phaedrus is dazzled by those points, those twinkling pirouettes which are the just pride of the extreme tips of Athikte's toes; he devours them with his eyes, he stretches his face toward them; he thinks he really feels their agile onyx flitting over his lips!—Don't apologize, dear Phaedrus. Don't be in the least abashed! . . . You have experienced nothing that isn't legitimate and obscure and therefore in perfect keeping with our mortal machine. Are we not an organized fantasy? And is not our living constitution an incoherence that functions and a disorder that works?—Do not events, desires, ideas shift about in us in the most necessary and the most incomprehensible manner? . . . What a cacophony of causes and effects! . . .

PHAEDRUS

Yes, you have admirably put what I was innocently feeling. . . .

SOCRATES

Dear Phaedrus, truly you were not moved without reason. The more I too watch this unutterable dancer, the more marvels I discuss with myself. I wonder how nature has been able to confine in so frail and slender a girl such a monster of strength and promptitude. Hercules transformed into a swallow? Does such a myth exist? And how can a head so small, and tight as a young fir-cone, give birth so infallibly to those myriads of questions and answers that pass between her limbs, and to those astounding attempts which she makes and re-makes and as constantly repudiates, receiving them from the music and returning them instantaneously to the light?

III

SOCRATES

Tell me then, son of Acumenes, O Eryximachus Therapeutes, you for whom the bitterest drugs and the obscurest aromatics have so few hidden virtues that you forswear their use; you then who possess as completely as any man in the world all the secrets of art and of nature, and yet never prescribe or recommend balms or boluses, or mysterious mastics; you, furthermore, who put no trust in elixirs, who do not believe in secret

192

philtres; O you who cure without electuaries, O you who disdain all the things—powders, drops, ointments, salts, flakes or gems or crystals—everything that bites the tongue, pierces the olfactory cavities, touches the springs of sneezing or nausea, kills or quickens; tell me, dear friend Eryximachus, of all iatrists the most learned in the *materia medica*, tell me, I pray: do you not know among so many active and efficient substances, among all these magisterial preparations which your learning considers as vain or hateful arms, in the arsenal of the pharmacopoeia, tell me, do you not know some specific remedy, some exact antidote for that evil among evils, that poison of poisons, that venom which is opposed to all nature? . . .

PHAEDRUS

What venom?

SOCRATES

Which is called: the tedium of living? I mean, understand me, not the passing ennui, the tedium that comes of fatigue, or the tedium of which we can see the germ or of which we know the limits; but that perfect tedium, that pure tedium that is not caused by misfortune or infirmity, that is compatible with apparently the happiest of all conditions—that tedium, in short, the stuff of which is nothing else than life itself, and which has no other second cause than the clear-sightedness of the living man. This absolute tedium is essentially nothing but life in its nakedness when it sees itself with unclouded eyes.

ERYXIMACHUS

It is very true that if our soul purges itself of all falseness, strips itself of every fraudulent addition to *what is,* our existence is endangered on the spot by the cold, exact, reasonable and moderate view of human life *as it is.*

PHAEDRUS

Life blackens at the contact of truth, as a suspicious mushroom blackens, when it is crushed, at the contact of the air.

SOCRATES

Eryximachus, I asked you if there were any cure?

193

Why cure so reasonable a complaint? There is nothing, no doubt, nothing more essentially morbid, nothing more inimical to nature than to *see things as they are*. A cold and perfect light is a poison it is impossible to combat. Reality, unadulterated, instantly puts a stop to the heart. One drop of that icy lymph suffices to slacken all the springs of the soul, all the throbbing of desire, to exterminate all hopes and bring to ruin all the gods that inhabited our blood. The Virtues and the noblest colors are turned pale by it in a gradual and devouring consumption. The past is reduced to a handful of ashes, the future to a tiny icicle. The soul appears to itself as an empty and measurable form. Here then are things as they are—a rigorous and deadly chain, where each link joins and limits the next. . . . O Socrates, the universe cannot endure for a single instant to be only what it is. It is strange to think that that which is the Whole cannot suffice itself! . . . Its terror of being what it is has induced it to create and paint for itself thousands of masks; there is no other reason for the existence of mortals. What are mortals for?—Their business is *to know*. Know? And what is *to know?—It is assuredly not to be what one is.*—So here are human beings raving and thinking, introducing into nature the principle of unlimited errors and all these myriads of marvels!

The mistakes, the appearances, the play of the mind's dioptric give depth and animation to the world's miserable mass. The idea introduces into what is, the leaven of what is not. . . . But truth sometimes shows itself, and sounds a discord in the harmonious system of phantasmagorias and errors . . . Everything straightway is threatened with perdition, and Socrates in person comes to beg of me a cure for this desperate case of clear-sightedness and ennui! . . .

SOCRATES

Well, Eryximachus, since there is no cure, can you tell me at least what state is the most contrary to this horrible state of pure disgust, of murderous lucidity and of inexorable clarity?

ERYXIMACHUS

In the first place, I see all the non-melancholic madnesses.

And then?

Drunkenness, and the category of illusions due to heady vapors.

Yes. But are there no intoxications which do not take their source in wine?

Certainly. Love, hate, greed, intoxicate! . . . The sensation of power . . .

All of that gives taste and color to life. But the chance of loving or hating, or acquiring very great possessions is bound up with all the hazards of reality. . . . Don't you see then, Eryximachus, that amongst all intoxications, the noblest, the most inimical to ennui, is the intoxication due to action. Our acts, and particularly those of our acts that set our bodies in motion may throw us into a strange and admirable state . . . the furthest removed from that wretched state in which we left the motionless and lucid observer we were imagining just now.

But if, by some miracle, this observer were to take a sudden passion for dancing? . . . If he wanted to stop being clear in order to become light; and if, trying to be infinitely different from himself, he attempted to change his liberty of judgment into liberty of movement?

Then he would teach us without more ado what we are now trying to elucidate. . . . But I have one other thing I still want to ask Eryximachus.

What you will, dear Socrates.

Tell me then, wise physician, who have sounded in your travels and your studies the science of all living creatures; great connoisseur that you are of natural forms and sports, you who have made yourself famous in the classification of remarkable animals and plants, (both the noxious and the benign; the harmless and the efficacious; the surprising, the frightful, the ridiculous, the doubtful; and those, finally, which do not exist), tell me then have you not heard of those strange animals which live and thrive in fire itself?

ERYXIMACHUS

Certainly! . . . Their appearance and habits, dear Socrates, have been thoroughly studied, although their very existence has recently been the subject of some discussion. I have often described them to my disciples; though I have never had occasion to see any with my own eyes.

SOCRATES

Well, don't you think, Eryximachus, and you, my dear Phaedrus, that this creature who is vibrating over there, and who is moving so adorably before our eyes, this glowing Athikte, who divides and gathers herself together again, who rises and sinks, who opens and shuts so swiftly, who seems to belong to other constellations than ours—does she not look as if she were living quite at her ease in an element comparable to fire,—in a highly subtle essence of music and motion, where she inhales inexhaustible energy, while she participates with her whole being in the pure and immediate violence of extreme felicity?—And if we compare our heavy and serious condition to that state of a sparkling salamander, does it not seem to you that our ordinary acts, caused successively by our needs, that our gestures and accidental movements are like some coarse material, like some impure stuff made for wear—while this exaltation and vibration of life, while this supremacy of tension, and this whirling into the greatest agility humanly possible, have the virtues and powers of flame; and that the shames, the worries, the sillinesses, and the monotonous fare of existence are consumed in it, making a shining light in our eyes of what is divine in a mortal woman?

Admirable Socrates! Look quickly! See how truly you are speaking! . . .
Look at that flickering creature! Dancing seems to come from her body
like a flame!

O Flame! . . .

—This girl is perhaps a fool?

O Flame! . . .

—Who can say of what superstitions and absurdities her ordinary self is
composed?

And yet, O Flame! . . . Living and divine! . . .

But what is a flame, my friends, if not *the moment itself?* All that is
mad and joyous and awful in the very moment itself! . . . Flame is the
act of the moment which is between earth and Heaven. O my friends, all
that passes from the state of heaviness to the state of subtlety, passes
through the moment of fire and light. . . .

And flame too, is it not the intangible and haughty form of the noblest
destruction?—What will never happen again happens magnificently before our eyes! What will never happen again is bound to happen as magnificently as possible!—As the voice sings passionately, as the flame sings
madly between matter and ether,—and rushes and roars furiously from
matter to ether,—so, is not great Dancing, my friends, the liberation of our
bodies, which are wholly possessed by the spirit of falsehood, and by music
which is falsehood too, and drunk with the denial of non-reality? Look at
that body leaping like flame replacing flame, look how it treads and tram-
ples on reality. How furiously and joyously it destroys the very place where
it happens to be, and how intoxicated it becomes with the excess of its
changes!

How it fights against spirit! Don't you see that it is struggling to surpass
its soul in swiftness and diversity? It is strangely jealous of that liberty
and ubiquity it believes the spirit possesses! . . .

Doubtless, the unique and perpetual object of the soul is what does
not exist: what was, and is no longer;—what will be and is not yet;—what
is possible, what is impossible,—that is the soul's concern, but never,
never, what is!

And the body which is what it is, see, it can no longer contain itself in space!—Where shall it bestow itself?—Where shall it come into being?— This *One* wants to play at being *All*. It wants to play at the soul's universality! It wants to remedy its identity by the number of its actions! Being a thing, it explodes in events!—It flies into transports!—And as thought, when excited, touches every substance, oscillates between pauses and instants, overleaps all differences; and as hypotheses are symmetrically formed in our mind, and as possibilities are arranged and numbered,— so this body exercises itself in all its parts, combines with itself, takes on shape after shape, and continuously leaves itself! . . . Now at last it has reached that state which is comparable to flame, in the midst of the most active exchanges . . . One can no longer speak of *'movement'* . . . Its acts are no longer distinguishable from its limbs . . .

That woman who was once there has been devoured by countless forms. . . . That body, with its bursts of vigor, inspires me with a quintessential thought; just as we ask of our soul many things for which it is not intended, and demand it to enlighten us, to prophesy, to forecast the future, adjuring it even to discover God, so the body there wants to attain complete possession of itself and reach a pitch of supernatural glory. . . . But it fares with the body as with the soul, for which the God, and the wisdom, and the depths that are demanded of it, are and can only be moments, flashes, fragments of extraneous time, desperate leaps out of its own shape. . . .

Translated by Dorothy Bussy

ON MYTHS AND MYTHOLOGY

. . . Myth is the term for everything which exists and subsists only on the basis of language. There is no speech so obscure, no gossip so fantastic, no remark so incoherent that we cannot give it meaning. One can always assume a meaning for the strangest language.

Suppose, for instance, that several accounts of the same event, or varying reports of the same incident are given by books or by witnesses, who, though equally trustworthy, do not agree. To say that they do not agree is to say that their simultaneous differences of opinion create a monster. Their disagreement gives birth to a chimera. . . . But a monster or a chimera, though not viable in the realm of fact, is thoroughly at home in the confusions of the mind. A combination of a woman and a fish is a mermaid, and the idea of a mermaid is easily acceptable. But is a living mermaid possible? I am not at all certain that we are already so expert in the natural sciences that we can deny existence to mermaids by demonstrative reasoning. Anatomy and physiology would have to go a long way to offer any other objection to them than this: In modern times no one has ever caught one!

Something that is destroyed by a little extra precision is a myth. Under rigorous inspection and the multiple convergent attacks of the queries and categorical interrogations with which the awakened mind is completely armed, you see myths die, and the buds of indeterminate things and ideas fading indefinitely away. . . . Myths vanish under the light in us which is generated by the combined presence of our bodies and of our highest perceptions.

See how a nightmare unites into one overpowering drama every variety of independent sensation which troubles our sleep. A hand gets caught beneath our bodies; a foot which is uncovered, and has escaped the blankets, gets cold independently of the sleeper; early morning passers-by cry out at dawn in the street; the empty stomach relaxes, and the intestines ferment; rays from the rising sun vaguely disturb the retina through the closed lids . . . so many separate and incoherent ingredients, and no one to reduce them to themselves and to bring them into the world we know, to retain some and discard others, to evaluate them and allow us to draw conclusions. But all these things are of equal value, and have to be equally satisfied. The result is a creation which is original, absurd, incompatible with the course of life, overwhelming, completely terrifying, and which has in itself no finality, no limit and no outcome. . . . So it is with the circumstances of our waking hours, but with even less coherence. The entire history of thought is nothing but the interplay of an infinity of little nightmares of great consequence, while sleep is composed of long nightmares of short duration and little consequence.

Our entire language is made up of short little dreams; and the delightful thing about it is that we sometimes fashion from them thoughts that are strangely exact and wonderfully reasonable.

Indeed there are so many myths in us, and such commonplace ones, that it is almost impossible to segregate completely in our minds anything that is not a myth. One cannot even talk about it without creating a myth, and am I not at the moment making a myth of the myth in order to satisfy the whim of a myth?

Yes, dear friends, I do not know what to do in order to escape from what does not exist! To such an extent does the spoken word govern us, and everything around us, that one cannot see how to set about foregoing the imaginary which cannot be dispensed with.

Consider the fact that tomorrow is a myth, and the universe as well; that numbers, love, reality as well as infinity, that justice, people, poetry . . . and the earth itself are myths! And that even the Pole is a myth, for those who claim to have gone there, only thought that they had for reasons inseparable from the spoken word. . . .

I am forgetting the entire past. . . . All history is nothing but myth, and is only composed of thoughts to which we give the essentially mythical value of representing what once was. Each moment fades each moment into the realm of the imaginary, and hardly are you dead before you are off, with the speed of light, to join the centaurs and the angels. . . . What am I saying? Hardly is our back turned, hardly are we out of sight, before opinion makes of us what it will.

I return to history. How imperceptibly it changes into a dream as it recedes from the present! Near us myths are still quite temperate, held in check by written words which are not entirely incredible, by material remains which curb our fantasies a little. But three or four thousand years before our birth, we are absolutely free. At last in the mythical void of a time, pure and unsullied by anything whatsoever which is similar to the things we know, the mind, certain only that there has been something, constrained only by the fundamental necessity of imagining precedents, 'causes,' evidence to support what is and what the mind is—creates times, states, events, persons, principles, increasingly ingenuous pictures and stories which make one think of, or are easily reduced to, that very sincere cosmology of the Hindus in which they place the earth on the back of an enormous elephant in order to hold it up in space; the elephant supported by a tortoise which in turn is floating in a sea contained in some sort of a vessel. . . .

The most profound philosopher, the most learned physicist, the geometrician best equipped with those means which Laplace calls "the resources of the most sublime form of analysis"—cannot and do not know how to give a better explanation.

That is why it happened that one day I wrote: in the beginning was the Fable!

Which means that any derivation and any beginning of things is of the same substance as the songs and stories which surround us in the cradle.

It is a kind of absolute law that everywhere, in every place, in every period of civilization, in every form of belief, by means of no matter what form of discipline, and in every respect—the false supports the true; truth has falsehood for an ancestor, as its cause, its author, and its point of origin, without exception and without recourse,—and the truth engenders this very falsehood by which it must be engendered itself. All antiquity, all causality, every human principle, are fabulous inventions and obey the simple laws of invention.

What would we be without the help of what does not exist? Not very much, and our very unoccupied minds would pine away if myths, fables, misunderstandings, abstractions, beliefs and monsters, hypotheses and the so-called problems of metaphysics did not people the darkness and the depths of our natures with abstract creations and images.

Myths are the very soul of our actions and of our loves. We can act only in pursuit of a phantom. We can love only what we create.

Translated by Anthony Bower

MAN AND THE NIGHT

Extract from "Variations on an Idea of Pascal"

I have sometimes tried to observe in myself, and to pursue into the realm of concrete thought, the mysterious effect that a clear night and the presence of stars generally has on men.

Then we only notice objects that have nothing to do with our bodies. We are strangely simplified. Everything that is near is invisible: every thing perceptible is intangible. We are carried far away from ourselves. We ourselves abandon our eyes to the prospect of a field of luminous manifestations, which they cannot help relating to each other by their spontaneous movements, as if they belonged to the same moment in time; tracing lines, forming images, which are theirs alone, which they impose on us, and which they introduce into the real scene.

And yet the pattern of all these points of light escapes us. We find ourselves overwhelmed, subdued, engulfed, and abandoned by this multifarious brilliance.

We can count these stars, and yet we cannot believe that we exist as far as they are concerned. There is no reciprocity between us and them.

We feel something that demands that we speak, and something that forbids it.

Since what we see in the sky, and what we find in the depths of our hearts are both equally removed from our actions, with the one shining far above our undertakings, and the other existing far beneath our expressions, a kind of relationship is formed between the thought we give to the most distant things and our most intimate introspections. They seem to be the extremes of our expectation which echo one another and resemble each other in hoping for some decisive event in the heavens or in the heart.

To this galaxy of stars which is stupendous to our eyes, the depths of our being opposes a dismayed feeling of being itself, of being unique,—

and, moreover, of being alone. I am all, and incomplete. I am all, and a part.

The darkness which surrounds us completely bares our soul.

This darkness is threaded through and through with inaccessible brilliance. With difficulty one refrains from thinking of houses where people are awake. Unconsciously we people the darkness with luminous, unidentifiable creatures.

This same darkness which banishes the outline of our bodies, in consequence lowers the sound of our voices and reduces it to an unspoken word, for we have a tendency only really to speak to people who are not very far away.

We experience a calm and strange uneasiness. Between the 'I' and the 'Not-I' there is no longer any distinction. In broad daylight our thoughts were bound to objects by our actions. We exchanged sensations for thoughts and thoughts for sensations and our actions served as intermediaries, our time served as the coin of exchange. But now there is no more exchange, the man of action, who is the measure of things, no longer exists. There are only two distinct presences, and two independent natures. There are only two adversaries who are face to face without understanding each other. The enormous increase of our perspective and the decrease of our powers are opposed. We lose for a little while the familiar illusion that things have meaning for us. We resemble a fly that cannot get through a pane of glass. We cannot remain in this moribund state. Sensibility knows no equilibrium. It could even be defined as a function whose role is to break down in human beings the entire equilibrium of their powers. Thus our mind must bestir itself to escape from its stupor and from that solemn, motionless surprise which gives it the feeling of being everything, and the evidence of being nothing.

Translated by Anthony Bower

SKETCH FOR "DESCARTES"

Descartes and his greatness are summed up for me in two points.

He made his personal concern those things which, up to his time, had been treated dogmatically and dominated by tradition. He decided that there was no authority that could prevail over the feeling it could engender of the vanity of its teachings; he wanted only evidence or carefully verified observation. That was to refuse to attribute to language a value which it derived only from people or from books. Thus he throws his very being into one scale of a balance of which the other was weighted with all the philosophy which had been contrived before his time. He finds that he triumphs. He feels very strong in being alone, and in being able to reply, with everything that he thinks and all that he has observed, or deduced, or defined himself, to that mass of doctrine, of formulae, and of purely verbal exercises which only have their existence in disputes between schools, and which are handed down from century to century like paper money that can never be converted into gold.

Descartes is, above all, a man of intentional actions. He wishes, above everything, to make the most of the store of intellectual ambition and vigor that he finds in himself—and he cannot want anything else. That is the important point, the key to the Cartesian position. It is futile to look for any other principle in his philosophy.

Whence comes that superb confidence that he shows in his strength of mind, that can be seen in his style and in his contempt, and that he is too lucid, as well as too prudent, to base on his hopes alone or on a visionary belief in its intrinsic value?

Descartes' belief in the power of his thought comes from the experiments he made with his talent for geometry. From them he had imbibed the intoxication of his superiority. He knew himself to be, in this branch of learning, the inventor of a method which seemed to him "as far beyond ordinary geometry as the rhetoric of Cicero is beyond the child's ABC."

These experiments of his youth dominated all his intellectual life. There is no doubt about his triumphs in this field, and he said to himself that the same man, with the same application of the intellect that obtained so happy and so considerable a success in the abstract analysis of space, must attack the physical world and could not fail to attain results of equal import.

Then he proceeds to invent a Universe and an Animal and imagines that he explains them. Whatever his delusions in this direction may be, his efforts have been of the greatest consequence. That is my second point. Even if the Cartesian universe has suffered the same fate as all the conceived or conceivable universes, nevertheless the world in which our 'civilization' lives still bears the marks of the way and manner of thinking of which I have spoken.

This world is imbued with applications of mathematical standards. Our lives are more and more regulated according to mathematical principles, and everything which escapes representation by numbers, all knowledge that cannot be measured, is judged with depreciation. The word 'Knowledge' is increasingly denied to anything which cannot be translated into figures.

And here is the strange observation on which this discourse will end: the predominant characteristic of this modification is objectivity, and impersonality—as unadulterated as possible—so that the truth for modern man, which is exactly related to his freedom of action over nature, seems more and more to be in opposition to everything that our imagination and our feelings would like to be true. But as I have already said, at the source of this prodigious transformation of the human world it is an 'Ego' that one finds, it is the bold and headstrong figure of Descartes, whose philosophy, perhaps, is of less value to us than the perception he gives us of a magnificent and memorable personality.

Translated by Anthony Bower

ON BOSSUET

Among writers, I see no one who stands above Bossuet; none more sure of his words, stronger in the use of verbs, more energetic or freer in all the shadings of speech, bolder or happier in syntax, and altogether more a master of language, that is to say of himself. This complete and singular gift which embraces familiar speech as well as supreme splendor, perfectly articulated precision as well as the most powerful and sonorous effects of the art, implies a perception and an extraordinary *prescience* of mind in regard to all the aspects and all the functions of words.

Bossuet says what he wants to say. He is essentially calculating, as are all those who are called *classic*. He proceeds by construction, while we proceed by accident; he gambles on the expectation he creates, while the moderns gamble on surprise. He sets out powerfully from silence, little by little grows animated, swells, rises, arranges his sentence, which is sometimes built up into an arch supported by lateral propositions marvellously arrayed around the nucleus, and which reveals itself and brushes aside its incidentals that are surmounted in order, at last, to reach the climax and to come back to earth again, after prodigies of subordination and equilibrium, to a definite termination and to the complete resolution of its strength.

As for the thoughts that are found in Bossuet, one must admit that, today, they hardly appear able to excite our minds profoundly. On the other hand it is we ourselves who ought to give them a little life by conscious effort and by means of a little erudition. Three centuries of very profound change and of every kind of revolution, and an enormous number of intervening events and ideas, necessarily render naive or strange, and sometimes even inconceivable to the posterity we represent, the substance of works from a time so different from ours. The majority of readers attribute to what they call the *content* an importance greater, and even far greater, than to what they call *form*. Some, however, are of a completely contrary opinion to this, which they regard as pure superstition. They boldly assume that the structure of the statement has a kind of reality while the meaning of the idea is but a shadow. The value of the idea is indeterminate; it varies with persons and with periods. What one person considers profound is for another insipidly obvious or insufferably absurd. Finally, one only has to look around to see that what still interests the moderns in the writing of the past is not in the nature of knowledge, but in the nature of examples or models.

For these admirers of form, form, though it is always called forth or demanded by some thought process, has more value and even more meaning than any thought. They appreciate in form the vigor and elegance of *action;* and they find in thought only the instability of *events.*

Bossuet is to them a treasure house of symbols and of co-ordinated ingenuity and performance. They can passionately admire his superbly styled compositions, much as they admire the architecture of temples, though the sanctuaries are deserted and though the sentiments and reasons which caused them to be built have long since faded away. The structure remains.

Translated by Anthony Bower

FROM A PREFACE TO MONTESQUIEU'S "PERSIAN LETTERS"

A

. . . A society raises itself from brutishness to order. In that barbarism is the period of *fact*, it therefore follows that the period of order should be under the sway of *fiction*,—for there is no authority capable of imposing order based on physical restraint alone. It must have fictitious powers.

B

Order therefore demands the *action of the presence of absent things* and results from the equilibrium between instincts and ideals.

A fiduciary or conventional system develops, which introduces connections or imaginary obstacles between men, the effects of which are very real. They are essential to society.

Gradually the *sacred*, the *just*, the *legal*, the *decent*, the *commendable* and their opposites take form and crystallize in the mind. The Temple, the Throne, the Tribunal, the Theater, monuments to co-ordination, and like geodesic symbols, appear in turn. Time itself is mapped out: sacrifices, audiences and public spectacles mark collective dates and hours. Rites, observances, and customs bring about the taming of the human animal, and curb or measure his immediate activities. Recurrences of his fierce or irrepressible instincts become, little by little, exceptional or negligible. But all this comes about only through the power of images and words. It is indispensable to order that man should feel himself on the point of being worthy of being a man. If he does not attach great value to this conception, very soon the whole structure will collapse.

C

The reign of order, which is the reign of signs and symbols, always arrives at almost total disarmament which begins by the abandonment of visible arms and gradually wins general consent. . . . Swords get smaller and disappear, characters are rounded out. Under the names of *foresight* and *tradition,* the future and the past—imaginary perspective—dominate and restrain the present.

The social structure seems to us as natural as nature, even though it is only held together by magic. Is it not, in reality, an edifice built of spells, this system which is based on writings, on words obeyed, on promises kept, on effectual images, on observed habits and conventions,—all of which are pure fiction?

D

This world of fiction seems to us, by habit, as stable and as spontaneous as the physical world; and although it is the work of man, meaning his indivisible and immemorial work, it seems no less complex or mysterious than the latter. I raise my hat, I take an oath, I do a thousand strange things whose origin is as obscure as that of matter. If one wishes to be born, to die, or to make love, any number of abstract and incomprehensible things become involved.

In the long run it comes about that the mechanism of a society becomes clogged with such indirect forces, with such confused memories and with such numerous interchangeable ideas that one gets lost in a web of prescriptions and inextricable relationships. The life of an organized people is a tissue of multiple threads most of which lead back into history and are only brought together in the most ancient times by circumstances which will never recur. No one knows their course and no one can obey their commands.

E

With order well established at last—that is to say with reality sufficiently disguised and with the beast sufficiently tamed—freedom of thought becomes possible.

With order the mind gradually becomes bold, and thanks to the disappearance of the necessity of having to find reasons for what one does, minds that are awakening and taking to their wings only perceive the obstacles and the peculiarities of the ways of society. Forgetfulness of the conditions and premises of the social order is achieved; and this oblivion is always the most rapid in those whom order has best served or most favored.

F

The mind, becoming freer of the basic demands of order as they are better applied to exempting it from thinking of them, becomes intoxicated by its relative freedom, and disports itself in its own clarity and in its pure ingenuity.

It dares to speculate without considering the infinitely complex system which makes it so independent of things and so detached from primitive necessities. Evidence conceals the heart of things. Thus reasoning is unleashed, and man believes himself to be a mind. From all sides, queries, doubts and theories spring up, all of them aspects of the possible, and unrestrained exercises in words as opposed to deeds. Criticism of the ideals which have given the mind the leisure and opportunity to criticize them breaks forth and flourishes everywhere.

Meanwhile the instincts of self-preservation and perpetuation are weakened or perverted.

G

Thus it is that, by the subterfuges of ideas, and in the confusion created by their interplay, disorder and the *state of fact* are bound to reappear and be reborn at the expense of order.

This return to a state of fact can sometimes come about in a way that could not have been foreseen, and man can become a new kind of barbarian as the unexpected consequence of his most perspicacious thoughts.

Certain people think today that the conquest of matter by positive science is going to lead us, or is leading us, back to barbarism, though of a circumscribed and laborious kind; but which is only more terrible than ancient barbarisms in being more exact, more uniform and infinitely more powerful. We shall return to the era of fact—but of scientific fact.

Now societies, on the contrary, are founded on *indeterminate things;* at least up to now they have rested on conceptions and entities mysterious enough for the rebellious mind never to be assured of being rid of them and to be hesitant of being afraid only of what it can see! A tyrant of Athens, who was a wise man, said that the gods were invented to punish secret crimes.

Could a society exist which had eliminated everything indeterminate and irrational in order to rely on the measurable and the verifiable? The problem exists and presses upon us. The entire modern age displays a continual increase in precision. Anything that is not perceptible cannot become precise, and in some way retards the rest. Inevitably it will more and more be considered vain and insignificant in contrast.

H

Order always weighs on the individual. Disorder makes him wish for the police or for death. These are two extreme circumstances in which human nature is not at ease. The individual seeks a completely satisfactory period in which he will be both freest and most looked after. He finds it toward the beginning of the end of a social system.

. . . .

J

. . . If the fates had given some free man the right to choose, from all known periods, the one that he would like best to live in, I am sure that that fortunate man would have chosen the exact period of Montesquieu. I am not without my weaknesses, I would do the same. Europe was then the best of possible worlds; in it authority and opportunity were reconciled; truth kept within certain bounds; matter and energy did not govern directly; as yet they did not reign supreme. Knowledge was already magnificent enough, and the arts were very exquisite; religion still existed. There was sufficient fantasy and enough discipline. The Tartufes, the idiotic Orgons, the sinister 'Messieurs,' the absurd Alcestes were happily buried; the Emiles, the Renés, the ignoble Rollas were still to be born. People were good-mannered even in the streets. Pedlars knew how to turn a phrase. Even revenue collectors, prostitutes, spies and beggars expressed themselves as no one does today. The public treasury made its demands gracefully.

The whole world was not yet completely explored; people lived at ease in a world of which the map was not without immense empty spaces waiting to be discovered in Africa, in America and in Oceania, which gave rise to dreams. Even the days were not crowded and hurried, but slow and free; timetables did not haunt one's thoughts and did not make people slaves of time and of one another.

People complained about the government; they always thought that things could be done better. But worries were not out of all proportion. There were a number of eager and sensitive men whose intelligence disturbed Europe and heedlessly harassed everything sacred or otherwise. Women were concerned about the nascent differential calculus, and about the bacteria, almost essential to love, which wriggled under the eye in the microscope; they leaned like fairies over the glass and copper cradle of infant electricity.

Even poetry tried to be exact and without nonsense; but that is an impossibility; it only succeeded in becoming impoverished.

K

There appeared at that time a type of mind so fine and so pure that every kind of libertinism seemed to it to be the inconsequential experiments of a creature so subtle that it would not allow itself to be caught by anything—not even by the very worst. Even the obscene did not ensnare it. People were so witty, so incredulous, so in love with enlightenment, that they felt themselves incapable of being soiled, or degraded or debased by ideas or even by the boldest theories, or the most hot-headed experiments. They went as far as the supreme artifice, which is to invent nature and to pretend to simplicity. This kind of fantasy always denotes the end of the scene and the last moment of good taste.

. . . .

Translated by Anthony Bower

ON MALLARMÉ

At the still tender age of twenty, and at the critical point in a strange and profound intellectual transformation, I suffered the shock of Mallarmé's work; I felt surprise and intimate, instantaneous dismay; and astonishment; and the breaking of the bonds that tied me to the idols of my age. I felt myself become a fanatic; I experienced the crushing advance of a decisive spiritual conquest.

The definition of beauty is easy; it is what leads to desperation. But you must welcome this kind of desperation which opens your eyes and enlightens you—and as old Horace said in Corneille—*which helps you.* . . .

I had written a few poems. I liked what one ought to have liked in poetry about 1889. The idea of 'perfection' still had the authority of law, though in a more subtle sense than the plastic and over-simplified meaning that the word had been given ten or twenty years before. People were not yet bold enough to attribute *values*—even infinite ones—to the immediate, unforeseen, unforeseeable, and—what am I saying—unimportant products of the moment. The principle that *you win at every throw* had not yet been enunciated, and, on the contrary, one only valued the *lucky throws,* or what one believed to be such. In a word, at that time one asked of poetry that it give a conception of itself completely opposite to that which the passage of time made attractive a little later on. (Which was bound to happen).

But what intellectual effect the least of Mallarmé's writings had on us at that time of revelation, and what moral effects! . . . There was something religious in the air at that period, when certain people were forming a passionate love and a cult for what they found so beautiful that it had to be called superhuman.

The *Herodiade, l'Apres Midi,* the *Sonnets*—the fragments of them that were found in Reviews—which were passed around, and which, by their interchange formed a bond, in sending them to each other, between initiates scattered all over France, much as the initiates of former times were united at a distance by the exchange of tablets and of lamellae of beaten gold—constituted for us a treasure house of incorruptible delights, very well self-defended against the barbarian and the infidel.

In this strange and apparently absolute work rested a magic power. By the mere fact of its existence it worked like a charm and like a sword. At one blow it divided the common herd from the human beings who knew how to read. Its appearance of enigma instantly excited the core of the literate intelligence. It seemed immediately, infallibly, to touch the most sensitive part of the cultivated mind, to overexcite the very center where there exists and is held in reserve some prodigious store of pride, and where *that which cannot bear not to understand* resides.

The author's name alone was enough to produce in people the most interesting reactions: stupor, irony, sonorous rages. There were some who invoked our *great classic writers*—who would never have imagined the kind of prose in which they were one day going to be called upon. Others played at laughing or smiling, and immediately regained (by those happy accidents of the facial muscles which guarantee us our freedom) all the immediate superiority which enables those people who are self-sufficient to live. Rare are the individuals who are not hurt by not understanding, and who accept the fact gracefully, as one accepts not understanding a language or algebra. One can live without those things.

The observer of these phenomena had the pleasure of seeing a fine contrast: a profoundly meditated work, the most calculated and the most conscious there ever was, giving rise to a number of *reflexes*.

That is to say that from the first glance given it, this matchless work touched upon and attacked the fundamental conventions of everyday language: *You would not read me, had you not already understood me.*

I am now going to make an admission. I confess, I agree, that all these good people who protested, who laughed, who did not perceive what we perceived, were in a quite legitimate position. Their opinion was quite in order. One must not be afraid to say that the kingdom of letters is only a province of the vast empire of entertainment. One picks up a book, one puts it aside; and even when one cannot put it down one very well understands that this interest is related to the facility of pleasure. That is to say that every effort of a creator of beauty or of fantasy should be bent, by the very essence of his work, on contriving *for the public* pleasure which demands no effort, or almost none. It is through the public that he should deduce what touches, moves, soothes, animates or enchants the public.

There are however several publics; amongst whom it is not impossible to find some people who do not conceive of pleasure without pain, who do not like to enjoy themselves without paying, and who are not happy if their happiness is not in some part their own contrivance through which they wish to realize what it costs them. Moreover it happens that a quite special public can be formed.

Mallarmé, therefore, created in France the conception of the *difficult author*. He introduced into art the obligation of intellectual effort. By this means he improved the condition of the reader; and with an admirable understanding of real reward chose for himself from amongst the whole world that small number of special connoisseurs who, once they had tasted him, could no longer bear impure, immediate, and undefended poems. Everything else *seemed naive and uncourageous after they had read him*.

His small, marvellously polished compositions imposed themselves as models of perfection, so very sure were the relations between words and words, between verse and verse, between movements and rhythms; to such an extent did each one of them give the impression of an object in some way absolute, thanks to the balance of its intrinsic strength, drawn by prodigious reciprocal combinations from those indeterminate fantasies of improvements and changes which the mind, as it reads, unconsciously conceives when confronted with the majority of texts.

The brilliance of these crystalline constructions, so pure, and so perfectly finished in every part, fascinated me. They have not the transparency of glass, no doubt; but in that they somehow break habits of mind on their facets and on their concentrated structure, what is called their obscurity is only, in reality, their *refraction*.

I tried to show myself the ways and the workings of their author's mind. I said to myself that this man had meditated on all words, and had considered and enumerated every kind of form. Gradually I became interested in the workings of a mind so different from mine—even more so perhaps than in the visible fruits of his efforts. I reconstructed for myself the author of such work. It seemed to me that this work must have been endlessly reflected upon in mental surroundings from which nothing was allowed to emerge that had not *lived* long enough in the world of presentiments, of harmonious patterns, of perfect forms and their reflections; a preparatory world where everything clashes with everything, and in which chance temporizes, takes its bearings, and finally crystallizes itself on some model.

A work can only emerge from a sphere so reflective and so rich in resonances by a kind of accident which ejects it from the mind. It falls headlong into time.

I came to the conclusion that there was an inner system in Mallarmé, a system which could be distinguished from philosophy, and moreover from mysticism; but not unanalogous to it.

I was perfectly disposed by nature, or rather by the change in my nature which had just taken place, to develop, in a strange enough way, the impression given by the poems which displayed to me such preparation for their beauty, that they themselves paled before the idea they gave me of this hidden work.

A short while before I had formed, and naively noted down, this opinion in the form of a vow: that if ever I should write, I should infinitely prefer to write entirely consciously, and with complete lucidity, something rather feeble, than to give birth, thanks to a trance and while outside myself, to the very finest masterpieces.

This was because it seemed to me that there were already many masterpieces, and that the number of works of genius was not so small that there was any great interest attached to wanting to increase it. I believed, rather more accurately, that a work resolutely thought out and sought for in the hazards of the mind, systematically, and through a determined analysis of definite and previously prescribed conditions, whatever its value might be once it had been produced, did not leave the mind of its creator without having modified him, and forced him to recognize and in some way to reorganize himself. I said to myself *that it was not the accomplished work, and its appearance and effect in the world, that can fulfill and edify us; but only the way in which we have done it.* Art and its difficulties increase our stature; but the Muses and good fortune only visit us to leave us again.

By this means I gave to the will and to the calculations of the *agent* an importance that I transferred from the *work.* This does not mean that I thought that the latter should be neglected; quite the contrary.

This dreadful thought, very dangerous to Letters (but about which I have never varied) was curiously allied, and opposed, to my admiration for a man who, in following his own line of thought, was going to do nothing less than deify the written word. What I liked best about him was the essentially calculating manner, the absolutist tendency, demonstrated by the extreme perfection of his work. Hard work, in literature, is manifested and accomplished by revisions. It can be said that it can be measured by the number of revisions. That if the study of the frequency and type of revisions was possible, it would be a capital source for intimate knowledge of the writer, since it would enlighten us about the secret discussion that takes place, at the time when the work is being done, between the temperament, ambition and foresight of the man, and, on the other hand, the excitements and the intellectual means of the moment.

The strictness of the revisions, the number of solutions rejected, and possibilities denied, indicate the nature of the scruples, the degree of conscience, the quality of pride, and even the reserves and diverse fears that are felt in regard to the future judgment of the public.

It is at this point that literature enters the domain of ethics; it is here that the conflict between the natural and the contrived is introduced, and here that it obtains its heroes and martyrs of the *resistance to the facile;* where virtue is manifested, and sometimes hypocrisy.

* * *

Mallarmé's "Coup de Dés"

I really believe that I am the first person to have seen this extraordinary work. Hardly had he finished it when Mallarmé asked me to come to his house. He took me into his room in the Rue de Rome, where, behind an antique tapestry, lay, until his death (a signal given by him for their destruction) his bundles of notes—the secret material for his great unfinished work. On his square, bow-legged table of very dark wood he placed the manuscript of his poem and started to read in a low, even voice, without the least 'effect' and almost to himself. . . .

I like this absence of artifice. The human voice seems to me so lovely in itself, taken as nearly as possible to its source, that professional speakers who claim to improve and interpret, when they only overload and corrupt the meaning and change the harmony of the text, are almost always unbearable to me,—particularly when they substitute their own lyricism for the real rhythm of the combined words. Is it not their real profession—

their paradoxical talent—to make the most slovenly verses seem momentarily sublime, but to make ridiculous, or to obliterate, most of the works which stand by themselves. Alas! I have sometimes heard the *Herodiade* and the sublime *Cygne* declaimed.

Mallarmé, having read to me in the simplest possible manner his *Coup de Dés,* as a mere preparation for an even greater surprise, finally made me consider the content. He seemed to me to have seen the outline of a thought which had found its place for the first time in our universe. . . . Here, in truth, infinity spoke, thought and gave birth to temporal forms. Expectation, doubt and concentration were visible things. My comprehension had to cope with embodied silences. I contemplated, at my leisure, incalculable periods of time; the fraction of a second during which an idea was born, shone forth, and was extinguished—the atom of time, the seed of psychological centuries and of infinite consequences—seemed at last like living beings completely surrounded by their nothingness made perceptible. Here were whispers, insinuations, thunder made visible, a spiritual tempest leading, page by page, to the ultimate in thought, to the ineffable breaking point; here the magic spell was woven; here on the very paper shone an indefinable, infinitely pure light from the farthest stars, in the same half-conscious void where, like a new kind of matter scattered in heaps, in tracks, in systems, coexisted Language.

This unparallelled concentration petrified me. The whole effect fascinated me as though a new star had appeared in the heavens; as if a new constellation had been formed which at last signified something.—Was I not taking part in an event of universal importance, and was it not in some way the visionary spectacle of the Creation of Language which was being displayed on this table, at this moment, by this entity—this brave man, so simple and so kind, so naturally noble and charming. . . . I felt myself delivered over to the diversity of my impressions; overcome by the novelty of the prospect, quite purged of doubt, completely detached from any further developments. I looked for an answer in the midst of the thousand questions I prevented myself from asking. I was a compound of admiration, resistance, passionate interest and of analogies to the state of being born, when confronted by this intellectual discovery.

And as for him, I think that he viewed my astonishment without astonishment.

*

On the 30th of March 1897, handing me the corrected proofs of the text which *Cosmopolis* was going to publish, he said to me with a wonderful smile, the embellishment of the very simple pride inspired in man by his understanding of the universe "Don't you think that this is an act of insanity?"

A little later, at Valvins, beside a window opening onto the placid countryside, he showed me the magnificent proof-sheets of the edition printed by Lahure (it was never published) and paid me the further compliment of asking my advice on certain details of the typographical layout, which was an essential part of what he was trying to do. I looked for, I offered, certain objections but with the sole object of making him reply to them. . . .

On the evening of the same day, as he was taking me to the train, the countless stars of the July night enclosing everything in a shining galaxy of other worlds, and while we walked, smoking in the dark, in the midst of the Serpent, the Swan, the Eagle and the Lyre—he seemed to me to be now involved in the very meaning of the silent universe: a text full of clarity and enigma; as tragic or as unimportant as one wants to make it; which speaks and does not speak; which embraces order and disorder; which proclaims a God as loudly as it denies one; which contains in its inconceivable entirety every period of time, each one associated with the distance of a heavenly body; which recalls the most evident and incontestable success of man, the fulfillment of his predications—to the seventh decimal place; and which crushes the living witness, the wise contemplator, beneath the futility of his triumphs . . . We continued our walk. In the depths of such a night between the remarks we exchanged, I thought of his admirable attempt; where Kant, naively enough perhaps, believed he understood Moral Law, Mallarmé undoubtedly understood the imperative of poetry; A Poetics.

This radiant dispersion; these pale pyrocanths; these almost spiritual causes, distinct but united; the immense question posed by this silence charged with so much life and with so much death; ought not all this, so glorious in itself and the strange sum of reality and of contradictory ideals, to suggest to someone the supreme temptation of reproducing its effect?

He had tried, I thought, to raise writing, at last, to the level of the starry heavens.

I saw Stephen Mallarmé for the last time on the 14th of July, 1898, at Valvins. When lunch was over, he took me into his study. Four paces long by two paces wide; the window opening onto the Seine and onto the forest through foliage rent apart by light, and the smallest movements of the shining river faintly reflected on the walls.

Mallarmé was worried about the finishing touches to the construction of the *Coup de Dés*. The inventor was contemplating and touching up with a pencil this new machine which the Lahure Press had agreed to construct.

Nothing had so far been undertaken—or even considered—to give the form of the text a significance and an effect comparable to those of the text itself. Just as the everyday use of our limbs makes us almost forget their existence and neglect the variety of their resources, and just as it happens that an artist in the use of the human body sometimes points out to us all their suppleness, at the cost of his life which he consumes in exercises and which he exposes to the dangers of his addiction, so the habitual use of language, the practice of reading at random, and the use of everyday expressions, weaken the understanding of these too familiar acts and banish the very conception of their power and of their possible perfection, unless some person survives and dedicates himself who is particularly disdainful of the easy ways of the mind, but singularly attentive to what he can produce that is most unexpected and most subtle.

I was in the presence of such a person. Nothing told me that I should never see him again. On this golden day there was no raven to foretell it. Everything was calm and certain. . . . But while Mallarmé was talking to me, with his finger on the page, I remember that my mind began to contemplate this particular moment. Absent-mindedly I gave it an almost absolute value. Near him while he was still alive, I thought of his destiny as already realized. Born for the delight of some and to the dismay of others, and to the amazement of all; for the latter a madness and an absurdity; for his own kind a marvel of pride, elegance and intellectual modesty, a few poems had sufficed for him to put in doubt the very purpose of literature. His work, difficult to understand and impossible to neglect, divided literate people. Poor and without honors, the nakedness of his condition disgraced all the advantages that others had; but he was assured, without having looked for it, of extraordinary loyalty. As for him, whose wise, disdainful victim's smile quietly disposed of the universe, he had never asked anything of the world but the most precious and rarest things it contained. He found them in himself.

*

We went into the country. The 'artificial' poet gathered the simplest flowers. Our arms were filled with corn-flowers and poppies. The air was on fire; the splendor absolute; the silence full of intoxication and communication; death impossible or unimportant; everything amazingly beautiful, afire and asleep; and the landscape trembled.

In the sun, in the immense arc of the cloudless sky, I dreamed of an incandescent space where nothing distinct exists, where nothing lasts, but where nothing ends, as if destruction itself was destroyed before it was accomplished. I lost my perception of the difference between being and not-being. Sometimes music gives us this impression, which is beyond all others. Is not poetry, I thought, the supreme pastime of transmuting ideas? . . .

Mallarmé pointed out to me the plain which summer was already beginning to turn to gold; "Look," he said, "it is the first drum-beat of autumn on the earth."

When autumn came, he was no more.

Translated by Anthony Bower

ON PAINTING

About Berthe Morisot

Is it absurd to think, if someday one had to undertake a very exact analysis of painting, that without doubt one should study at close proximity the painters' vision? That would only be to begin at the beginning.

Man lives and moves in what he sees, but he only sees what he wants to see. Try different types of people in the midst of any landscape. A philosopher will only vaguely see phenomena; a geologist, crystallized, confused, ruined and pulverized epochs; a soldier, opportunities and obstacles; and for a peasant it will only represent acres, and perspiration and profits. . . . But all of them will have this in common, that they will see nothing as simply a view. They will only get from their sensations the shock necessary to carry them on to something quite different, to what they are familiar with. They all experience a certain arrangement of colors; but each one immediately transforms them into *symbols,* which mean the same thing to them as the conventional colorings of a map. These strangely arrayed yellows, and blues and greys fade in the space of a moment; memory dispels the present; the useful dispels the real; the meaning of objects dispels their form. We only immediately see hopes or regrets, properties and potential values, promises of harvests, signs of maturity or mineral deposits; we only see the future or the past, but no trace of the actual moment. Absolutely anything colorless is forever substituted for the chromatic present, as if the substance of the non-artist had absorbed the appreciation of it and would never again relinquish it—having evaded it on account of its consequences.

The opposite of this abstraction is the artist's abstraction. Color speaks to him of color, he replies to color with color. He lives in his object, in the very midst of what he seeks to find and of perpetual temptations, defiance, examples, problems, analysis and intoxication. It may well be that he does not see what he imagines, and imagines what he sees.

His very means are a part of the compass of his art. Nothing is more provocative to the eyes than a box of paints or a palette. Even a piano is less exciting to the vague desire to 'produce,' for it is but silence and expectation, while the delightful display of lacs and terras, oxides and aluminas already sings, in all its tones, the prelude to what can be done ar᠎ enchants him. I can only compare it to the teeming chaos of pure and luminous sound which comes from an orchestra while it is tuning up, and seems to dream before the music begins; each instrument trying to find its note, sketching its own part in the confusion of all the other sounds, in a disorder full of promise and more general than all music, which stimulates with delightful anticipation all of the sensitive soul and all the very roots of pleasure.

Digression. It is a universal and ageless opinion that there exists an 'interior life' from which actual things are excluded and to which they are harmful, for which scents, colors, images and, perhaps, even ideas are handicaps and disturbances to its perfection; and in consequence one would like the people who consume themselves in the desire, the enjoyment or the secret commerce of their incommunicable perceptions, to feel them to be even more alive and get from them even more real results, the more advanced they are in their profundity and in their detachment, and the more removed they are from the external or what they believe to be the external.

To the life that employs definable senses and which is satisfied with their illusions, they readily oppose a certain 'life of the heart' or of the soul, or even a life of the pure intellect; all withdrawn from the superficial disturbances caused by what can be felt and seen. One finds that many wise men hold the formal opinion that the senses are allies of the enemy and that the essential organs should be treated as panders. *"Odoratus impedit cogitationem"* said Saint Bernard—amongst other things. I am not so sure that private meditation and personal renunciation are always innocent, nor that the recluse always increases in purity within himself. If some sensual desire is, inadvertently, confined with the soul in these mental retreats, it sometimes happens that it will grow as in a hot-house, with incomparable luxuriousness and fury. But though it is generally accepted and supported by very great men, this hostile doctrine to the senses is not so reliable that one cannot, at times, maintain and enjoy the exact opposite. Why do we want the essence, the supposed essence of ourselves, the semblance of essence that we find in ourselves, by accident or by indefinite waiting, to be more important to observe—if we really believe it to be so in pursuing it—than the appearance of this world. Is what we perceive when we are so alone and so uncertain, with so much difficulty, and as though by chance or by fraud, necessarily more worth while knowing, higher in degree, or nearer to our deepest secret than what we can see distinctly? Is not this abyss where venture the most credulous and the most inconstant of our senses, on the contrary, the place and the product of our most vain, most senseless and most clumsy impressions, those which are confused and the farthest removed from the precision and co-ordination found in others whose masterpiece we call the Exterior World? We despise this perceptible world for overwhelming us with its perfections. It is the domain of coincidence, of distinctions, of references and recoveries, where the whole range of our senses and the multitude of our enduring elements are brought together and unified. Let us make a very easy supposition, in order to understand this better. Let us imagine that the sight of the things that surround us is not familiar, that it is only allowed us as an exception, and that we only obtain by a miracle, knowledge of the day, of human beings, of the heavens, of the sun, and of faces. What would we say about these revelations, and in what terms would we speak of this infinity of wonderfully adjusted data? What would we say of this distinct, complete and solid world, if this world only appeared very occasionally, to cross, to dazzle, and to crush the unstable, incoherent world of the solitary soul?

Mysticism consists, perhaps, in rediscovering an elementary, and in some ways, primitive sensation—the sensation of pursuing life on an uncharted course which has been set through an already completed life which seems already to *have happened*.

Translated by Anthony Bower

AN UNPUBLISHED LETTER TO PIERRE LOUYS

Saturday 13/9/15

My dear Pierre, this morning (and for the last few days) I am in an ultra-vibratory nervous state, very unsuitable to regulated and sustained psychic activity. Nothing consumes more time than a galloping nervous system.

I cannot read your letter *coherently*. It awakens ideas in me at random— from all sides. For me as I am this morning, it is a town by night, form- less, with lights in every window on all the unknown floors, and planes and distances.

And I answer it in the way I am thinking: at random. Two words in this letter loom large and seem like ineradicable monsters in a dream.

Their task is to guard their meaning. And I cannot pass. It's no use. Impossible to enter.

What are these monster-words? One big and one small.

The big one is called SIMULTANEOUS. I see it in the form of a key- board.

The small one is called *I* or *Me*. Even more formidable.

I and *Simultaneous* are appalling and at the same time familiar to me.

I shall not enter into your letter for they would devour me first. And that is understood. We are quite used to it. They to devouring me, and I to being devoured by them.

I can even give you this example—at any rate for today.

Imagine a mind. Or rather a system of the nervous type. (I don't like the mind alone: I don't believe in it.)

As we know nothing about this system, we are allowed to regard it as a myriad of milliards of . . . little separate workers.

Each one of them only does and only knows how to do what he always does. Whatever happens, he is limited to doing or to not doing his own particular task. And he starts or stops doing it without knowing why. Apart from that he knows nothing—if he did know something, that would amount to supposing that he himself contained a thousand milliard other workers. And so forth.

Thus this ignorant multitude works or rests, but its work does not belong to it, is never returned to it. The work is lost somewhere, in another 'world' the strange state of which is similar to that of the workers. I mean that in it nothing reveals the infinitesimal industry of which it is part and parcel.

Let us leave this other world and come back to the first. I see something like a Milky Way. On every star some activity. Here, in order to be able to continue, I am obliged to make a coup d'état. I am obliged to choose some star in order to be able to consider the others from it. I am obliged to put myself somewhere—and yet I haven't the right. Necessity should oblige me to suppress myself to leave room for My Multiplicity. It's all very difficult.

Here I am on one of these points of light. What do I see? In what state do I see the others?—Certainly not in the state in which they *are,* but in the state in which they were.

I see Sirius as it was in the year X . . .

And now what does Simultaneous mean?

What does the word Present mean to an element of the mind or of the marrow whose own modifications are transmitted to one another by means of time?

If I could think about your letter, I think that I should say this: your Simultaneous and your I contradict each other. In my opinion there is no such thing as a simple I—(simplex)—'I' signifies at least a division into two. And if my sensibilities were better trained, if *I* perceived myself, or if *I* perceived *itself* without confusion or evasions, it is not a triplex that we would have, but a milliardiplex, still more disturbing.

One more word—or rather a clumsy image of these ramblings: You look at yourselves in the mirror, you gesticulate, you stick out your tongue . . . Alright.

Now suppose that a malicious god plays a game of enormously diminishing the speed of light.

You are forty centimetres from your mirror. At first you saw your reflection after 2,666 millionths of a second. But the god has amused himself by making the ether more dense. And now you see yourself after a minute, a day, a century, *ad libitum*.

You see yourself being slow to obey yourself. Compare this with what happens when you look for a word, a 'forgotten' name.

This slowness is all of psychology,—which we can qualify paradoxically as: What takes place between something . . . and itself.

We were that something and we did not know it. We know *now*, but we are it no longer.

Your
P. V.

Translated by Anthony Bower

ANALECTA

MY BODY

This "my-body" occupies a volume. But in the interior of this volume a singular connection seems to reign.

The interior distances are not of the same kind as ordinary distances. Sensations, local movements, although localized,—do not seem to be at different points as far as *distance* is concerned.

For two points of the body taken at random, distance has no meaning.

For two points that can never come into contact naturally and that have no individual relation, distance does not exist.[1]

Far and *near* are also altogether special. A distant limb seems to obey without any intermediary; and to be, on that account, nearer than a less distant but non-tractable and non-mobile spot.

In interior corporal distances it is found that the question of interval between different parts of the body is tied up with the mobility of those parts and the time necessary to set them in motion. The most mobile is the eye.

One might thus roughly classify: eye, fingers of the hand, tongue and lower jaw, head, toes, hand, forearm, feet, lower limbs, loins, torso, shoulders, all this extremely approximate—and variable.

Degree of mobility?

This mobility is very complex. It depends on innervation, on the musculature and its insertions, on the mass, on the moment of inertia of the part, on the position of the body, on the degree of alertness, and also on *phase,* that is on the immediately preceding states.

The body is a mass or a space permeated with sensibilities as a stone is veined with iron, or as a sponge is filled with water: permeated with

[1] *The fundamental postulate of exterior distance $ab + bc = ac$ has no meaning in the perception of the inside.*

228

will in a less subtle fashion. Sensibility and will, leaving between this network where they exist, insensible and inert parts, whose size is delimited by the fineness of these divisions.

There are regions where will does not exist and which are purely local. The dimensions of these regions are *discernible according to our knowledge and possession of ourselves.*[2]

Curious analogy. Thought too is made up of regions into which it cannot penetrate. There are distinctions that it fails to fathom, durations it does not subdivide. It penetrates something, but only to a certain degree.

The substance of our body is not on our scale. The most important phenomena for us, our life, our feelings, our thoughts, are intimately linked to events smaller than the smallest phenomenon accessible to our senses, or that can be used by our actions. We cannot intervene directly— seeing what we are doing. Medicine is an indirect intervention—the other arts too, as a matter of fact. In this minuteness, any conceivable action of ours has no longer any meaning.

The nervous system, among other properties or functions, possesses that of linking very different orders of magnitude. For example: it joins what belongs to the chemist with that which belongs to the mechanic.

Physics today considers *masses* so infinitely small that even light has nothing to do with them. Whatever images we may conceive of them *have no bearing, can have none,* on what they are supposed to represent. The notion of *form* in connection with them has no sense, is entirely foreign to objects so tiny that one cannot even conceive of their enlargement, for that presumes the existence of similarity.

ORDER, DISORDER AND ONESELF

I have found this note-book again. It had not been mislaid. On the contrary. I had put it away so carefully that I did not recognize myself. It had departed from my ways. I had lost my divining rod, my "disorder." But my own, personal, and familiar disorder.

Not to lose things, you must always put them where you would naturally put them without thinking. One does not forget what one is in the

---

[2] *That is, my presence is more or less dense according to the region of my body under consideration.*

habit of doing. Real disorder is the upsetting of that rule of a sort, *the derogation of frequency*. It is to put things in a place laboriously decided upon,—found after gropings, combinations, deviations, or *successive steps away from tendency,* like a discovery, a new world, an unusual solution . . .

Then, in order to find the object again I am obliged to find a certain train of thought again, with nothing to lead me back to it.

But if it has been put somewhere without premeditation I only have to find myself again, myself whole and in bulk,—that is, *I only have to be.*

If your rule is disorder, you will pay dearly for having put things in order.

Follow your rule.

A man in agony dares not move—either his body or his mind—just as a man in his bath, if he stir in the water, would feel the cold. The former would feel his fear.

Movement makes one's sensibility more acute. After a shock, one dares not move. It is a strange *nexus* in which ideas, movements, varying sensations are curiously confused.

Abrupt Changes in a Selfsame Thing

Sometimes our attention is strangely and abruptly arrested by an idea, a recollection, a corner of some piece of furniture. All at once, it seems as though we were seeing something for the first time that we have seen a thousand times; or we perceive the coming of age—the puberty of an impression.

An idea in its sudden force seems more real; and yet we have thought of it many times before, and even close-up, even with deliberation;—but this time it is, as it were, *tangible*. This face looks at me. In the same way it often happens that we understand something only long afterwards: an intention, a text, a person,—oneself. We discover the significance of a look addressed to us twenty years ago by someone now dead; and the meaning of a phrase; and the beauty of a line of poetry we have known by heart since childhood.

So, it is said, the grain of wheat found in a hypogeum germinates after three thousand years of arid slumber.

The name Body corresponds habitually to several very different needs for expression. One might say that each one of us has in his mind the idea of *Three Bodies—at least*.

This, I am going to explain.

The first is the favored object that is ever present, although our knowledge of it may be variable and subject to illusions—like everything that is inseparable from the moment. Everybody calls this object *My-Body;* but we do not give it a name in *ourselves:* that is *in it*. We speak of it to others as a thing which belongs to us; but for us it is not altogether a thing; and belongs to us less than we belong to it. . . .

For each one of us it is essentially the most important object in the world and is in opposition to this world on which it is aware of being dependant. We can say with equal truth, by simply changing the *accommodation* of our mental vision, that on it the world rests and that this world adapts itself to it, or else that it is itself only a kind of infinitely negligible and changeable event of this world.

But neither the word "object" I have used, nor the word "event," is the proper word here. There is no name to describe the feeling we have of a substance of our presence, of our actions and our emotions which are not only actual but also imminent or deferred or purely possible—something more withdrawn and yet less intimate than our secret reservations: we find in ourselves a capacity for modification almost as varied as the surrounding circumstances. This object obeys or disobeys, carries out or hampers our plans; we derive from it the most surprising powers and weaknesses connected with either the whole or some part of this more or less sensitive mass, which at times is suddenly charged with impelling forces that make it "act" by virtue of some unknown inner mystery, and which, at others, seems itself to become the most crushing and immovable weight.

Furthermore this thing is formless: we know by sight only a few mobile parts that can be brought within range of the seeing region of the space of this My-Body, this strange asymmetric space where distances have unparalleled relations. I have no conception of the spatial relation between "My Forehead" and "My Foot," between "My Knee" and "My Back."

. . . This has strange consequences. My right hand is a stranger to my left hand. When one hand takes hold of the other it is taking hold of a *non-me* object. These singularities must play a part in sleep and, *if dreams exist,* must organize them and provide infinite combinations.

This thing, so much mine and yet so mysteriously, and at the same time, and always in the end, our most formidable antagonist, is the most insistant, the most constant, and the most variable thing in the world: all constancy and all variation belong to it. Nothing moves before us without its making a sort of corresponding modification, following or imitating the movement it has perceived; and nothing stops moving without a similar cessation occurring in some part of it.

It has no past. This word is without meaning in respect to something which is the very present itself, all composed of events and possibilities. Sometimes certain parts or regions stand out, are lighted up, take on an importance before which everything else fades, and which instantly impose their charm and their incomparable rigor.

*

Our *Second Body* is the one others see, and that is more or less revealed to us in the glass or in portraits. It is the one which has a form and which the arts apprehend; the one on which we hang stuffs, ornaments and armor. It is the one Love sees or longs to see, anxious to touch it. It is ignorant of pain, knowing only the grimace of pain.

It is this body, indeed, that was so dear to Narcissus, but that is the despair of so many people, and saddens and depresses almost every one of us when, the time having arrived, we are forced to admit that this old creature in the glass has a shockingly close resemblance, although incomprehensible, to that which is looking at it and rejecting it. We refuse to consent to being this ruin. . . .

But the knowledge of our *Second Body* never gets beyond the sight of a surface. One can live without ever having seen oneself, without knowing the color of ones skin; it is the fate of the blind. But it is that of all of us to live without life ever imposing on us the necessity of knowing what it is that this, practically uniform skin of our *Second Body,* covers. It is remarkable that the living, thinking, acting human being has nothing to do with his interior organization. He is not qualified to know it. There is nothing to make him suspect he has a liver, a brain, kidneys and all the rest: this information would, moreover, be totally useless to him since, in the natural state of things, he has no way of controlling these organs. All his powers of action are directed toward the "exterior world," to such an extent that "exterior world" might be defined as the world that is effected by our means of action: for example whatever I *see* can be transformed by *my movement:* I act on my environment, but I do not know by means of what mechanisms.

*

There is then a Third Body. But this one, except in our mind, lacks unity, since we only know it from having divided it and taken it to pieces. It must be drawn and quartered before it can be known. Out of it flow scarlet or pale or hyaline liquids, often extremely viscous. Out of it are removed masses of various dimensions which have been fitted in rather neatly: these are sponges, vessels, tubes, filaments, articulated bars. . . . All this, reduced to very thin slices or to drops, reveals under the microscope the shapes of corpuscles which look like nothing at all. We try to decipher these histological cryptograms. We wonder how this fiber could produce motive power? And what relation there can possibly be between these tiny constellations with delicate radicles, and sensation and thought? But what would a Descartes, a Newton have done, ignorant as they were of electromagnetism, induction, and all the scientific discoveries since their time, if a dynamo had been presented to them for inspection, and they had been told only its effects? They would have done what we do with a brain: they would have taken the apparatus apart, would have unwound the coils, would have made a note of the presence of copper here, carbon there, and steel there, and would finally have had to admit themselves defeated, incapable of divining how this machine that they have been told accomplishes the transformations we all know, functions.

*

Among these *Three Bodies* I have just given you, there necessarily exist innumerable connections which it would be interesting, although rather laborious, to try to make clear. I prefer now to have recourse to pure fancy.

*

I maintain that for each one of us there is a *Fourth Body* which I might indifferently call either the *Real Body* or the *Imaginary Body*.

This body is regarded as inseparable from the unknown and unknowable sphere of which physicists give us an inkling when they harry the sensible world and, by the circuitous way of stage within stage, produce phenomena whose origin they place far above and beyond our senses, our imagination and, finally, even beyond our intellection.

From this inconceivable sphere my *Fourth Body* is as indistinguishable as a whirlpool is indistinguishable from the liquid in which it is formed. (I have a perfect right to dispose of the inconceivable as I see fit.)

This *Fourth Body* is not any one of the *Three Bodies,* since it is not My-Body, nor is it the Third Body that belongs to scientists, since it is made of what they know nothing about. . . . And let me add that the knowledge acquired by means of the intellect is a product of what this Fourth Body *is not.* Everything that is, masks for us, necessarily and irrevocably, *something that may be. . . .*

But why here introduce such an utterly vain notion? Just because an idea, even a perfectly absurd idea, is never without value; and because an expression, an empty sign, will invariably serve as a spur to the mind. But where did it come from, this term *Fourth Body?*

As I was considering the idea of the Body in general and my *Three Bodies* just mentioned, vaguely I seemed to hear, in the dim recesses of my mind, the voice of the time-honored problems awakened by these themes. I confess that I usually keep them at a distance from the most sensitive and instant point of my attention. I never ask myself what the origin of life and of the living species may be; I do not ask whether death is a simple change of climate, costume and habits, whether the mind is, or is not, a by-product of the organism; whether our acts can at times be, what is called, free (without any one ever having been able to tell exactly what that means); etc.

It is against this background of jaded problems that my absurd and luminous idea appeared: "I call *Fourth Body,*" I said to myself, "the unknowable object *the knowledge of which would, at a single stroke, resolve all those problems, it being implicit in them.*"

And while a protest was beginning to stir in me, the Voice of the absurd added: "Just consider for a moment: where else do you hope to find answers to those philosophic questions? Your images, your abstractions

234

are derived solely from the nature and experiences of your *Three Bodies*. But the first offers you nothing but moments; the second, a few visible shapes; the third, at the price of appalling acts and complicated preparations, a quantity of figures more undecipherable than Etruscan texts. Your mind with its language triturates, composes, arranges all this: I concede that out of it all it does, by means of its well-known and endless questionings, extract those famous problems; but it cannot give them the ghost of a meaning unless it presupposes, without admitting it, some Inexistence of which my Fourth Body is a kind of incarnation."

Translated by Louise Varèse

FRAGMENT FROM "AN EVENING WITH MR. TESTE"

Stupidity is not my strong point. I have seen many persons; I have visited several nations; I have taken part in divers enterprises without affecting them; I have eaten nearly every day; I have tampered with women. I now recall several hundred faces, two or three great events, and perhaps the substance of twenty books. I have not retained the best nor the worst of these things. What could stick, did.

This bit of arithmetic spares me surprise at getting old. I could also add up the victorious moments of my mind, and imagine them joined and soldered, composing a *happy* life . . . But I think I have always been a good judge of myself. I have rarely lost sight of myself; I have detested, and adored myself—and so, we have grown old together.

Often I have supposed that all was over for me, and I would begin ending with all my strength, anxious to exhaust and clear up some painful situation. This has made me realize that we understand our own thought too often in terms of the *expression* of other people's! Since then, the thousands of words that have buzzed in my ears have rarely reached me with what they were meant to mean. And all those I have myself spoken to others, I could always feel them become distinct from my thought—for they were becoming *invariable*.

If I had thought as most men do, not only would I have believed myself their superior, but would have seemed so. I have preferred myself. What they call a superior man is one who has deceived himself. If we are to marvel at him, we have to see him—and if we are to see him, he has to show himself. And what he shows me is that he has a silly obsession with his own name. Every great man is thus flawed with an error. Every mind considered powerful begins with the fault that makes it known. In exchange for a public fee, it gives the time necessary to make itself knowable, the energy spent in transmitting itself and in preparing an alien satisfaction. It even goes so far as to compare the crude game of glory to the joy of feeling oneself unique—the great private pleasure.

These ideas came to me during October of '93, at those moments of leisure when thought practises simply existing.

I was beginning to think no more about them, when I made the acquaintance of Mr. Teste. (I am now thinking of the traces a man leaves in the little space through which he moves each day.) I heard that he lived on modest weekly speculations at the Bourse. He used to take his meals at a small restaurant on the Rue Vivienne. Here, he would eat as if he were taking a purgative, with the same rush. From time to time he would go elsewhere and allow himself a fine, leisurely meal.

Mr. Teste was perhaps forty years old. His speech was extraordinarily rapid, and his voice quiet. Everything about him was fading, his eyes, his hands. His shoulders, however, were military, and his step had a regularity that was amazing. When he spoke he never raised an arm or a finger: he had *killed his puppet*. He did not smile, and said neither hello nor goodbye. He seemed not to hear a "How do you do?"

His memory gave me much to think about. Signs that I could judge it by led me to imagine in him unequalled intellectual gymnastics. It was not that this faculty (his memory) was excessive—it was rather trained or transformed. These are his own words: "For twenty years I have not had a book. I have burned my papers also. I scribble in the flesh . . . I can retain what I wish. That is not the difficulty. *It is rather to retain what I shall want tomorrow!* I have tried to invent a mechanical sieve. . . ."

Thinking about it convinced me that Mr. Teste had managed to discover laws of the mind we know nothing of. Surely he must have devoted years to this research: even more surely, other years, and many more years, had been given to maturing his findings, making them into instincts. Discovery is nothing. The difficulty is to acquire what we discover.

The delicate art of duration: time, its distribution and regulation—how to spend it on well-chosen objects, to give them special nourishment—was one of Mr. Teste's main preoccupations. He watched for the repetition of certain ideas; he watered them with number. This served to make the application of his conscious studies in the end mechanical. He even sought to sum up this whole effort. He often said: "Maturare!" . . .

This man had early known the importance of what might be called human *plasticity*. He had tried to find out its limits and its laws. How deeply he must have thought about his own malleability!

On certain days I can recover him quite clearly. He reappears in my memory, beside me. I breathe the smoke of our cigars, I listen to him, I am wary. Sometimes, in reading a newspaper I encounter his thought, which some event has just justified. And I try again some of those experiments in illusion that used to delight me during our evenings together. That is, I imagine him doing what I have not seen him do. What is Mr. Teste like when he is sick? How does he reason when he is in love? Is it possible for him to be sad? What would he be afraid of? What could make him tremble? . . . I wondered. I kept before me the complete image of this rigorous man, trying to make it answer my questions . . . It faded.

He loves, he suffers, he is bored. People all do alike. But in his sigh, in his elemental moan, I want him to put the rules and forms of his whole mind.

Exactly two years and three months ago this evening, I was at the theater with him, in a box someone had offered us. I have thought about this all day today.

I can still see him standing with the golden column at the Opera; together.

He looked only at the audience. He was *breathing in* the great blast of brilliance, on the edge of the pit. He was red.

An immense copper girl stood between us and a group murmuring beyond the dazzlement. Deep in the haze shone a naked bit of woman, smooth as a pebble. A number of detached fans were living their own lives in the crowd that foamed up, dim and clear, to the level of the top lights. My sight spelled a thousand little faces, settled on a sad head, ran along arms, over people, and finally flickered out.

Each one was in his place, with room for slight movement. I tasted the system of classification, the almost theoretical simplicity of the audience, the social order. I had the delicious sensation that everything breathing in this cube was going to follow its laws, flare up with laughter in great circles, be moved in rows, feel as a mass *intimate,* even *unique* things, secret stirrings, be lifted to the unavowable! I strayed over these layers of men, from level to level, in orbits, fancying that I was bringing together in some ideal relation all those having the same illness, the same theory, or the same vice . . . One music moved us all, swelled, and then became quite small.

It disappeared. Mr. Teste was murmuring: "We are *beautiful,* extraordinary, only to others! *We* are eaten by others!"

The last word stood out in the silence created by the orchestra. Teste drew a deep breath.

His fiery face, glowing with warmth and color, his broad shoulders, his dark figure bronzed by the lights, the form of the whole clothed mass of him propped by the heavy column, took hold of me again. He lost not an atom of all that became perceptible at each moment in that grandeur of red and gold.

I watched that skull of his making acquaintance with the angles of the capital, his right hand refreshing itself among the gilt ornaments; and, in the purple shadow, his large feet. From distant parts of the theater his eyes came back toward me; his mouth said: "Discipline is not bad . . . It is at least a beginning . . ."

I did not know what to answer. He said in his low quick voice: "Let them enjoy and obey!"

He fixed his eyes for a long time on a young man opposite us, then on a lady, then on a whole group in the higher galleries—overflowing the balcony in five or six burning faces—and then on everybody, the whole theater, full as the heavens, eager, fascinated by the stage which we could not see. The stupidity of them all revealed to us that something or other sublime was going on. We watched the brightness dying from all the faces in the audience. And when it was quite low, when the light no longer shone, there remained only the vast phosphorescence of those thousand faces. I felt that this twilight made these beings passive. Their attention and the darkness, mounting together, formed a continuous equilibrium. I was myself attentive, *necessarily,* to all this attention.

Mr. Teste said: "The supreme simplifies *them.* I bet they are all thinking, more and more, *toward* the same thing. They will be alike at the crisis, the common limit. Besides, the law is not so simple . . . since it does not include me—and—I am here."

He added: "The lighting is what holds them."

I said, laughing: "You too?"

He replied: "You too."

239

"What a dramatist you would make," I said to him. "You seem to be carrying on some experiment beyond the limits of all the sciences! I would like to see a theater produce your meditations."

He said: "No one meditates."

The applause and the house lights drove us out. We circled, and went down. The passers-by seemed set free. Mr. Teste complained slightly of the midnight coolness.

.   .   .   .

Translated by Jackson Mathews

FRAGMENT OF "A LETTER FROM MRS. EMILIE TESTE"

. . . It is now time for our daily walk. I am just going to put on my hat. We shall walk slowly down through the terribly stony and crooked little streets of this old city, which you know somewhat. We usually end by going down where you would like to go if you were here, to the ancient park where all men of thought, care, and monologue go toward evening, as water goes to the river, and gather necessarily together. There are scholars, lovers, old men, the disillusioned, and priests, all *absent* men of every kind. They seem to be seeking mutual loneliness. They must like to see and not know one another, and their separate disillusionments are accustomed to meeting. One drags his illness with him, another is pursued by his anxiety; they are shadows running from themselves and each other; but there is no other place to run from others than here, where the same notion of solitude irresistibly draws each of these absorbed beings. In a short while we shall be there in that place worthy of the dead. It is a botanical ruin. We shall be there a little before twilight. You can imagine us, walking with short steps, giving ourselves to the sun, the cypresses, and the cries of birds. The wind is cold in the sun, and the sky, at times too beautiful, grips my heart. The hidden cathedral rings out. Here and there are round pools, built up as high as my waist. They are full to the brim with black impenetrable water, on which are fixed the enormous leaves of the Nymphaea Nelumbo; and the drops that venture onto these leaves roll and shine like mercury. Mr. Teste muses over these large living drops, or perhaps strolls slowly among the 'beds' with their green labels, where specimens of the vegetable kingdom are more or less cultivated. He enjoys this rather ridiculous order and delights in spelling the baroque names:

Antirrhinum Siculum
Solanum Warscewiezii!!!

241

And the *Sisymbriifolium*, what jargon! . . . And the *Vulgare*, and the *Asper*, and the *Palustris*, and the *Sinuata*, and the *Flexuosum*, and the *Praealtum!!!*

"*This is a garden of epithets*," he said the other day, "*a dictionary and cemetery garden . . .*"

And after a while, he said: "*Learnedly to die . . . Transiit classificando.*"

Please accept, kind sir, all our thanks and good wishes.

Emilie Teste

Translated by Jackson Mathews

TWO FRAGMENTS FROM "A LETTER TO A FRIEND"

Suddenly I felt *in Paris,* some hours before I was there. I was clearly recovering my Parisian spirits, which had been somewhat dissipated in my travels. They had been reduced to memories; now they were again becoming living values and resources to be used at every moment.

What a demon is the demon of abstract analogy! (You know how he torments me sometimes!) He whispered to me that I should compare this indefinable alteration occurring in me to a rather abrupt change in certain mental *probabilities.* Such and such response, such and such movement, such and such contraction of the face, all of which, in Paris, may be the instantaneous effects of our impressions, are no longer so natural when we are alone in the country, or in the society of a fairly remote place. The spontaneous is no longer the same. We are not ready to respond except to what is *probably at hand.*

This could produce curious consequences. A daring physicist willing to include the living, and even hearts, in his experiments, might perhaps go so far as to define separation as a certain inner distribution . . .

I am very much afraid, dear old friend, that we are made of many things that do not know us. And it is for that reason we do not know ourselves. If there is an infinite number of such things, then all meditation is useless. . . .

So, I felt myself gripped by another scheme of life, and I knew my return as a kind of vision of the world to which I was returning. A city where verbal life is more powerful, more diverse, more active and capricious than in any other, began taking shape in my mind as a sparkling confusion. And the train's harsh murmur added to my image-filled distraction the accompaniment of a beehive's noise.

It seemed to me that we were moving toward a cloud of talk. A thousand glories evolving, a thousand titles of books *per second* appeared and perished away in this swelling nebula. I could not tell whether I was seeing or hearing this mad stir. There were written books that cried out, spoken works that were men, and men that were names. . . . Nowhere on earth, I thought, does language have more frequency, more resonance, less reserve, than right in Paris where the literature, the science, the arts, the politics of a great country are jealously concentrated. The French have piled up all their ideas within the walls of this one city. And here we live in our own fire.

Tell; retell; foretell; contradict; slander. . . . All these verbs together summed up for me the humming of this paradise of the word.

What could be more tiring than to conceive the chaos of a million minds? Each thought in this tumult has its like, its opposite, its antecedent, and its sequel. So many similarities, so much unforeseen, discourage thought.

Can you imagine the incomparable disorder that can be maintained by ten thousand essentially singular beings? Just imagine the *temperature* that can be produced in this one place by such a great number of *prides,* all comparing themselves. Paris contains and combines, and consummates or consumes most of the brilliant failures summoned by destiny to the *delirious professions.* . . . This is the name I give to all those trades whose main tool is one's opinion of oneself, and whose raw material is the opinion others have of you. Those who follow these trades, doomed to be perpetual candidates, are necessarily forever afflicted with a kind of delusion of grandeur which is ceaselessly crossed and tormented by a kind of delusion of persecution. This population of uniques is ruled by the law of doing what no one has ever done, what no one will ever do. This is at least the law of the *best,* that is to say, of those who have the courage to want, frankly, something absurd. . . . They live for nothing but to have, and make durable, the illusion of being the only one—for superiority is only a solitude situated at the actual limits of a species. Each one founds his existence on the non-existence of others, but from them he must extort their consent not to exist . . . Please notice that I am only deducing what is contained in what is seen. If you doubt, just ask yourself where an effort leads to, which cannot be made but by one particular individual, and which depends on the particularity of men? Think of the real meaning of a hierarchy founded on rarity. I sometimes like to apply an image, taken from physics, to our hearts, intimately composed as they are of an enormous amount of injustice and a bit of justice, in combination. I imagine in each of us an atom more important than the others, and composed of two *grains of energy* wanting to be separated. These energies are contradictory but indivisible. Nature has joined them forever, although they are furious enemies. One is the eternal movement of a large *positive electron,* and this movement generates a series of grave sounds which the inner ear, with no trouble at all, makes out to be a deep monotonous phrase: *There's only me. There's only me. There's only me, me, me.* . . . As for the small, radically *negative* electron, it screams at the extreme pitch of shrillness, piercing again and again in the cruelest fashion the other's egotistical theme: *Yes, but there is so-and-so . . . Yes, but there is so-and-so . . . And so-and-so, and so-and-so!* For the name changes, often . . .

A bizarre kingdom where all the beautiful things growing there are bitter food for all souls but one. And the more beautiful they are, the bitterer their taste.

Or again. It seems to me that every mortal possesses, very nearly at the center of his mechanism, and well placed among the instruments for navigating his life, a tiny apparatus of incredible sensitivity which indicates the state of his self-respect. There we read whether we admire ourselves, adore ourselves, despise ourselves, or should blot ourselves out; and some living pointer, trembling over the secret dial, flickers with terrible nimbleness between the zero of a beast and the maximum of a god.

****

You know, dear You, that my mind is of the most shadowy kind. You know by experience, and better still for having heard it said a hundred times. There are plenty of people, learned, and benign, and well disposed, who are waiting until I am translated into French, to read me. They complain of me to the public, they expose before it citations of my verse which I confess must perplex them. They even take a righteous pride in not understanding something; a fact others might hide.—*"Modeste tamen et circumspecto judicio pronuntiandum est,"* said Quintilian, in a passage that Racine has taken care to translate, *"ne quod plerisque accidit, damnent quae non intelligunt."* But for my part I am extremely sorry to grieve these lovers of light. Nothing really attracts me but clarity. But alas, friend of mine! I assure you that I find almost none at all. I whisper this close into your ear; do not spread it about. Guard my secret excessively. Yes, for me clarity is so uncommon that over the whole extent of the world—and particularly of the thinking and writing world—I see it only in the proportion of diamond to the mass of the planet. The darkness people find in me is vain and transparent beside that I discover almost everywhere. Happy are those who agree among themselves that they understand one another perfectly! They write or speak without fear. You can sense how much I envy all those lucid beings, whose works make us dream of the sweet facility of the sun in a crystal universe. . . . My bad conscience sometimes suggests that I should defend myself by attacking them. It whispers to me that only those who seek nothing never run into obscurity, and that we should tell people only what they know already. But I look into my depths, and I am forced to agree with what so many distinguished persons say. It is true, my friend, I have an unfortunate mind, one which is never quite sure that it understands what it has understood without realizing it. I have great difficulty in distinguishing what is clear without reflection from what is positively obscure . . . This failing is no doubt the principle of my darkness. I distrust all words, I have reached the point, alas, of comparing those words on which we so lightly traverse the space of a thought, to light planks thrown across an abyss, which permit crossing but no stopping. A man in quick motion can use them and get away; but if he hesitates the least bit in the world, this fraction of time breaks them down, and all together fall into the depths. He who hurries has *caught on;* he must not dwell heavily: he would soon find the clearest speech to be a tissue of obscure terms.

All this might very well lead me into a long and charming inquiry, which I spare you. A letter is literature. There is a strict law in literature that we must never go to the bottom of anything. This is also the general will. Just look around, everywhere.

Translated by Jackson Mathews

THEATER

SKETCHES OF "MY FAUST"

FRAGMENT OF "LUST, OR THE CRYSTAL MAIDEN"

Act II—Scene 5

Faust comes in from the garden, holding a rose.

FAUST

I'm coming, Mademoiselle . . . Here, here is a rose for you . . . But please find something to write with quickly . . . I'm going to dictate here . . . Ideas are crowding in on me.

LUST

Thank you, mon Maître! It is so very fresh. One would like to spend a lifetime, with eyes closed, drawing up from this flower all its softness and intoxication . . . Oh, it's so strong and yet so sweet!

FAUST

Yes . . . But ideas won't wait. Are you ready? Put the flower down over there.

LUST

I have everything I need—paper, pencils . . . (*She attaches the rose to her dress.*)

FAUST

Good, let's begin. I'm going to dictate without any plan. Ideas cost nothing. It's the form. But we must seize them . . .

LUST

I'm ready, Maître.

FAUST

Good. Good . . . But now I'm not. (*There is a pause.*) How heavenly it is, this evening . . . (*Lust writes it down.*)

LUST

(*reading back*) ". . . heavenly . . . this evening . . ."

No, no . . . I'm not dictating . . . I'm just existing. It's heavenly to-night. It's too good, too sweet, even too beautiful . . . The earth is tender . . .

LUST

Shall I stay? Perhaps you'd rather be alone.

FAUST

No . . . It's too much for one person alone. Sit there . . . You must stay. You must enjoy with me, and as I do, the fresh scent of the damp earth and the precious emanations that the end of day draws from all my flowers. For me these perfumes are promises. Pure promises—nothing more. Because nothing is more delicious than a promise. Nothing more . . .

LUST

You really don't want to work?

FAUST

We'll work later on. It is often wise to begin with the reward. This moment is of such great price . . . It possesses me like those harmonies of sound which go beyond the limits of desire of hearing, that make one's being dissolve and return to the first happy confusion of its strengths and weaknesses. Everything around us is singing. The beauty of this day is singing before it dies.

LUST (*con amore*)

But it's you who are singing, mon Maître . . . You're like a god this evening . . . You're doing more than living . . . You seem to be, in yourself, one of those miraculous moments full of all the powers that confound death. Now your face is the most beautiful of your faces. It offers to the rich light of the setting sun the most spiritual and most noble thing the sun can illumine. No, I have never really seen you before, before now I have never seen this superb compassion and that glance which goes beyond what we see. Is it . . . you aren't about to die, are you? Your eyes seem to be contemplating the whole universe in this little garden—which to them is like the small pebble a savant picks up, that tells him, as it lies in the palm of his hand, about a whole epoch of the world's history.

FAUST

The universe means nothing to me, and I'm thinking of nothing.

How do you know?

I tell you that I'm not thinking about anything. But soon now, something is going to be decided, and I know it precisely for this reason—that I'm not thinking of anything.

But what is it?

Something and perhaps . . . something else . . . But my body does not yet know what it is, and my mind does not tell me. There is only this —this moment singing the profusion of the evening.

It's strange . . . I, I'm not thinking of anything either.

It's just too beautiful this evening. There's nothing more one can think about. How old are you?

I could have been married for five years.

I could have been dead for a long time, a very long time. I was young once, Lust.

But I'm sure you were never more beautiful.

I was young, Lust. And I have been old. And then I was young again. I've run through more than one world . . . But I've weighed my desires and my experiences in solitude.

In the desert?

Why? Solitude is something that can be made anywhere.

And . . . now?

I've weighed everything. The total weight is nothing. I've done good.

And I've done evil. I've seen good come out of evil, and evil come from good.

LUST

The whole circle, then?

FAUST

Yes.

LUST

And . . . now?

FAUST

And now, here I am what I am, and I don't think I am something else. It took so many hopes and so much despair, so many triumphs and disasters to reach this point . . . But here I am . . . With a little more intelligence, I might have gotten to it by intelligence alone.

LUST

Maître, I don't hear everything that you're saying. You're talking to yourself, not to me. But I don't need to understand. This evening I can't follow an idea anyway. It's your voice which makes me follow, like a band in the street. It carries me along . . . to the brink of tears . . . Oh, say everything that you want to. It is almost unbearable . . . I want to feel unhappy from feeling so wonderful. I'm too happy, and I'm suffocating . . . I can't find the words, or anything else, that can relieve my heart of this abundance . . . of myself. Oh! And then those terrible birds so high in the sky whose piercing calls cut through my happiness . . .

FAUST (to himself)

Am I perhaps at the summit of my art? I am alive. And I'm doing nothing else but live. There is a work of art . . . At last what I have been has ended by creating what I am. I no longer have any importance. Now I'm the present itself. My personality is completely wedded to my presence, in perfect harmony with whatever may occur. Nothing more. No further depths. The infinite has been defined. What doesn't exist no longer exists. If knowledge is what the mind must produce, so that what is may be, then here you are now, Faust—knowledge full and pure, plenitude, accomplishment. I am who I am. I'm at the crest of my art, at the classic moment of the art of living. Here is my work of art: being alive. Isn't that everything? But I must know it . . . It's no good finding oneself on this high plateau of existence and not knowing it. How

252

many adventures and causes, how many dreams and mistakes to achieve the liberty of being what one is, and nothing but what one is! What is perfection if not the suppression of everything we lack? What we lack is always too much . . . But now the least sight, the faintest sensation, the least, the smallest actions and movements of life, take on for me the same dignity as the intentions and inner voices of my thought . . . It is a supreme state, where everything reforms itself in living, and which refuses every question and every answer with a smile . . . Living! . . . I feel and breathe my masterpiece. I am born every instant for that instant. Living! . . . I breathe. Isn't that the whole of it? I breathe. I open wide each time, and each time for the first time, those inner wings which mark the true passage of time. They carry him who is, from the he who was, to the he who will be . . . I am! Isn't that extraordinary? To hover above death like a stone suspended in space? It's unbelievable . . . I breathe, and nothing more. The imperious perfume of my flowers commands me to breathe, and the smell of the fresh earth enters into me, ever more desired, ever more desirable, acting upon the power of my breathing. I breathe; and nothing more, because there is nothing more. I breathe and I see. This place is good to look upon . . . But what does this place mean? And what is the meaning of what I see? To see is enough, and to know that one is seeing. Therein lies a whole science. I see that pine tree. And what does that pine tree itself mean? Couldn't it just as well be an oak? I would see it just the same. And that roof of gleaming slate might just as well be a mirror of calm water. I would see that. And as for the shape of those distant hills which haphazardly enclose the landscape, I feel in my hands the power to redesign their long soft line according to my own taste . . . To see is then, as well, to see something else; to see what is possible as well as what is. And what then are those extraordinary visions which the ascetics seek compared with this prodigy of seeing whatever it may be. The soul is a beggarwoman. If I close my eyes and concentrate, here I am between mind and soul . . . What poverty! Where are the precise shapes, the nuances, the perspective which the least movement changes? What price in weariness must I pay now, beneath my eyelids, for the duration, the exactness and the brilliance of the objects I try to form for myself? And what intense faith, what stubborn mortifications or what excess of prayer could ever create a sun like this one, which glows and pours out so generously its purple blood for everyone?

(*to one side but coming closer to Faust from behind, with care, and as if moved by a power outside herself*) I can't stay so far away. It would be like being far away from myself . . . What would he say if I kissed his hand? What would he do?

FAUST

I breathe and I see . . . But what is perhaps more immediate in the immediacy is this: I touch . . . (*He strikes the arm of the bench on which he is seated.*) And with one single blow I find and create reality . . . My hand feels itself touched as it touches. That's what reality means. And nothing more.

LUST (*behind him, speaking softly*)

He speaks and I speak to myself; and there is no exchange between our words. And yet it can't be that there is no resemblance between what he feels and what I feel myself . . . living. The moment is too ripe, too laden with the ripe fruit of a day full of splendor, for it to be possible that two people, even as different as we are, should not be at the end of their resistance to the force of things in the same way . . . Both overcome in the same way as they must be, both in the same way too rich, as if charged with an almost unbearable force of happiness, which cannot find its expression, its natural limit, its activity, its end . . . a kind of death . . .

FAUST

Yes. What could be more real? Am I touching? I am touched. An old author once said: Only bodies by themselves can touch and be touched . . . (*There is a silence. Lust gently places her hand on his shoulder.*) Someone is touching me . . . Who is it? Is it you, Lust? I thought you had gone.

LUST

Yes, it's I . . . But why did you call me "tu"?

FAUST

Because you touched me . . . Why did you touch me?

LUST

I was afraid you would fall asleep while you were dreaming . . . It's not a good thing to do, you know . . .

I've nothing to fear from a sun that is setting . . . Leave your hand there.

No. Why should I leave it?

Because there's no longer any reason . . . Take it away.

No.

Why not?

Because it came there of its own accord . . . Really I don't know why it came, or why it should stay there on your shoulder, or why it should go away? Why? That's quickly said. Do you know yourself, wise as you are, why you called me "tu" just now? That happens of its own accord like everything that is very important. (*She takes away her hand.*)

Well that was born from you and me, and not from me or from you. Your hand and my calling you "tu," they make something, a sort of being. We know no more about it than people who make a child know about the child they are making. Sometimes intimacy is born from nothing, from something done without thinking, from a shared blunder . . . And sometimes that nothing resolves into nothing; sometimes it carries everything with it . . . Take away your hand, Mademoiselle.

But, Maître, I did take it away.

I thought I still felt it resting ever so lightly on my shoulder . . . But now, give me your hand . . . I need it. A kind of languor that is too pleasant keeps me from getting up. (*She gives him her hand; he makes a movement as if to pull her down to him; but immediately he drops and pushes away the hand he was holding.*) No . . . It's no good . . . Thank you. Don't help me. If you gave it to me . . .

What then?

FAUST (*getting up*)

The whole thing would follow.

LUST (*lowering her head, in a trembling voice*)

You're going back?

FAUST

Not yet. I still want to work a little here. We still have nearly an hour of daylight. One would say the light was sorry to leave us. But my work hardly goes forward. Will you get your notebook? Something is troubling you. You look as if you were going to cry.

LUST

Oh no! That's just a way I have of looking now and then, Maître. I don't know what does that to my face. I must be awfully ugly . . . But a woman wouldn't be fooled by it. She would see at once that I'm not thinking of anything that leads to tears. Men never know how to read on our faces the little things that might sometimes be of the greatest importance for them.

FAUST

Say rather: the importance they give to women.

LUST

I mean the importance they give to a particular woman. That one is lucky.

FAUST

You too, I see, believe in happiness—that word for women—and you define it as the feeling of being the only concern, the sovereign and eternal concern of another person . . . who knows? So be it. But since you have no desire or reason to cry, I'm glad of it, and I beg you to get ready for our dictation . . . Where you please. Good . . . And now will you read back to me the last sentence?

Translated by J. Laughlin and Anthony Bower

Some New Directions Paperbooks

Walter Abish, *Alphabetical Africa.* NDP375.
  In the Future Perfect. NDP440.
  Minds Meet. NDP387.
Ilangô Adigal, *Shilappadikaram.* NDP162.
Alain, *The Gods.* NDP382.
David Antin. *Talking at the Boundaries.* NDP388.
G. Apollinaire, *Selected Writings.*† NDP310.
Djuna Barnes, *Nightwood.* NDP98.
Charles Baudelaire, *Flowers of Evil.*† NDP71,
  Paris Spleen. NDP294.
Martin Bax. *The Hospital Ship.* NDP402.
Gottfried Benn, *Primal Vision.*† NDP322.
Wolfgang Borchert, *The Man Outside.* NDP319.
Jorge Luis Borges, *Labyrinths.* NDP186.
Jean-François Bory, *Once Again.* NDP256.
E. Brock, *The Blocked Heart.* NDP399.
  Here. Now. Always. NDP429.
  Invisibility Is The Art of Survival. NDP342.
  The Portraits & The Poses. NDP360.
  The River and the Train. NDP478.
Buddha, *The Dhammapada.* NDP188.
Frederick Busch, *Domestic Particulars.* NDP413.
  Manual Labor. NDP376.
Ernesto Cardenal, *Apocalypse & Other Poems.*
  NDP441. *In Cuba.* NDP377.
Hayden Carruth, *For You.* NDP298.
  From Snow and Rock, from Chaos. NDP349.
Louis-Ferdinand Céline,
  Death on the Installment Plan. NDP330.
  Guignol's Band. NDP278.
  Journey to the End of the Night. NDP84.
Jean Cocteau, *The Holy Terrors.* NDP212.
  The Infernal Machine. NDP235.
M. Cohen, *Monday Rhetoric.* NDP352.
Robert Coles. *Irony in the Mind's Life,* NDP459.
Cid Corman, *Livingdying.* NDP289.
  Sun Rock Man. NDP318.
Gregory Corso, *Elegiac Feelings.* NDP299.
  Happy Birthday of Death. NDP86.
  Long Live Man. NDP127.
Robert Creeley, *Hello.* NDP451.
Edward Dahlberg, *Reader.* NDP246.
  Because I Was Flesh. NDP227.
Osamu Dazai, *The Setting Sun,* NDP258.
  No Longer Human. NDP357.
Coleman Dowell, *Mrs. October . . .* NDP368.
  Too Much Flesh and Jabez. NDP447.
Robert Duncan, *Bending the Bow.* NDP255.
  The Opening of the Field. NDP356.
  Roots and Branches. NDP275.
Richard Eberhart, *Selected Poems.* NDP198.
E. F. Edinger. *Melville's Moby-Dick.* NDP460.
Russell Edson. *The Falling Sickness.* NDP389.
  The Very Thing That Happens. NDP137.
Wm. Empson, *7 Types of Ambiguity.* NDP204.
  Some Versions of Pastoral. NDP92.
Wm. Everson, *Man-Fate.* NDP369.
  The Residual Years. NDP263.
Lawrence Ferlinghetti, *Her.* NDP88.
  Back Roads to Far Places. NDP312.
  A Coney Island of the Mind. NDP74.
  The Mexican Night. NDP300.
  Open Eye, Open Heart, NDP361.
  Routines. NDP187.
  The Secret Meaning of Things. NDP268.
  Starting from San Francisco. NDP220.
  Tyrannus Nix?. NDP288.
  Who Are We Now? NDP425.
F. Scott Fitzgerald, *The Crack-up.* NDP54.
Robert Fitzgerald, *Spring Shade.* NDP311.
Gustave Flaubert, *Dictionary.* NDP230.
Gandhi, *Gandhi on Non-Violence.* NDP197.
Goethe, *Faust,* Part I. NDP70.
Allen Grossman. *The Woman on the Bridge.*
  NDP473.
Albert J. Guerard, *Thomas Hardy.* NDP185.
John Hawkes, *The Beetle Leg.* NDP239.
  The Blood Oranges. NDP338.
  The Cannibal. NDP123.
  Death Sleep & The Traveler. NDP393.
  The Innocent Party. NDP238.
  John Hawkes Symposium. NDP446.

The Lime Twig. NDP95.
  Lunar Landscapes. NDP274.
  The Owl. NDP443.
  Second Skin. NDP146.
  Travesty. NDP430.
A. Hayes, *A Wreath of Christmas Poems.*
  NDP347.
H.D., *End to Torment.* NDP476.
  Helen in Egypt. NDP380.
  Hermetic Definition NDP343.
  Trilogy. NDP362.
Robert E. Helbling, *Heinrich von Kleist,* NDP390.
Hermann Hesse, *Siddhartha.* NDP65.
C. Isherwood, *All the Conspirators.* NDP480.
  The Berlin Stories. NDP134.
  Lions and Shadows, NDP435.
Philippe Jaccottet, *Seedtime.* NDP428.
Alfred Jarry, *The Supermale.* NDP426.
  Ubu Roi, NDP105.
Robinson Jeffers, *Cawdor and Meda.* NDP293.
James Joyce, *Stephen Hero.* NDP133.
  James Joyce/Finnegans Wake. NDP331.
Franz Kafka, *Amerika.* NDP117.
Bob Kaufman,
  Solitudes Crowded with Loneliness. NDP199.
Hugh Kenner, *Wyndham Lewis.* NDP167.
Kenyon Critics, *G. M. Hopkins.* NDP355.
H. von Kleist. *Prince Friedrich of Homburg.*
  NDP462.
P. Lai, *Great Sanskrit Plays.* NDP142.
Tommaso Landolfi,
  Gogol's Wife and Other Stories. NDP155.
Lautréamont, *Maldoror.* NDP207.
Irving Layton, *Selected Poems.* NDP431.
Denise Levertov, *Collected Earlier Poems.*
  NDP475.
  Footprints. NDP344.
  The Freeing of the Dust. NDP401.
  The Jacob's Ladder. NDP112.
  Life in the Forest. NDP461.
  O Taste and See. NDP149.
  The Poet in the World. NDP363.
  Relearning the Alphabet. NDP290.
  The Sorrow Dance. NDP222.
  To Stay Alive. NDP325.
  In Her Own Province. NDP481.
Harry Levin, *James Joyce.* NDP87.
Enrique Lihn, *The Dark Room.*† NDP452.
García Lorca, *Five Plays.* NDP232.
  Selected Poems.† NDP114.
  Three Tragedies. NDP52.
Michael McClure, *Gorf.* NDP416.
  Antechamber. NDP455.
  Jaguar Skies. NDP400.
  September Blackberries. NDP370.
Carson McCullers, *The Member of the
  Wedding.* (Playscript) NDP153.
Thomas Merton, *Asian Journal.* NDP394.
  Gandhi on Non-Violence. NDP197.
  My Argument with the Gestapo. NDP403.
  New Seeds of Contemplation. NDP337.
  Raids on the Unspeakable. NDP213.
  Selected Poems. NDP85.
  The Way of Chuang Tzu. NDP2776.
  The Wisdom of the Desert. NDP295.
  Zen and the Birds of Appetite. NDP261.
Henry Miller, *The Air-Conditioned Nightmare.*
  NDP302.
  Big Sur & The Oranges. NDP161.
  The Books in My Life. NDP280.
  The Colossus of Maroussi. NDP75.
  The Cosmological Eye. NDP109.
  Henry Miller on Writing. NDP151.
  The Henry Miller Reader. NDP269.
  Just Wild About Harry. NDP479.
  The Smile at the Foot of the Ladder. NDP386.
  Stand Still Like the Hummingbird. NDP236.
  The Time of the Assassins. NDP115.
  The Wisdom of the Heart. NDP94.
Y. Mishima, *Confessions of a Mask.* NDP253.
  Death in Midsummer. NDP215.
Eugenio Montale, *New Poems.* NDP410.
  Selected Poems.† NDP193.
Vladimir Nabokov, *Nikolai Gogol.* NDP78.
  Laughter in the Dark. NDP470.

The Real Life of Sebastian Knight. NDP432.
P. Neruda, The Captain's Verses.† NDP345.
  Residence on Earth.† NDP340.
New Directions in Prose & Poetry (Anthology).
  Available from #17 forward. #38, Spring 1979.
Robert Nichols, Arrival. NDP437.
  Garh City. NDP450.
  Harditts in Sawna. NDP470.
Charles Olson. Selected Writings. NDP231.
Toby Olson. The Life of Jesus. NDP417.
George Oppen, Collected Poems. NDP418.
Wilfred Owen, Collected Poems. NDP210.
Nicanor Parra, Emergency Poems.† NDP333.
  Poems and Antipoems.† NDP242.
Boris Pasternak, Safe Conduct. NDP77.
Kenneth Patchen, Aflame and Afun. NDP292.
  Because It Is. NDP83.
  But Even So. NDP265.
  Collected Poems. NDP284.
  Doubleheader. NDP211.
  Hallelujah Anyway. NDP219.
  In Quest of Candlelighters. NDP334.
  The Journal of Albion Moonlight. NDP99.
  Memoirs of a Shy Pornographer. NDP205.
  Selected Poems. NDP160.
  Wonderings. NDP320.
Octavio Paz, Configurations.† NDP303.
  Eagle or Sun?† NDP422.
  Early Poems.† NDP354.
Plays for a New Theater. (Anth.) NDP216.
J. A. Porter, Eelgrass. NDP438.
Ezra Pound, ABC of Reading. NDP89.
  Classic Noh Theatre of Japan. NDP79.
  Confucius. NDP285.
  Confucius to Cummings. (Anth.) NDP126.
  Gaudier Brzeska. NDP372.
  Guide to Kulchur. NDP257.
  Literary Essays. NDP250.
  Love Poems of Ancient Egypt. NDP178.
  Pavannes and Divagations. NDP397.
  Pound/Joyce. NDP296.
  Selected Cantos. NDP304.
  Selected Letters 1907-1941. NDP317.
  Selected Poems. NDP66.
  Selected Prose 1909-1965. NDP396.
  The Spirit of Romance. NDP266.
  Translations.† (Enlarged Edition) NDP145.
James Purdy, Children Is All. NDP327.
Raymond Queneau, The Bark Tree. NDP314.
  The Flight of Icarus. NDP358.
  The Sunday of Life. NDP433.
Mary de Rachewiltz, Ezra Pound. NDP405.
M. Randall, Part of the Solution. NDP350.
John Crove Ransom, Beating the Bushes.
  NDP324.
Raja Rao, Kanthapura. NDP224.
Herbert Read, The Green Child. NDP208.
P. Reverdy, Selected Poems.† NDP346.
Kenneth Rexroth, Beyond the Mountains.
  NDP384.
  Collected Longer Poems. NDP309.
  Collected Shorter Poems. NDP243.
  New Poems. NDP383.
  100 More Poems from the Chinese. NDP308.
  100 More Poems from the Japanese. NDP420.
  100 Poems from the Chinese. NDP192.
  100 Poems from the Japanese.† NDP147.
Rainer Maria Rilke, Poems from
  The Book of Hours. NDP408.
  Possibility of Being. NDP436.
  Where Silence Reigns. (Prose). NDP464.
Arthur Rimbaud, Illuminations.† NDP56.
  Season in Hell & Drunken Boat.† NDP97.
Edouard Roditi, Delights of Turkey. NDP445.
Selden Rodman, Tongues of Fallen Angels.
  NDP373.
Jerome Rothenberg, Poems for the Game
  of Silence. NRP406.
  Poland/1931. NDP379.
  Seneca Journal. NDP448.
Saikaku Ihara, The Life of an Amorous
  Woman. NDP270.

Saigyo. Mirror for the Moon.† NDP465.
St. John of the Cross, Poems.† NDP341.
Jean-Paul Sartre, Baudelaire. NDP233.
  Nausea. NDP82.
  The Wall (Intimacy). NDP272.
Delmore Schwartz, Selected Poems. NDP241.
  In Dreams Begin Responsibilities. NDP454.
Kazuko Shiraishi, Seasons of Sacred Lust.
  NDP453.
Stevie Smith, Selected Poems, NDP159.
Gary Snyder, The Back Country. NDP249.
  Earth House Hold. NDP267.
  Myths and Texts. NDP457.
  Regarding Wave. NDP306.
  Turtle Island. NDP381.
Gilbert Sorrentino, Splendide-Hôtel. NDP364.
Enid Starkie. Rimbaud. NDP254.
Stendhal, The Telegraph. NDP108.
Jules Supervielle, Selected Writings.† NDP209.
W. Sutton, American Free Verse. NDP351.
Nathaniel Tarn, Lyrics... Bride of God. NDP391.
Dylan Thomas, Adventures in the Skin Trade.
  NDP183.
  A Child's Christmas in Wales. NDP181.
  Collected Poems 1934-1952. NDP316.
  The Doctor and the Devils. NDP297.
  Portrait of the Artist as a Young Dog.
  NDP51.
  Quite Early One Morning. NDP90.
  Under Milk Wood. NDP73.
Martin Turnell, Art of French Fiction. NDP251.
  Baudelaire. NDP336.
  Rise of the French Novel. NDP474.
Paul Valéry, Selected Writings.† NDP184.
P. Van Ostaijen, Feasts of Fear & Agony.
  NDP411.
Elio Vittorini, A Vittorini Omnibus. NDP366.
  Women of Messina. NDP365.
Vernon Watkins, Selected Poems. NDP221.
Nathanael West, Miss Lonelyhearts &
  Day of the Locust. NDP125.
J. Williams, An Ear in Bartram's Tree. NDP335. •
Tennessee Williams, Camino Real, NDP301.
  Cat on a Hot Tin Roof. NDP398.
  Dragon Country. NDP287.
  Eight Mortal Ladies Possessed, NDP374.
  The Glass Menagerie. NDP218.
  Hard Candy. NDP225.
  In the Winter of Cities. NDP154.
  One Arm & Other Stories. NDP237.
  The Roman Spring of Mrs. Stone. NDP271.
  Small Craft Warnings. NDP348.
  Sweet Bird of Youth. NDP409.
  Twenty-Seven Wagons Full of Cotton. NDP217.
  Vieux Carré. NDP482.
  Where I Live, NDP468.
William Carlos Williams.
  The Autobiography. NDP223.
  The Build-up. NDP259.
  Embodiment of Knowledge. NDP434.
  The Farmers' Daughters. NDP106.
  I Wanted to Write a Poem. NDP469.
  Imaginations. NDP329.
  In the American Grain. NDP53.
  In the Money. NDP240.
  Paterson. Complete. NDP152.
  Pictures from Brueghel. NDP118.
  The Selected Essays. NDP273.
  Selected Poems. NDP131.
  A Voyage to Pagany. NDP307.
  White Mule. NDP226.
  W. C. Williams Reader. NDP282.
Yvor Winters, E. A. Robinson. NDP326.
Wisdom Books: Ancient Egyptians, NDP467;
  Wisdom of the Desert, NDP295; Early
  Buddhists, NDP444; English Mystics, NDP466;
  Forest (Hindu), NDP414; Jewish Mystics,
  NDP423; Spanish Mystics, NDP442; Sufi,
  NDP424; Zen Masters, NDP415.

Complete descriptive catalog available free on request from
New Directions, 80 Eighth Avenue, New York 10011   † Bilingual